C000273600

"GRANDDAD'S WAR"

THE FIRST WORLD WAR EXPERIENCES OF PRIVATE HERBERT BARNES

BY

TED BARNES – HIS GRANDSON

Published by

MELROSE BOOKS

An Imprint of Melrose Press Limited
St Thomas Place, Ely
Cambridgeshire
CB7 4GG, UK
www.melrosebooks.co.uk

FIRST EDITION

Cover designed by Hannah Belcher

ISBN 978-1-908645-26-5

Printed and bound in Great Britain by:
CPI Antony Rowe, Chippenham, Wiltshire

FSC
www.fsc.org
MIX
Paper from
responsible sources
FSC® C013604

This book is dedicated to Mary Hughes, eldest Granddaughter of Herbert Barnes and a much loved sister to me.

She has always been there for me.

It is also dedicated to all of Herbert's Grandchildren – Connie, Anne, David, John, Barbara, Nancy and Brian, who always held him in such high regard.

CONTENTS

AUTHOR'S NOTES

Granddad's War is factual in all its detail. It traces the story of my Grandfather, Herbert Barnes, a private soldier in the First World War. At the age of 34, this Norfolk man with a wife and 4 children was plucked from the comfort of his home and sent to fight in the bloodiest conflict in our country's history. Like thousands of others, he witnessed scenes of unspeakable horror. He fought in battles that are now household names – at The Somme, at Arras and at Ypres. He was wounded three times, twice within an inch of his life, shipped back to hospitals in England to be patched up and sent back to the trenches. He served as an infantryman and later as a stretcher bearer. He survived to bring up a large family.

He was one of 4 brothers who were Tommies in the First World War. In an amazing way, the paths of these 4 Norfolk boys repeatedly crossed as they moved around the battlefields in France. The relationship between the 4 brothers and how they kept meeting one another as the war progressed is a secondary theme of the story.

Back home in Norfolk, Herbert's wife, Rose, was bringing up 4 children without the support of the man of the house. Like thousands of others, theirs was a one parent family. She struggled to feed, care for, educate and discipline a young growing family in war stricken England. A third theme of the story is her experiences and ultimate triumph.

The book has been meticulously researched using public records and private family archives. I have visited the battlefields where Herbert fought many times as well as spent time investigating the many military hospitals in the U.K. where he recovered from his wounds. Military accuracy has been achieved using battalion diaries and consulting with experts. The story is generously supported by photographs and maps taken by myself and from other publications.

The story is told, not because Herbert was in any way exceptional but rather because he was so very typical. His story epitomises the experiences of so many and as such, captures for the reader what it must have been like in those days now so largely forgotten. And, of course, he was a much loved Grandfather.

TED BARNES

ACKNOWLEDGEMENTS

I have never written a book before. Indeed it was never my intention to write this book. It happened in large part by accident. It was a project that "grew like Topsy".

My first stimulation was itself an accident of circumstance. I have been involved for some years in a local Heritage Society, created some 10 years ago, which records and fosters the heritage of the village in which I live. Amongst other activities, the Society supports a programme of events for the benefit of its members. A few years ago one of these events, operated in conjunction with Nottingham University, was a three day visit to the Somme Battlefield. Like most amateur historians, I knew a little about the First World War but my knowledge was considerably less than extensive. However, while walking in the peace and quiet of Delville Wood on a bright and sunny summer's day, I recalled that many years before, my Grandfather had made one of his very rare references to the "War". He had told me he had fought in "Devil's Wood", as he called it. I started to wonder exactly where he had been and what he had done. Had he trod exactly the same ground as I was treading now? Had he been in "Princes Street" or "Buchanan Street"? What had he experienced here? My curiosity was aroused and my interest sparked. That visit to Delville Wood began an extended period of research and investigation that involved many enjoyable trips to Northern France and visits to locations all over the United Kingdom. My intention was merely to satisfy my curiosity as to where this most loved of Grandfathers had gone while he was a Tommy. As the research continued, a story began to unfold – a story which was supported by documentary evidence. It was a story about the hardships, not only of Herbert Barnes but also a story about his wife, Rose Barnes, left at home back in England to raise a large family without the support of her husband. It became clear that it was a captivating story worthy of recording if only as a family archive.

As time went by, however, the idea of a book was born.

A second stimulant was Herbert and Rose Barnes themselves. The reader, as he or she leafs through these pages, will quickly learn that they were both much loved by their family and by the community in which they lived. They were in no way special, except of course to the people who knew them and to the family they fostered. They were not the sort of people who would ask for a memorial and they would never have dreamed of asking for recognition for anything they had done. However, like millions of others, they lived through a very difficult period in our country's history and they triumphed through their determination and good nature. So, yes, this book is a memorial to them and, in a modest way, a thank you for their lives.

The third stimulant was much more self-centred. All my adult life I have been interested in military history. For me battles have a morbid fascination. They have been, through time, the moments of schismatic political change; of massive shifts of power brought about sometimes by the vagaries of fortune. But my fascination does not end there. As one who has never been asked to take up arms, I have always had this question of myself: How would I perform in the heat of a battle? What would I do? Would I march fearlessly towards the guns or would I cower in a foxhole trying to dodge the bullets? What was being a Tommy in the trenches really like? Out of that question is born a deep respect for the common soldier in wartime who faced the ultimate danger. Out of that question is also born an undying gratitude for those who paid the ultimate price. I am not talking about just how we all feel on Remembrance Sunday on the 11th hour of the 11th day of the 11th month. I am talking about a continuous thankfulness for what they all did for us. So, yes, this book is a tribute to the common soldier, of whom Herbert Barnes was just one.

The research for this book was extensive and I have met and been helped by many kind people along the way. I cannot mention them all but some went well beyond the call of good neighbourliness.

My heartfelt thanks go first of all to Mr Dick Rayner of Spixworth near Norwich. Dick is a remarkable man. Educated at Hammonds School in Swaffham, he is a Norfolk man through and through just as Herbert Barnes was. Dick has spent many years researching and recording the history of the 8th Battalion the Norfolk Regiment. His knowledge of the Norfolk Regiment in general and the 8th Battalion in particular is very extensive. Dick has the uncanny ability to view the catastrophic events of the First World War from the viewpoint of the common soldier. He has developed the ability to cut through what may be the considered wisdom of a later age and to identify the concerns and emotions of the soldiers on the ground. This narrative of the wartime service of my Granddad has been hugely helped by his advice and patient support. I am deeply grateful.

I would also like to record my thanks for the support and co-operation from Kate Thaxton and her staff at the Norfolk Regiment Museum in Norwich. Complete access to the Battalion diaries of the Norfolk Regiment was essential in piecing together the detail of Granddad's war. She has also been most kind in allowing me on occasions to park myself in the Regiment Museum offices.

My thanks also go to my sister Mary Hughes to whom I have dedicated this book, and her husband Brian. She is the first born of Herbert Barnes's many Grandchildren and she loved him dearly. Mary has patiently and diligently reviewed each chapter as it has developed and has given much valuable input. She has given me advice drawn from her own experiences and memories. She has also kept me going during the frequent periods when my enthusiasm has waned a little. Brian also has reviewed each chapter and given valuable input and advice. I suspect I would not have got to the end of the road without them.

My thanks also go to two more of Herbert Barnes' Grandchildren, Barbara Speller (Phyllis's daughter) and Nancy Hatley (Bert's younger daughter). Both are amateur family historians who have justifiably earned from me the loving nickname of Squirrels. It reflects their determination to chase down even the most obscure details of our family heritage.

My thanks also go to my good friend Valerie Stout who has given up her time to read the drafts and to correct and modify the many misspellings and grammatical errors to which the author is prone.

Others have given me valuable assistance. Mrs Elaine Donnelly of Crosshouses in Shropshire has written a history of the Berrington War Hospital where Herbert Barnes was treated after his wound at Arras. She has been very generous in her help. Mr Timothy Ewatt-Lonsdale of Calverhall in Shropshire is a direct descendant of Lord Kilmorey of Shavington Hall and has shown me great hospitality in sharing his childhood reminiscences and allowing me access to the Shavington Hall visitor's book. Mr Richard Weymss of Weymss Castle in Fife was equally generous in allowing me access to the grounds of his wonderful home. Mr McDonald, his estate manager, also gave up a day of his very valuable time.

In compiling Herbert's story, I have accessed the work of many others. I am particularly grateful to Peter Barton and the Imperial War Museum for allowing me to make liberal use of their many excellent publications

I would also like to record my thanks to the staff of the following establishments all of whom gave me valuable assistance. The National Archives at Kew, The Imperial War Museum, The Commonwealth Graves Commission, The Thiepval War Memorial in France, The South African Memorial at Delville Wood, The Arras War Memorial, The Ypres War Memorial, the Kings Lynn Library, the Swaffham Library, the Swaffham Museum, the Norfolk Record Office at Norwich, the Surrey Record Office at Woking, the Suffolk Record Office at Bury St Edmunds, Ely Library and Epsom Library. These hard working archivists and librarians are the unsung heroes of any piece of research. Their expertise and support is always very much appreciated.

I would also like to thank Mrs Anne Dolan for typing and transcribing my scribbled thoughts, for preparing the manuscript, for transposing the photographs and appendices and for diligently working long hours to bring this book to fruition. Most of all I thank her for her patience and tolerance. Both qualities she has in abundance and both have, from time to time, been required to get us through the day.

In spite of the assistance of so many people, it may well be that there are errors that I have made as the story of Herbert Barnes unfolds. These errors are my responsibility and mine alone. There are also many occasions in the story where I have attempted to give my own insights into how he felt about the situations in which he found himself. These observations are the fruits of my own empathetic imagination and may not be factually accurate. They do however attempt to delve a little into his inner mind.

Last, but certainly not least, I would like to thank my wife Lillian for her continuous support and undying encouragement as well as for a never ending supply of hot tea and biscuits. Teamwork comes in many different forms and she is never found lacking in any respect.

CHAPTER 1

INTRODUCTION

On 22 November 1915, Herbert Edward Barnes (Bogey to his friends), father, husband, qualified tailor living and working in the small market town of Swaffham in Norfolk got out of bed. It was a cloudy overcast day with a stiff breeze blowing from the south-west. It was unusually cold. His wife of eight years, Rose, was up and about some time before him. She had hustled her four children out of bed and was thinking about putting breakfast on the table. It was a familiar routine that they had followed for most of their married life. Their eldest child, Alf, was eight years old; capable of washing and dressing himself as was his sister, Phyllis, who was six. His two younger brothers, Bert aged four and Ted aged two, had to be dressed and fed, a task that would inevitably fall to Rose. Later, the two youngest children could play in the yard at the back of the small cottage in Spinks Yard, off Ash Close. The two eldest children would go off to school.

Their breakfast would have been sparse. Herbert's menial wages as an "all round" tailor in Mr Fayers' clothes shop a few yards from the house further down Ash Close kept the family living at a level marginally above poverty. Herbert was 34½ years old and approaching what in 1915 could be called his "middle age".

Everything that morning appeared normal – an average day in a very normal life. But this 22 November was far from being a normal day. It was the day that Herbert Bogey Barnes was going off to war.

After breakfast, the children said an emotional farewell to their father. No doubt there were tears all around although Herbert was a robust man who did not readily let his feelings show. Both Alfie and Phyllis were old enough and

1

aware enough to know the significance of that day. They would have heard in and around the town of the mounting casualties being incurred on the Western Front and in the Middle East. They would have heard of men from Swaffham and the villages around who had been killed in the Battle of Loos which was just finishing. The names Gallipoli and Mesopotamia would have been uttered in hushed tones. They would have heard the scuttlebutt around the town of Swaffham of men who had lost limbs, been shot or been gassed. They would have known, even at their tender age, that there was a chance that their father might not return. They both loved him dearly. He was a fun-loving dad who busied himself with his children. He laughed a lot and was always ready for a game or two. It was a very hard day for them all. They were old enough to know that their life with their mother was going to be very different.

On the other hand, Bert and Ted were far too young to be concerned. It is likely that, to them, this was indeed just another day.

After breakfast, the children were ushered to their Grandparents' house which was situated three doors away in Spinks Yard. Rose wanted them out of the way. Grandfather Drake, Rose's father, was in his 60s and lived with Rose's elder spinster sister, Emma. He was a jolly, upbeat man and the children were used to spending happy days in his house. Mid-morning, Herbert packed a few belongings and at the allotted time he and Rose walked 350 yards or so to Swaffham railway station. Arm in arm, they strode purposefully up Ash Close, turned right into Spinners Lane and onto Station Road. As they went they nodded courteously to people they knew along the way, but did not stop to talk. Some wished Herbert good luck but this was not a time for cheery conversation. They passed the Chapel where Rose sang in the choir. They passed The Norfolk Hero, the pub where Herbert had had a beer or two. They did not dwell in either. Herbert was catching a train to Norwich.

They said goodbye on the station platform. It started a pattern that would be followed for the next three years on the few occasions when Herbert would come home on leave. Rose would accompany him to the station. She would see him onto the train. She would also meet him at the station when he returned – the children left playing in their Grandfather's house. This was Rose and

2

Herbert's private moment, away from the children and family, and what was said is known to them alone.

However, on the station platform they were not alone. Some weeks before, a recruiting officer had visited Swaffham and had addressed the men of the town from the bandstand in the market square. It was part of a huge drive which had stretched the length and breadth of the country. The challenge – to raise one million men for Field Marshal Lord Kitchener's "New Army", an army of volunteers that would win the war for King and Country. The recruiting officer had impressed upon the Swaffham men that their country needed them and that it was their duty to join the armed forces. It was time for them to fight and die. On the station at Swaffham were other men who had decided to volunteer at the same time as Herbert. So amidst the swirling smoke of the engines and the clanking of the carriage wheels, other couples like Rose and Herbert were saying their private farewells.

The journey from Swaffham to Norwich is short – less than one hour. Herbert disembarked at Norwich's Thorpe Station. He walked the three quarters of a mile to the Britannia Barracks, home of the Norfolk Regiment. The barrack buildings were imposing and rather austere, many times bigger than any structure he had ever seen in Swaffham. They stood proud, high on Mousehold Heath, overlooking the city. (The same Mousehold Heath where William Kett had led a rebellion against his king hundreds of years before.) The grand and imposing façade of the building still stands to this day. When Herbert arrived in 1915, the area was teeming with hundreds of soldiers and civilians all busy supporting the massive war effort.

On arrival, he completed attestation papers – papers which survive (see Appendix Four). He wrote down his name and his address. He filled in his date of birth. He detailed the name of his wife, to whom his belongings should be sent, should he be killed. He filled in the names and ages of his children in his neat flowing handwriting. He outlined his trade or "calling" as the document called it. He declared that he had never been a soldier before. He gave them permission to vaccinate him and finally he agreed to be enlisted into general service for the duration of the war. He also agreed that, if His Majesty required it, he might be retained in the armed forces after the hostilities were over. He swore an oath of allegiance to His Majesty King George V and to his heirs and successors. Lastly, he agreed to obey all orders, whatever they were.

He immediately went for a medical examination. He was 5 ft 6 ins tall. His chest size was 35½ inches with an expansion range of an additional two inches. He was described as a fine, fit man and given a clean bill of health.

He went into the barracks and took off his civilian clothes. He wrapped them in a brown paper parcel, tied them with a piece of string and scrawled his home address in Ash Close. They would be posted back to Rose. He had already picked out soldier's uniform that approximated to his size and he now put this on.[1] By the middle of the afternoon on 22 November 1915 he was Private Herbert Edward Barnes, number 22345 of the Norfolk Regiment. For the next one thousand, three hundred and sixty-four days his well-being, his movements, his life itself would be in the hands of the British Army. He now belonged to them. From a quiet, peaceful family life in a rural Norfolk town he was to be pitched into the bloodiest conflict in the history of the western world. He was a confused, bewildered and frightened man. He was totally unaware and unprepared for what lie ahead of him. Nevertheless he was resolved and determined to do his duty.

Ours is a fortunate generation. I was born in 1944 at the end of the Second World War. My generation has never seen a major conflict which totally engulfs our country, our families and our loved ones. As I grew up, I worried about schooling and marriage and children and mortgages and earning a living, confident that, as certain as one day follows another, our lives would proceed in a regulated manner. I do not mean to minimise the conflicts in Korea, Cyprus, the Falklands, Iraq and Afghanistan. Nor do I mean to minimise the bravery and the dedication of the British men who have fought and have died in those theatres. But, in the great scheme of things, these were small, local conflicts

---

1   It is possible that he was not given his uniform until his arrival at Felixstowe, but for the sake of this narrative, it is assumed it happened at the Britannia Barracks.

fought by small numbers of forces of largely professional soldiers who had voluntarily signed up to do just that.

My parents' and grandparents' generations were not so lucky. Twice in the span of 25 years, the world was plunged into conflicts that surpassed in death and destruction anything that had gone before. Both involved the conscription of all able-bodied men in our nation. There were a few reasons why a man need not be called to arms, but exceptions were few. The well-being of every family was disrupted. Fathers, who up until this time had led normal family lives, went away, many never to return. Millions of children were brought up in what we now call one-parent families. Streets and villages and towns were impacted in a way that had never happened before. Theirs was a glorious but unfortunate generation.

Herbert Edward Barnes was a part of this exodus. On 22 November 1915 he was 34 years and 6 months old. He was approaching middle age. He had been married for eight years. He had four young, healthy and boisterous children. He had a regular job. His life was set. And yet he went to war. He was wrenched away from the life he knew and the family he loved.

He lived in Ash Close in the small market town of Swaffham. As the story unfolds, we shall see that nearly every other house in that small street sent men off to the Western Front and the Middle East. Through volunteering and, after 1916, through conscription, family upon family was ruptured. No conflict in our history has ever had such an all-pervasive impact on the life of our nation.

We shall see that Rose Barnes, Herbert's wife, had a husband, two brothers, four brothers-in-law, three cousins and two nephews all fighting at the front at the same time in 1916. Many did not survive. Many families at home received the dreaded telegram. And many who did survive were wounded in a way that would affect the quality of their lives for ever. It is difficult in the comfort of the age in which we live to put ourselves in the places of our ancestors' generation and to envisage the devastating impact of the First World War on the towns and villages of our nation.

It is equally difficult to put ourselves in the place of the men who fought in that war. They were, for the most part, ordinary men living peaceful ordinary lives – men like Bogey Barnes. Most had never seen a gun before, much less used one in anger. They were suddenly shipped from that way of life and plunged into a living hell for which they were poorly prepared. Their experiences were harsh. They witnessed the horror of death and mayhem all around them. The pain inflicted upon them by what they saw and what they had to do was extreme. The survivors often had difficulty coming to terms with these experiences. The way in which many thousands reacted was to refrain from discussing or talking about what they had done and seen. The killing and maiming, the smashed bodies, the hardship and deprivations were not for public consumption. It was their way of burying their trauma deep inside them. There developed almost a conspiracy of silence amongst the men who were lucky enough to return to their families.

Herbert Edward Barnes followed this pattern. He was to live a long and fulfilled life after the war was over. He was a much-loved husband, father and grandfather. He played a full part in the community in which he lived. But the period from 1915 to 1919 was a secret. He did not discuss it with his wife. His children knew very little about what he went through. His family knew of perhaps only six or seven incidents that he might have mentioned in passing. We had no idea what he did in the Battle of the Somme. Some of us were not sure that he had been there at all. We did not know that he had fought in the Battle of Arras. There was no discussion about the hell that was Third Ypres. We were vaguely aware that he was wounded but where and how and how often and how severely was not a subject of conversation. We did not know that twice he came to within an inch of death. We knew that he spent months in hospitals all over the British Isles but were unsure as to which hospitals. Nobody knew that he was an infantryman who retrained as a stretcher-bearer and that he eventually became a member of the Royal Army Medical Corps. His family knew none of these things because he did not discuss them. For him, they were best left buried in the mud of Flanders.

It was not until I visited the battlefields of France and recalled my Grandfather mentioning, in passing, the name of Delville Wood (or Devil's Wood as he called it) that my curiosity was stimulated. I was lucky that

Herbert Barnes' records in the National Archives at Kew were comprehensive and complete. His was not one of the 60 percent of soldiers' records lost, ironically, during the Second World War. If that had been the case, I suspect his story would have remained locked inside him and would never have seen the light of day.

With the help of many people I have been able to piece together day by day the story of Herbert Edward Barnes` days as a Tommy in the British Army. The story that he never told to anyone himself can now be told. The story is a tribute to him from me – a tribute to a grandfather who was dearly loved and hugely respected by all his family. It is, in a way, a thank you for his survival.

But it is much more than that. It is a way of saying from my generation to a previous generation that fought and died in their hundreds of thousands, thank you for your sacrifices, thank you for your commitment, thank you for your service. You believed that you were fighting for King and Country. This story is a way of saying to my Grandfather and to all the Tommies,

We will remember you.

CHAPTER 2

A MAN FROM NORFOLK

1881–1915

Herbert was a Norfolk man through and through.

He was born on 6 May 1881, the third of 13 children.[2] His father and mother lived in a rented two-up-two-down house at 18 Kirby Street in the Victorian back streets of Kings Lynn (see Photo 4).

The street still exists but the old houses have long since been demolished and replaced by modern homes. In the 1880s each side of the narrow road was lined by a long terrace of workers' dwellings with outhouses attached to the back. The street ran south from Norfolk Street, a main thoroughfare from the town centre eastwards. Along it would rattle the horse-drawn wagons and coaches that brought people and products from the surrounding countryside. A growing mischievous boy could jump on the carts and hitch a ride to the large, impressive Tuesday market square, with or without permission from the carter. At the southern end of Kirby Street were extensive cattle pens where cows, sheep and horses were kept, awaiting sale in the nearby cattle market. And just to the east of Kirby Street was a public park, much beloved by the Victorians, where a young lad could kick a football or run and play. Herbert's home was in a busy bustling part of Victorian Lynn.

---

2   It appears that he was actually born on May 4 but the birth was not registered until some time later and May 6 was what appeared on his birth certificate. He therefore always celebrated his birthday on that day.

The house was conveniently situated for Herbert's father's work. Alfred George Barnes was an "engine man" or what we now call a train driver. He had worked for most of his adult life for the Great Eastern Railway Company, firstly as a stoker (or fireman). He had worked his way up to take command on the footplate. This was the golden age of the railways, a time when this new fast form of transport was changing the economy of Victorian England. Indeed, it was changing the nature of life in agricultural Norfolk as well, more than halving the travelling time between the market towns dotted all over the county. Engine drivers in the 1880s were viewed a little like airline pilots in the 1960s. It was a job which had a little glamour attached to it. Alfred was still working class, of course, but he was better paid and had more status than the agricultural labourers with whom he had grown up. His photograph reveals a distinguished looking man, upright, straight backed with a tailored moustache – a man who took himself seriously. He was a father who would not stand too much nonsense.

He travelled all over Norfolk on the county railway lines. The network was extensive – all the market towns and many of the villages had their own stations. Sometimes he drove the train down the main line to London. From time to time, he called in at Ely Station on the Kings Lynn to Cambridge line. It was there that he met and married Hannah Negus, a local girl who would become Herbert Barnes' mother. Hannah always answered to the name of Elizabeth although there is no mention of that name on her birth certificate. The name change was to distinguish her from a close maiden aunt who was also called Hannah. To Herbert, she was always simply Mother.

Her family lived in a small terraced house in Annesdale in the ancient city of Ely (see Photo 3). Annesdale in the 1880s was somewhat of a separate community to the rest of Ely, dwarfed by the massive structure of Ely Cathedral high above it on the hill. Annesdale fronts onto the river Great Ouse just where the railway line crosses the river and near where Ely Station is situated. Of course, in the 1880s the river was a major artery for boat traffic which still plied the Fenland waterways and Ely was a significant river port. The barges and lighters competed and would eventually be eclipsed by the new fangled railway system. Here was the busy industrial hub for sedate Ely. As well as the docks and railway station, the area was home to the brewery, the gasworks, the waterworks, and the coal yard. The Cutter Inn down by the river was the pub where railwaymen, boatmen, traders and merchants would congregate to exchange stories and drink warm ale. It is highly possible that this is where the dashing railwayman met Elizabeth and swept her off her feet. They married and he took her off to live in Kings Lynn.

A few days before Herbert was to be born, a heavily pregnant Elizabeth took the train from Kings Lynn back to Ely and returned to her sister's house in Annesdale where she had grown up. She had followed the same practice with her first two children. Both had been born in Annesdale even though the family home was in Kings Lynn. With her husband constantly away on his job, she found comfort in being with her family during her labour and delivery, especially with her sister Jane with whom she was very close.

On 4 May 1881, Herbert Edward Barnes came into this world. This man of Norfolk, who would live in Norfolk all his life and was so proud of his Norfolk heritage, was actually born in the Isle of Ely, then a separate county. It was a fact to which he very rarely referred unless it be in an almost inaudible voice. A few days later, mother and child returned back home to Kirby Street, again by train.

Not much is known about Herbert's early life. Until the age of 10 he grew up with the town of Kings Lynn as his playground. His home was close to the open ground that was the cattle pens, now long since knocked down and replaced by a modern shopping centre. The railway station was on his doorstep too, as was St James' Park and The Walks, public open ground with grass and space for kicking and throwing a ball. And then there were the maze of small streets that surrounded his house which would offer captivating opportunities for an inquisitive boisterous youngster. At the age of five, the young Herbert went to the Board School of St Margaret's in the Fleet, a few hundred yards away from his home. He was an intelligent lad without being academically brilliant. He developed a very neat, almost deliberate handwriting which would serve him well all his life (it made the research for this book many times easier). He was not an avid reader, neither was he particularly artistic, but he acquired a very sound educational grounding under the watchful eye of his mother and the strong discipline of his father. To his father, education was important. It was a way for working class people to improve the quality of their life, perhaps even to escape the daily drudge that was their lot. He would see that his son took his studies seriously.

Herbert was very much a boy's boy. Sport was his passion. He was always on the move, running here, running there. He could cover the ground, sprinting at an alarming pace. For him, the centre of the town was no more than a few minutes away. He played cricket with his mates in the park but his real love was football. He spent as much time as possible with his brothers and friends kicking the ball around the park and in the streets. He was later to say that perhaps he should have been doing other things, like the three Rs. However his father was "away on the trains" for much of the time and he and his brothers indulged their love of sport.

What we do know is that the family grew around him. His sister Mary, the eldest of the clan, was to become a second mother to him. She was a "serious" girl who spent time helping to look after the demanding family. He worshipped his elder brother Alfred, an outgoing, somewhat eccentric character who shared Herbert's love of sport. Alfred, like Herbert, always enjoyed a joke and laughter was never far away. As Herbert was growing up, there were new additions to the family. His brother John (who answered to the name of Jack) had been born in 1883. Charlie followed in 1886 and Jane in 1888. There were now six children with Alfred and Elizabeth in the tiny house in Kirby Street (See Family Tree - Appendix One). Family life was very strong and bonds were formed that would last a lifetime. Herbert developed a strong sense of family and family values that he would live by all his life. Indeed he would pass them on to his own family and children. His brothers and sisters, especially his brothers, were his mates, relationships forged by close proximity and common experience. The boys, Alf, Herbert, Jack and Charlie, grew up together. They looked like one another. They were all avid sportsmen. They even talked like one another in a strong rural West Norfolk accent. They were interested in the same things.

They were very close. (The author remembers seeing them all together when they were all in their 70s sitting together in the parlour of Alfred's house in Stowmarket.) They were all men of Norfolk.

Herbert was therefore always comfortable with, and keen to be with, children. He helped to bring up his younger brothers. He played with them. He sometimes taught them. Sometimes he fought with them. He always supported them. He became a strong family man. And of course many years later it was what made him so beloved by his own grandchildren.

Years later, in the trenches, Herbert would find himself as "the old man" surrounded by younger, more inexperienced soldiers. He would naturally drop into the role that he knew so well during his upbringing, a role of protecting and caring and looking after as far as he could the younger men around him. It was his natural way.

But in 1891, when he was 10 years old, young Herbert's life, and those of all the family, were to change and change quite significantly. His father decided to leave Kings Lynn. The decision to move to the lovely little Norfolk market town of Swaffham, 13 miles distant, might have been brought about because the family had outgrown the house at 18 Kirby Street. It is more likely, however, that he moved because of the demands of his job. It was at about this time that he became a fully qualified engine driver on the Great Eastern Railway. Whatever the reason, in May 1891, his family were living temporarily at 38 Austin Street in Kings Lynn, a few hundred yards from Kirby Street, while "Father" was staying in rooms at the old pub, the Norfolk Hero, in Swaffham.[3] The Norfolk Hero, named after the county's most famous son, Admiral Lord Nelson, was a hotel and tavern next to Swaffham railway station, the same station that would witness so many tearful farewells a few years later. No doubt he was working out of Swaffham station and also searching for a house to rent. A few weeks later the family upped and moved. Herbert said goodbye to his friends, to the back streets of Kings Lynn he knew so well, to all those haunts of his childhood. He set about making a new life in Swaffham.

---

3   This is how they all appear in the 1891 census.

The house that Alfred and Elizabeth moved to in Swaffham was in Ash Close, just off the market square. Although he did not know it at the time, the move triggered an association with Ash Close that was to have a major influence on Herbert's life for the next 32 years. His teenage years would be spent there; he would find a wife there; he would live in the same street as a married man; his children would grow up there and from that very same street he would go away to war. He would return to Ash Close after he had survived the mayhem of the trenches. Ash Close was to figure large in his and his family's life.

The new house was not very much bigger than the one they had left in Kings Lynn. It was another two-up-two-down but with the luxury of an outhouse extension on the ground floor. The close family life continued in Swaffham as it had in Kings Lynn with Mum and Dad, the four boys and the two girls all closeted together.

Ash Close was a long narrow street, not much more than an alleyway. (See Appendix Two – Map of Swaffham.) It is still there today although with many new houses on either side. At its southern end it opened right into the centre of Swaffham, to the wide open spaces of the market square which is where the small town lived and breathed. Its northern end leads to Spinners Lane beyond which in 1881 was open countryside, ideal for walking and exploring for adventurous young boys.

Herbert would always think of himself as a Swaffham man. In his mind it was his home. Although he was 10 before he moved there, all his formative years would be spent in the town. He would be 42 years old before he left it. He would become completely socially integrated into the town. His love of football resulted in him having considerable prowess as a goalkeeper. For four years he played for Swaffham Whippets (see Photo 5), the town's premier football side, as indeed did two of his brothers (Alf and Jack). He was, at 5 ft 6 ins tall, slightly above the average height of a man at that time without ever being as tall as would be required by goalkeepers in the modern game. When he was old enough he liked a pint of beer although he rarely drank to excess. He frequented firstly the Oddfellows Arms a few yards away from his home in Ash Close. But the Greyhound in the market square was his local. He sometimes went to the Norfolk Hero. He became competent at many of the pub games played in the evening at that time. He was a dab hand at dominoes, and even late in life, never lost the ability to hold a "full set" in his two hands. He learnt and mastered the game of crib which he enjoyed all his life. All his children would be taught to play and all their children after them. If he had a dozen or more in his hand, he would chuckle heartily, the chuckle getting progressively louder as he laid out his score. "Fifteen two, fifteen four, two is six and six is twelve," he would announce and rap his knuckle on the table if he had one for his knob as well.

His father took on an allotment down Shouldham Lane (see Appendix Two). The allotments are still there, although at the time of writing poorly tended. At that time an allotment was a very important asset indeed to a working man, supplementing the family fare with fresh vegetables and fruit. The young Herbert spent many happy hours with his father learning the ropes. When he grew up, he would have an allotment of his own and all his life would be a very keen gardener, spending hours growing every variety of vegetable imaginable, most of which he would give away.

He became a member of the Baptist Church on Station Road, just a few hundred yards from his home, but he was not a heavily religious man. His religious views were to be overtaken by the emergence at this time of working class political movements, set up to improve the lot of the lower classes. His father had decidedly left wing views which he would pass on to all his children, most of whom would become active in working men's causes. Herbert was somewhat the exception and was never hugely political. His chapel attendance was, I suspect, more to please his mother than through any deep religious conviction. In later life, the experiences of the war years were to eclipse any deep religious conviction.

But we are running ahead in Herbert's story.

On moving to Swaffham, he made pals at his new school down London Road, a few hundred yards from his home. The school took in all the girls and boys from the his part of Swaffham. One of the girls he met there, a year younger than him, was called Rose Drake whose father and mother also lived in Ash Close. Herbert first knew Rose when he was 10. She was one of many children with whom he played and no doubt teased unmercifully. What he thought of her at the time is not recorded. Although he did not know it, little Rose was to play a very large part in his life.

After the family had been living in Swaffham for two years, space in the small terraced house became even more precious. Elizabeth announced that she was pregnant again. She gave birth to her seventh child, christened George, the last of the family. The sixth child, Jane, was by this time five years old, so it is likely that George was what, in those days, was called "an afterthought".

Herbert developed a special relationship with his youngest brother George. He was 12 years old when George was born. George grew up to be a boisterous, spoilt and somewhat mischievous but nevertheless serious thinking young man. Herbert spent a lot of time with him; the elder brother was a playmate to the younger lad. They played football of course, but it is likely that Herbert also protected George against the other boys of the town when that was needed. It was a relationship that was to have poignancy during the dark days of the First World War.

At the age of 14 in 1895, Herbert left school to start work. He was a bright lad, with a rounded education for a working class boy. He could read and write well and had a good grasp of the subjects taught. He always had a very healthy view, picked up from his father, of the power of education in improving the lot of the working poor. But in 1895 any further education was out of the question. It was not even an option. A working class boy needed to learn a trade which would put bread on his table and eventually feed a family. His father was an engine driver and earned a good wage by the standards of the time, and he knew the importance of having a "trade". Herbert's eldest sister Mary, a very bright girl indeed, had not gone into service as was usual for young girls at that time but had stayed at home to become an apprentice to a local dressmaker. His eldest brother, Alf, also still lived at home, and although he was an errand boy, he too would soon pursue a very exotic career indeed.

So Herbert stayed living at home and was apprenticed to a local tailor. Mr Tom Fayers had a tailors shop in Swaffham – that too was in Ash Close, a few doors from Herbert's home. At that time, bespoke tailoring was a very popular sort of tailoring and there was no reason to believe that it would not always be that way. There was no reason to doubt that tailoring would provide a solid income for Herbert all his life. So for the next few years, he, an active, dynamic man, would sit cross-legged at a bench at the back of Fayers' shop in poor light with needle and thread in his hand. He would learn all the skills of tailoring and buttonholes became somewhat of a speciality.

How he hated it. Not for one moment did it give him very much satisfaction. His love was sport and the outdoors. Being cooped up in Fayers' shop must have been "a sort of hell" for him. It was no way for an active young teenager to spend his days.

But this was 1895, in a small agricultural Norfolk town. There was little future in joining the ranks of the agricultural labourers, the lot of most of the young lads that Herbert knew. Being apprentice to a well respected local tailor was a much better option. Little did he know that he would do this for the next 20 years of his life.

In 1899 when Herbert was 16 years old and still living with his parents, his eldest brother, Alf, announced that he would join the army and become a regular soldier. Alf had figured large in Herbert's life up to this time. As his elder brother, most of his growing up had been done with him. They were playmates and confidants. They were brothers and buddies. Alf leaving home affected Herbert a great deal. Alf was a lively lad with a laugh on his lips and a twinkle in his eye. He was fun to be with and all his life would be a leader of men through both his actions and his personality.

It may be that the lack of a trade was a factor in Alf's decision to join up. Maybe it was the effect of the Boer War that was raging in the southern tip of Africa. Maybe the motivation was purely financial. Whatever the reason, Alf not only left home but was very quickly on the other side of the world. For the next seven years, he would see service in India, in Mesopotamia (modern day Iraq) and Malta. He would distinguish himself in India by taking on the role of "teacher" to the children of married soldiers serving there and also to some of the children of government administrators. He would rise to the rank of

Sergeant, no mean achievement for the son of a working class family. Alf had gone from Herbert's life to far-off places, but not forever. In 1905 Alf was to return again to Swaffham. But more dramatically Herbert and Alf would meet in the mud of the Somme and the hell of the trenches of Passchendaele. Their destinies were to be intricately entwined.

In the meantime, Herbert took on the mantle of "eldest son" with all that that entailed. His teenage years and early twenties were happy years spent enjoying the country life in Swaffham. He was of course a regular member of the Swaffham football team, he had a regular if low paid job, he lived with a large supportive family, and he had a large number of friends and acquaintances in the town and the villages around. Money was not abundant but his mother and father made ends meet. His Norfolk life was good.

After 1903 however his life took on some new directions. It was in this year that romance came his way, a romance that was to sustain him for the rest of his days. Rose Drake, or Rosa as Herbert insisted on calling her during their early days together, was a Swaffham girl through and through. We have already observed she went to the same local school as Herbert. She had been born in the town in 1882 and when the romance started she was 21 years old. Her father was Alfred Drake. He was both illegitimate and illiterate and became a self-employed agricultural worker, a somewhat unusual status in a time when all agricultural labourers were employed by the large estates in the area. Alfred was an odd job man who could turn his hand to just about anything, and did. As well as working in the fields, on what we would now call a freelance basis, he was known to dash walnuts from the local trees, or help on thrashing machines, or hire out his horse and cart that he kept in a nearby barn. He was a skilled thatcher and sheep clipper and was a familiar figure on Swaffham market selling walnuts and mellow pears He also tended an allotment.[4]

---

4   His obituary in the *Eastern Daily Press* in 1942 read as follows –

Born at Wyndham in 1850, Alfred could remember the last train leaving the station with open carriages. He worked in Middlesbrough in a chemical works and had been a navvy, farm labourer, thatcher and sheep clipper. He was a familiar figure on Swaffham market place where he sold walnuts and "mellow pears". He married when earning only 10 shillings a week and had 14 children of which only four survived him. He helped in the construction of the railway from

Alfred Drake was a character, a free spirit, beholden to nobody. He earned a satisfactory living nevertheless, at a time when agricultural labourers were poor and struggled to support their families. He had married Alice Alexander from the nearby village of Beachamwell. Local gossip suggested that Alfred Drake had married above his station (Alice's brother was the butler at Beachamwell Hall) but that would not have bothered Alfred very much. They had five children that survived infancy, Arthur, Ted, Rose, Emma and Maud. All were to play important parts in Herbert's life and in Herbert's war.

Rose was a small, almost diminutive young lady. She had a very pretty, round face and was slim in build. She was a gentle soul, with a very strong artistic tendency. In later life she would write and publish poetry. She would sing in choirs and tell stories to the children. But beneath the soft exterior was a very strong backbone indeed. In the family, it would be Rose that would be the one that would discipline the children, take care of the house, watch over their education, and set the standards. Her outward appearance belied an inner strength. Her parents, in their own way, had passed onto her a soft, gentle demeanour and a powerful determination.

On leaving school Rose had "gone into service" as did most young girls at that time. We are fortunate that she kept many of the postcards that she received so there is a beguiling and complete record of her early life. She worked as a maid at various country homes, Kelling Heath, Wells-next-the-Sea and at Panworth Hall in the nearby village of Ash Hill. She went home to Swaffham to be with Herbert whenever she could.

She starts referring to Herbert in endearing terms in 1903 and they were boyfriend and girlfriend in Swaffham for the next four years. It was a remarkably long courtship by contemporary standards. Whether Herbert was dragging his heels about popping the question; whether his life as a bachelor in an active

---

Swaffham to Watton and helped to lay the first pavements in Swaffham. He often talked of cock-fighting and bare fist fighting. He remembered when inn floors were covered with straw and how two bears once killed a number of sheep at Mundford. His grandmother used to drive geese from Ashill to London for the Christmas market by road, the journey taking a fortnight each way.

lively country town was too good to give up; whether Rose did not want to rush things; we shall never know.

Meanwhile other events were overshadowing Herbert's life. In 1906, his mother died of cancer of the womb. Elizabeth had been in bad health for some time. Almost continuous childbearing over the last 12 years had taken its toll. Before her death, Alfred took Elizabeth and the family away from Ash Close in Swaffham and moved 20 miles north to Wells-next-the-Sea, a very attractive small seaside town on the North Norfolk coast. Elizabeth's health might have been a factor in the move but it is more likely that it was motivated by Alfred's job as Wells was on the local railway line. Herbert did not go. Instead he took digs with Mr Fayers, his employer. He rented a room above the shop where he could stay close to his job and be close to Rose.

And so for the first time since those far away days in Kings Lynn, the family was beginning to separate. Alf was abroad, and Herbert was living away from his Mum and Dad. He was independent, on his own, in charge of his life. And he was courting his Rosa.

His mother finally succumbed to her cancer. The impact of his mother's death on Herbert is not recorded. His father was the dominant figure in his early life but there is no reason not to believe that he had much love for his Mum. She had cared well for her growing family and had been ever present in family life on the many occasions when Alfred's job took him away from the house.

A few months after his mother's death, Herbert had another surprise of a very different kind. Rose let it be known that she was pregnant. She confided firstly to her sister Emma with whom she was very close and then informed Herbert. It was some time before Rose plucked up the courage to tell her parents. It must have been a bombshell. In 1906 pregnancy out of wedlock was not uncommon but, unlike today, carried a huge social stigma which could blight a young girl's life for years to come. Even less acceptable was a child born outside of marriage. A baby born illegitimately – the word itself tells its own story – could carry a mark for the rest of its life. In a small country town like Swaffham this was especially true and there would be no escape from wagging tongues.

19

Herbert himself would want to "do the right thing". Parents, especially his father, would have also had a very strong "point of view". So in March 1907 Herbert Barnes married Rose Drake at somewhat short notice.

In spite of this inauspicious start, the marriage was to be strong and last for 53 years.

There were no cameras at the wedding at Swaffham church so we have no pictures of the smiling bride, of the very proud bridegroom or of the extensive Barnes and Drake family gathered around the happy couple. Or of the many young men and women of Swaffham who came along. It might well be that there was nobody who owned a camera. It is much more likely that as Rose was six months pregnant the wedding had been arranged somewhat hurriedly and it was decided to forego an official photographer.

1907 was very much "a year of weddings" for Herbert. Later the same year, his father, no doubt feeling the loneliness of a widower, married his housekeeper Ethel Catchpole. He was 54 years old, she was only 31. Herbert would no doubt have been surprised and possibly offended that someone had taken his mother's place so quickly but Aunt Ethel, as she would now be called, was a vivacious, fun loving woman and Herbert quickly warmed to her. Their relationship would always be good. Amazingly, Herbert's father and his second wife would enjoy a very long marriage which provided another seven children over the next 14 years, all of them half-brothers and half-sisters to Herbert. The family even by Edwardian standards was now very large indeed, although the second family in Wells would always be separate and more distant to Herbert than his own brothers and sisters.

Equally amazingly, the marriage ceremony was a "double wedding". Herbert's younger brother John, now called Jack by one and all, also tied the knot on the same day in the same church at Wells. He married Alice Mitchell, a local girl. So father and son were married together in the same ceremony. There is no obvious explanation for this occurrence other than one of practicalities. Weddings were joyous occasions but they were also expensive for working class families. It was probably convenient and economical for all concerned to share the expense of the family event.

And it did not end there. Before the year was out, Herbert's elder and much beloved brother, Alf, had also tied the knot. He had returned from India in 1906 with his Sergeant's stripes on his arm and had left the army after seven years service to take up the trade of a painter and had met and married Florence Bullen, yet another Swaffham girl. But Alfred, ever the leader, had his own ceremony. There was to be no sharing there.

So 1907 had seen the beginning of married life for Herbert, Herbert's brothers Alfred and Jack, and the beginning of a second marriage for Herbert's father. It was a time for settling down, for bringing up children, for a stable and steady life. The boys who had grown up together in Kings Lynn and Swaffham had now all married and set up households of their own, all in Swaffham. The future stretched ahead of them in a very planned way. It meant having a family, holding down a manual job, earning a living and enjoying the many pleasures of family life. That is what their parents had done and that is what they would do. They had no way of knowing, neither was there any indication, that within a few years a very dark storm cloud indeed would darken their lives.

Rose and Herbert began married life in White Hart Lane, now called Cley Road, which they took over from Rose's parents who moved to Ash Close. The married home was very small but situated only 20 yards from the bustling market square. And of course within three months the first child was born. Herbert was delighted for it was a boy. As was customary for the age, boys were held in higher esteem than girls and Herbert was a man of his time. Naming him was easy as Herbert's father was Alfred and Rose's father was George – so Alfred George it was. Everybody was happy and satisfied.

There was little understanding or practice of contraception at this time, so Rose was quickly pregnant again but this time the happiness of the young married couple was severely dented. The new baby was a girl, christened Ruby, but she was a sickly child and died within a week of birth from influenza, a virulent killer at the time. The couple must have been grief-stricken even though infant mortality at the turn of the century was more commonplace than it is today. They had lost their second born. For the rest of his life Herbert rarely talked about the loss and Rose referred to the whole episode only with pain and distress.

However, Rose was soon pregnant again and in 1909 Phyllis was born (see Photo 7). She was, thank God, a healthy robust little girl. The family was growing and Herbert and Rose moved back to their beloved Ash Close. They rented a small house in a yard off Ash Close called Oddfellows Yard because it was situated behind the Oddfellows Arms. The yard was also called Spinks Yard after the surname of the landlord at the pub. There, in quick succession, two more children were born. Bert who was named after his father and Ted named after his Uncle. Herbert named the boys with well-established family names – while Rose named the girls with "names she liked". It was a fine illustration of their differing characters.

Life was now set for Herbert. He had a regular job, a loving wife, and four growing healthy children. He was by now in his 30s, with a happy family living in a small town that he knew very well. He had a wide circle of friends and the support of a large and loving family. He was content.

Not being a man who wrote much at all, Herbert never recorded his memories of this period of his life. However his third child Bert did. Bert was a fun loving character with a wonderful mischievous sense of humour and was perhaps Herbert's favourite child. Father and son had many similar traits. Later in life he captured what family life in Ash Close before the First World War was like and committed it to paper. It is perhaps worth dwelling on Bert's recollections as they draw a picture of Herbert's happy family life before the War:

I was born in Ash Close, Swaffham in the year 1911 in a little 4 roomed cottage at the bottom end of Oddfellows Yard, or Spinks Yard as it was usually called. The Oddfellows Arms public house stood at the entrance to the yard and the landlord was one Tom Spinks. I have no real memory of him, but I remember his wife. I had an extreme dislike of her as whenever we were unlucky enough to kick our ball over the high back doors she would keep it, and they were hard to come by in those days. The yard consisted of a row of cottages, 8 in all I think. Our family was fortunate in having a front and back yard which gave us a certain prestige. The rent was 2s/6d per week which I know took a bit of finding. Ash Close had 2 other yards, Well Yard and Cock Yard and to venture into either of these invited danger.

My father, Herbert Barnes, was apprenticed as a tailor with Mr Tom Fayers whose business was in Ash Close. Mr Fayers was a huge fellow and his wife a tiny woman. We all liked her. She would give me a penny now and again. There was a son, Ben Fayers who ran a wood business in the close. Sometimes my father would take me round to the workshop and I would sit on a little stool watching the tailors sewing away up on the bench, and take cotton reels home to play with as toys.

Life was hard for us in Ash Close; we lived in a state of semi poverty. My father was never very highly paid and my mother was ever at her wits end to find us all enough food and clothes. Most of the responsibility of bringing us up fell upon her. She would mend our boots and shoes. I would go to the saddlers for 6 pennorth of leather enough for 2 pairs and he would give me a few clates for heels and toes. She would cut our hair and alter clothes given to her by charitable people and even did the whitewashing and distempering. She worked from morning to night. We would hear the sound of her hammering away at our boots sometimes after midnight. She was a very good cook and knew how to utilise every scrap in the way of food. A sheep's head was 6d, a few scraps from the butcher for 2d and a bucket of pigs belly's we could collect free. Every Saturday night she would send one of us to the confectioners for 6d of stale buns. The lady would give us a generous bag full. We always had plenty of vegetables, that was one thing my father did really well, he was a good gardener. His allotment was down Gashouse Lane. I would spend many happy hours with him there. In those early days a close bond grew between us which was to last until he died. Every year he grew a long row of sweet peas which mother would bunch with a few carrot leaves for decoration and I tramped round the houses Saturday morning selling them at 1d per bunch.

Mother would sing to us in the evening after washing us and getting us ready for bed. We were always clean and tidy. She had a good singing voice and managed to have a few evenings out at the Baptist Chapel singing in the chorus and this must have been a great outlet for her. She wrote poetry and could recite beautifully.

My father would play games with us before he went out for the evening. We liked the ringboard. There was an unending supply of rings taken from potted meat jars. Halma and draughts were played. And with him we had to play hard. He would have no messing about. He was a keen sportsman and played in goal for Swaffham Whippets. He played quoits which was popular before bowls took over. He often brought home joints of meat, given by local butchers as prizes, and which my mother must have welcomed.

We were all avid readers and all loved reading Childrens Newspaper and My Magazine. I remember some of the stories to this day. Our parents never bought us comics but we usually managed to get hold of copies of Rainbow and Tiger Tim from somewhere.

You can just imagine how crowded we were in our tiny living room, sometimes 6 of us and when the chimney smoked as it often did, we would cough and splutter. The front room was out of bounds all week but on Sundays we had tea in there and father played his penny whistle and accompanied us for singing hymns.

Our highlight was to walk round to Grandfather Drake's house Sunday evenings. We were only allowed one at each visit so had to take turns. He had a grandfather's clock standing in the corning of the front room and it seemed so cosy with the clock ticking away and watching the flames flickering from the wood fire. Grandfather liked a game of dominoes. He couldn't read or write but he knew his dominoes. He owned a piece of land in Ash Close with sheds and a stable and a white pony which looked all skin and bone. I remember riding on his pony and cart to the Dry Mare down the Cley Road to bring home a load of hay.

My Uncle Alf, my father's brother lived in Ash Close then and I remember sitting in his back garden during the summer evenings listening to his gramophone. It had a huge horn and it needed winding up for each record. I would be completely enraptured and still enjoy listening to those tunes even now.

Another entertainment that gave us great pleasure and excitement was our "magic lantern" which consisted of a coloured tin box which contained a small paraffin lamp and magnifying glass. The glass slides depicted various scenes and comical characters and mother would invite children from the yard to form an audience in our living room always a great event.

I have several clear memories of life in Spink's Yard. Like having the photographer call to have our "likenesses" taken, a very rare occasion as our parents couldn't afford that luxury too often. Pushing an old pram to the coal yard at the station to get coal brick made chiefly of coal dust and some kind of cement. Gathering conkers from the horse chestnut trees around the recreation ground. Attending the Baptist Chapel in Station Street. A cormorant alighting on the weather vane of Swaffham Church remaining there for quite a while and attracting a great deal of attention. A large van parked on the marketplace advertising the attractiveness of emigrating to Canada, and giving out brochures with beautiful pictures. And most of all, the summer Sunday School treat held on a field on Mr Larwood's farm down Sporles Road. That was a great day with sports and swings on the trees and tea on the grass. But the most thrilling, never to be forgotten experience of all my childhood in Ash Close, without any doubt, was the first Sunday School outing to Hunstanton.

Herbert and Rose were settled in Ash Close. Bert's description of family life with his mother and father, brothers and sisters is far from idyllic but nevertheless captures the happiness and contentment of the family. No daily newspaper was delivered to Ash Close and as far as we know there was no radio set in the home at this time. So Herbert would have taken some time to hear about the assassination of a member of the Hapsburg Royal family in a far off place called Sarajevo. And even if he had heard he wouldn't have cared much; he would have thought it had nothing to do with him or his family or his way of life in a small market town called Swaffham in Norfolk.

He would have been very wrong.

CHAPTER 3

THE MAKING OF A TOMMY

NOVEMBER 1915–APRIL 1916

Herbert's first night as a soldier was spent in a bunk in the austere surroundings of the Britannia Barracks. It was a very cold night, the temperature dropped to close to freezing and sleep came somewhat fitfully. There was no fragrant Rose next to him now. The regular breathing of his four children in the next room was replaced by the sounds of hundreds of men sleeping, snoring and grunting their way through the night. He knew that some of them would become his pals. As he lay there, feeling homesick for Swaffham and feeling apprehensive about his future, he might well have been reviewing in his mind why he had enlisted in the first place. There was no obligation for him to do so. He could have stayed in Swaffham. Why had he taken such a momentous decision?

Herbert Barnes was a volunteer. The British Army in November 1915 could boast upwards of one and a half million men and all were volunteers. It was by far and away the largest volunteer army in the history of our country. So what on earth persuaded a 34-year-old father of four to leave his home and family and go fight for his King and Country, possibly never to return?

The war was 15 months old. The euphoria of 1914 and "it will all be over by Christmas" had long since faded. The army had recruited young, fit men, to fight a short war. As Christmas 1914 passed, the news from the Western Front had been almost uniformly bad. Germany had successfully invaded France. Her troops had only been halted as they knocked on the door of Paris. A line of trenches stretched 250 miles from the Channel coast to Switzerland. The two sides confronted each other across a no-man's-land only a few hundred yards wide. The armies supported by the industrial might of Germany, France and Britain dug into defences which were unprecedented in their depth and strength. By the summer of 1915 a sort of stalemate had been achieved.

In September–October 1915 the British attempted to break through the German front line at Loos. They incurred some 50,000 casualties, and the British High Command learnt a salutary lesson. They came to realise that this was going to be a long war. It was going to be a war of attrition, and what's more, a war won by the side which could get the most, best supported, soldiers into the front line. It was going to take at least a million more men.

Kitchener's drive to recruit a million-strong volunteer army – known as the "New Army" and often referred to as "Kitchener's Army" – is well documented and there is no need to recount it here. Recruitment officers were sent to every part of the country – to market places, to town halls and to football grounds. Indeed to anywhere and everywhere that they could get their message across. They reached into the far flung corners of the British Empire, to India, Australia, New Zealand, South Africa and Canada. Never before had there been a recruitment drive quite so extensive. The famous poster of the crusty old Lord Kitchener pointing his finger at the man in the street and commanding "your country needs you" is indelibly printed into the national consciousness. But of course it was not the only poster – there were many hundreds of them – on billboards, lampposts, notice boards and in newspapers (see Photo 8). The posters were persuasive. Some of them were very direct. All of them demanded that it was the duty of every able-bodied man to enlist. Many of them went even further. They hinted that able-bodied men in civilian clothing were guilty of cowardice or were in some way unpatriotic. They commanded that "every fit Briton should join our brave men at the front". The pressure was intense.

Herbert listened to the recruitment officer when he addressed the townsmen from the Cross in Swaffham market square. He saw all the posters. He read the billboards. He felt the intense pressure of the campaign and the loud call for him to do his national duty.

The social impact of the campaign was equally intense. By the end of 1915, public opinion did not look favourably on able-bodied men under the age of 40 who were not in uniform. In every town, the length and breadth of the nation, whispering campaigns were afoot. As the casualties of the war increased, it was not uncommon for civilian men to be spat upon on the street or cursed as they passed by. The white feather was in evidence in the big cities. Men who refused to join the army for conscientious reasons, or "conshies" as they were called, were universally vilified and sometimes physically attacked. The social pressure to volunteer was evident to all.

Herbert felt that pressure. Over a pint of beer in the Greyhound pub in Swaffham marketplace or in the Baptist Church on Station Street, or down at the Whippets Football Club, tongues would be wagging. Most of the younger men in the places that Herbert frequented had already left and gone to war. Most of his friends who lived in Ash Close had already left for the front. Of course Herbert was older than all of them but it gave him much food for thought. Neighbours were asking questions.

Perhaps the most overriding influence on Herbert's decision came from his own family. By June of 1915, three of his brothers and his two brothers-in-law were already in uniform. At the outbreak of the war in 1914, his elder brother Alf (see Photo 9) had rejoined the Suffolk Regiment that he had left in 1907 and was now a part of the 8th Battalion. As an experienced soldier with military training who had seen service abroad, he had immediately rejoined at the outbreak of the war. Herbert's youngest brother George (see photo 10) had volunteered on the first day war was declared. He was 20 years old. He had joined the Norfolk Regiment but in 1915 was posted to the Gloucestershire Regiment. In early 1915 Jack (see Photo 11) the third of the four boys, volunteered and enlisted into the 8th Battalion the Norfolk Regiment. Only Charlie had stayed a civilian as he was an engine driver, just like his dad, and as such was in a reserved profession. Of the five brothers who had grown up together and had been so close, three were already in the trenches. That fact alone would have played on Herbert's mind.

Rose did not want him to go. As a mother of four young children her every wish would be to keep Herbert at home and safe. Two of her three brothers had already enlisted (see Appendix One). Ted was a machine-gunner with the Royal Field Artillery on the Western Front. The youngest, Alexander, who everybody called Alec, had joined the Horse Artillery and had already been posted to Egypt. Only her eldest brother Arthur had not joined up for the tragic reason that he had contracted dropsy (oedema) and died in Kings Lynn Hospital in 1914. However, his son, Cecil, Rose's nephew, was old enough to enlist and was on his way to France. It did not end there. Rose's sister Maud had married and her husband, a man by the name of William (Bill) Brundle, was already in France. All the men in Rose's family with a very few exceptions had "gone to war".

Even so, she did not want Herbert to go.

Once Herbert had made up his mind, Rose's opinion did not count for much. This was 1915 – it was a man's world where decisions for all the family were made by men. Rose had to accept whatever Herbert decided. After they had said their tearful goodbyes at Swaffham Station, she trudged back to Ash Close with lowered head and a sad countenance. The impact of losing the man she loved, perhaps temporarily, perhaps for ever, stayed vividly in her mind for the rest of her life. Many years later she wrote a poem which captured the confused and troubled thoughts she had at this poignant moment (see Appendix Three).

Herbert perhaps also knew that his going to war was inevitable. Conscription was indeed introduced in the early months of 1916 and was being extensively discussed at the time Herbert made his decision. He must have known that sooner or later he would be called. The tugging loyalties between family and duty had swung firmly to the side of duty. Certainly, had he discussed his decision with his father, he would have been firmly pointed in the direction of the Britannia Barracks.

Next morning, Herbert fell in on the drill square armed with nothing more than an elongated piece of wood. He had begun the process that would over the next six months transform him from being a gentle, loving, family man with four children, to a combat soldier capable of killing an enemy in hand to hand fighting. It was, as one would say today, a big ask. He would find it arduous in the extreme and at times extremely distasteful. Killing was against every value that he held – every value that he had been taught by his parents in his upbringing. Caring for others and obeying the law were part of his make-up. It was the ethic of his family. How could he possibly now, at his age, go and kill another man? Training these new recruits was a challenge that the British Army in 1915 needed to confront. Like thousands of other men, Herbert needed to be trained to kill.

That first morning, he was told that he would become part of the 3rd Battalion of the Norfolk Regiment. This was one of the regiment's two training battalions to which all new recruits were sent. It was based over the border in Suffolk at the coastal town of Felixstowe. Herbert was on the move.

The next day, he set out to cover the one mile to Norwich's Thorpe Station. He was catching another train. But this time he did not stroll in civilian clothes as he had two days before. He marched in step, in strict order, through the streets of Norwich – down Ketts Hill and along Riverside Road to the station. He was in uniform, with officers barking orders and a kit bag on his shoulder. People watched as they marched by. It was a sight to which the people of Norwich were well used. Some might have clapped, or shouted an encouraging word. Most paid little attention. He boarded the train. It was most likely crowded with new recruits mixed with civilians going about their wartime business. He probably stood in the corridor as the train chugged through the South Norfolk countryside. It passed through Diss and then to Stowmarket, through Ipswich and finally to Felixstowe. He was used to trains. That was something he knew about. His father had spent half his life on them. It was just as well. In the next three years he was to experience many uncomfortable and painful train journeys.

The 3rd Battalion of the Norfolk Regiment was part of the Harwich Garrison. It was based at the old Landguard Fort which protrudes into the estuary of the Stour and Orwell rivers. The battalion was part of the special reserve brigade which also included battalions from Suffolk, Essex, Bedford and Lancashire. Herbert was meeting new people – men who came from all over the country. He was, for the first time in his life, mixing with men who spoke differently to him – men who had very different backgrounds and came from all walks of life. He was getting to know the good, the bad and the ugly of British manhood. Over the next three years his homely, small country town attitudes would change –

he would become worldly, more aware, more rounded. He would get a little tougher.

The 3rd Battalion had two purposes. The first was to lend a hand in the defence of the nation against possible invasion by German forces. Such garrisons were positioned around the country, nearly all in coastal locations. Harwich's area of patrol was the Suffolk and Essex coast north and south of the old fort. It seems almost silly now, given the stalemate of the Western Front, to think that the high command considered an invasion a possibility, but in 1915 the fear was very real. The coasts of this island had to be defended.

Indeed, while Herbert was at Felixstowe, a great daylight bombing raid took place on the fleet anchored in Harwich Harbour. Seventeen German aeroplanes swooped low over the area, the first major airborne attack on this nation. Casualties were incurred amongst both soldiers and civilians. Ten days later the Germans came again in a second and much more severe raid. More casualties were incurred although the men from Norfolk escaped into their defences and were largely untouched. For Herbert this was a totally unexpected and premature introduction to the risks of war.

Most of the duties of the battalion consisted of the tedious task of building and reinforcing coastal defences and marshalling the population. Much of the coastal area was lined by deeply dug trenches, the first line of defence against an attack by the Boche. Herbert must at times have thought that he had reverted to being a Norfolk agricultural labourer with spade, shovel and pickaxe. It was hard physical labour and Herbert was determined to keep up with much younger men in his platoon. He did not yet know that digging trenches and excavating foxholes was to be critical to survival in the months to come.

The second role of the battalion was that of training new recruits to go to war. To quote the official history of the Norfolk Regiment:

> ... the role of the training battalions during the period of the war is a
> monotonous one. It took men, trained men and sent men to the various theatres
> of war. And all the time it had to maintain itself as a defensive fighting unit in

case the coast was invaded. Many of these men, it was destined never to see again, unless, returning maimed and worn out, they drifted back to Felixstowe.

Herbert was one of thousands. He was one of the many new recruits to pass through Felixstowe. The 3rd Battalion, the Norfolk Regiment alone trained over 700 officers and nearly 19,000 other ranks for service in France, Mesopotamia and Gallipoli and other theatres around the world. Not all the men came from Norfolk. Many were from London and the West Country where enlistment offices were being overwhelmed and men were sent to Norwich for purely practical reasons. But come they did, the product of the biggest recruitment drive in the history of the British Army. If the accusation of "cannon fodder" is in any way justified, then the training battalions were where the fodder seed was grown.

In November 1915, the Harwich Garrison was home to over 10,000 soldiers, sailors, airmen. The area was a hive of activity with men and their equipment hustling and bustling from fort to dockside, from camps to billets, from recreation huts to canteens. Herbert had never seen so many people, so much activity, and so much machinery. Felixstowe harbour was the most secure deep water harbour between the Thames and the Humber, and the biggest Royal Navy destroyer base on the east coast. Hundreds of boats were riding at anchor in the bay. Felixstowe was also a seaplane base. It is very possible that Herbert had never seen a plane before and if he had, certainly not in these large numbers. He was wide-eyed and incredulous. It was a long way indeed from Swaffham where the biggest crowd he had ever seen was a few hundred men gathered around the Cross in the market place.

As the train pulled into the station, he saw and sensed the quickening of the pace of his life. The new recruits were marched to one of the major temporary camps on the east side of the town quite close to Landguard Fort itself. He could not help but notice that the fort itself was bristling with heavy guns pointing out to sea and across the harbour. How long he stayed in these temporary huts is not clear – they were crowded and extremely uncomfortable – but what is clear is that he was quite quickly billeted to live with a local family (see Photo 12). This was common practice at the time. Many thousands of soldiers were parcelled out at night to stay with families who lived in the back streets of the town. Unfortunately, we have no record of where he stayed or with whom he stayed but we do know that his billets were to the north of Felixstowe in the suburb of Walton. The area was very reminiscent of his first home in Kirby Street in Kings Lynn – long terraces of two-up-two-down houses with outhouses to the rear. Herbert spoke very fondly of his days in billets. In comparison to the mass anonymity of the large huts and camps, the friendliness and homely care of an ordinary bed in an ordinary home was very acceptable. A little home cooking and freshly laundered sheets never went amiss and it reminded him of home. But there was scant comfort in it all. Everybody knew that this was the lull before the storm. These were the last home comforts that he would have for some little time. The ladies who provided billets knew that too and most went out of their way to give their men hearty food even in war-torn Britain. For many, it would be the last they would ever have.

With so many soldiers gathered together in one place, it is not surprising that the army made every effort to entertain and distract the men from the peril of their situation. Herbert knew that this was not France, but it was a staging point to going to France. He frequented the YMCA recreational huts that had been erected for the troops. There were four of them in the Felixstowe area. They were large, single storey structures that could provide entertainment for 200 to 300 men at a time. The YMCA organised soccer matches, darts competitions, domino and card evenings, whist and beetle drives – exactly the sort of thing that Herbert was used to doing back in Swaffham. It was not the Greyhound but it was the next best thing. He enjoyed the competition, he liked the camaraderie. He developed friendships. His initial apprehension began to fade a little. He learnt that in their shared hardship, the men bonded together very quickly, and with one or two exceptions supported and helped one another. Herbert learnt that he was not alone. He was one of many, all of whom had to confront their own demons in the best way they knew how.

The YMCA also provided refreshment for the soldiers when they were not on duty – a sort of home from home. The Salvation Army was also there in force. They too had huts (see Photo 13) and huge marquees to provide entertainment and comfort for the men. They provided of course devotional activities – the men needed to look after their souls – and they also organised recreational evenings in a number of locations around the town. Herbert was not much interested in the Salvation Army church services but he did frequent the huts to play games and to attend concerts. He loved the sing-alongs and was popular because he could knock out a tune on his penny whistle. He also found that being a competent tailor, a trade that he had never really liked, now had real benefits. A man who was skilled in sewing was always in demand. When his colleagues ripped off buttons or tore their uniforms, they knew that Bogey Barnes could fix them. His mending skills, together with his ability to play a dab hand of crib, meant that Herbert was never short of tobacco for his pipe.

For the next six months in Felixstowe and the surrounding countryside Herbert was trained to be a soldier and his training was intense and comprehensive. It has been argued that Kitchener's New Army was an untrained army. It is just not true. Of course, it was inexperienced – the new recruits had never performed under fire before. However it was very well trained, at least in the theory of land warfare as it was understood at that time. Nearly all the men received upwards of six months' training before they went into action. Only men with special skills who were urgently required in the trenches – drivers, engineers, sappers – were hurried across to France. The rest were trained first to be a soldier and then afterwards to fight and kill. Herbert Barnes was no exception.

The methodology of training men for war was remarkably straightforward and, some would argue, had changed little over the years. Admit it or not, basic training was aimed at breaking the will of the new recruit so that he would follow orders without question or hesitation. The technique was nothing short of humiliation – a deluge of verbal abuse and derogatory remarks. The objective was that the soldier should subjugate his own will to that of the unit he was in and the commander who commanded it. The success of the platoon, or company, depended on the men acting together quickly and effectively against a defined objective.

There is no doubt that Herbert found this very hard. He was a man who had his own self-respect. He had belief in his own capabilities and values. What's more, he was 34 years old, and the head of a household. At this stage in his life, to bury his own emotions, to subjugate his own free will, to put aside his own judgement was challenging in the extreme. To have a non-commissioned officer hold his face a few inches away and yell orders at him was gruelling. And not to respond – well that was something that was very difficult to get used to. The first few weeks at Felixstowe were miserable.

But get used to it he did. His records show that he adapted remarkably well. As far as is known, there were no issues with Herbert Edward Barnes. He gradually became a competent, effective soldier by the standards of the time. The transformation in a few months was remarkable. He had very little option and he knew that. He had to subject his own individual will to the collective "esprit de corps". He had to conform each time and every time. He was in the British Army.

Discipline was further imposed by the constant repetition on the drill square. Herbert, along with his new colleagues, spent hour after hour square bashing until he thought he would lose his mind. He repeatedly went on forced marches across the Suffolk countryside with the constant vocal bombardment of the drill sergeant in his ears. He became very fit, and he shed excess weight. His chest expanded by around two inches. He became more muscular. His diet improved and he became stronger. He got used to the unending rota of fatigues. He learnt to clean, to scrub, to polish, to wash. (In later life, his family never saw him in anything other than sparkling boots in which you could "see your face".) It must have been hard. He was a man who had never taken naturally to household chores back in Ash Close. He had definitely viewed all that as women's work. Rose would no doubt not have believed that such a change could take place. But the army was the army and Herbert quickly learnt to do what he was told and to do it well.

He would have very much endorsed a description given by a soldier colleague of Herbert's in a letter sent home from Felixstowe in 1916:

We are always scrubbing floors, forming fours, doing 160 paces per minute in the square, brushing boots every hour from 5am until 7.30pm when we are free to write up notes until 9.30pm. We are called miscellaneous names by sergeants who know nothing. It is a dog's life. Many men stated that they would prefer to be in France in the trenches.

Part of the methodology was to provoke constant frustration and harassment amongst the recruits, keeping them busy, always giving men just that little bit less time than they felt they needed, engendering discipline through routine. Herbert would get used to hearing "come on, quick, quick, quick, you're on parade in two minutes, rush, rush, rush". He was always being rushed, pushed like mad to get things done. He never had a moment's peace. How he must have hated it and how hard he must have had to work on his own state of mind in order to become a good productive soldier. How he must have struggled with himself, and to have yearned for the peaceful loving life he had had at Swaffham.

Of course the men doing the training knew very little of the conditions in France. A contemporary photograph of the officers of the 3rd Battalion (see Photo 14) shows a group of stern-faced, unsmiling, unsympathetic, upper class gentlemen, most of them in their 40s. They were nearly all retired officers and NCOs called back into the army. Very few had seen action and for those that had, it was in the Boer War, 16 years previously. So the drill and tactics were seriously out of date. The blind were definitely leading the blind. It was not until later that men returned from the trenches were able to bring more reality to the training battalions. They had the experience to update the training manuals to reflect conditions on the real battlefield.

But in 1915 Herbert did not know that. He just did as he was told – and hated every minute of it.

Photo 1: *Herbert and Rose Barnes in the front garden at Burntstalks.*

Photo 2: *Herbert Barnes in his postman's uniform braving a snowdrift outside Burntsalks in Docking.*

Photo 3: *The Cutter Inn on the river front at Ely during the floods of 1918. The house in which Herbert was born is just to the left of this view.*

THE OLD makes way for the new in Kirby Street, Lynn, as a bulldozer gets to work. (OC 7891).

All change in Kirby St

FAMILIES who moved out of their homes in the Kirby Street area of Lynn to make way for demolition will be given the chance to move back to the area when it has been redeveloped.

The area of terraced houses comprising Kirby Street, part of Stanley Street, Bedford Street and part of Marshall Street is a slum clearance area.

The site will be redeveloped with a building of 28 two-storey units which will probably be similar in design to the Queen Street flats.

A spokesman for West Norfolk Council said that promises have been made to people who moved out of the Kirby Street area that they can be rehoused in the new scheme.

A general brief has been given to the architects who will put forward a scheme or schemes for the council to consider.

When the council decides on a definite scheme it is expected that work will start in March 1977. The contract will last 18 months.

The scheme will provide accommodation for old people and there will also probably be provision for single people.

Photo 4: *The demolishing of Kirby Street in Kings Lynn in 1976 as reported in the Kings Lynn Advertiser. Herbert's childhood home stood approximately where the digger is positioned.*

Photo 5: *Swaffham Whippets football team in 1902. Herbert stands at the back. His younger brother, Jack, is seated on the right.*

Photo 6: *Herbert as an auxiliary postman in 1922. The photograph was taken on Empire Day at the entrance to Spinks Yard. Herbert's youngest daughter Ivy is on his shoulders.*

Photo 7: *Rose Barnes with her children Alfred and Phyllis. This picture was taken in 1911 in Spinks Yard.*

Photo 8: *A selection of posters from 1915 exhorting young men to enlist in the volunteer army.*

Photo 9: *Sergeant Alfred Negus Barnes of the 8th Suffolks, Herbert's elder brother and mentor.*

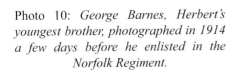

Photo 10: *George Barnes, Herbert's youngest brother, photographed in 1914 a few days before he enlisted in the Norfolk Regiment.*

Photo 11: *Private John (Jack) Barnes, Herbert's younger brother photographed in 1915 in the uniform of the Norfolk Regiment.*

Photo 12: *Soldiers billeted in Walton, a suburb of Felixstowe. Herbert Barnes spent 6 months in billets such as these during his time with the 3rd Battalion, the Norfolk Regiment.*

Photo 13: *The Salvation Army's Soldiers Rest at Felixstowe where Herbert spent many happy hours before being shipped to France.*

Photo 14: *The Officers of the 3rd Battalion the Norfolk Regiment photographed in 1916. These were the men who trained Herbert to be a "Tommy".*

Photo 15 – Open Wagon troop trains: *Troops en route to the front in open wagon troop trains. Herbert used this form of transport on his first journey to the front line.*

Photo 16 – Railway embankment at Ovillers: *A modern view of the railway embankment at Aveluy where Herbert and the 7th Battalion Norfolk Regiment took cover on 1 July 1916.*

But square-bashing, doing fatigues, and cleaning boots "does not a soldier make". Learning and accepting army discipline is one thing, becoming an effective fighting man quite another. The second stage of training for Herbert at Felixstowe was aimed at turning him into an effective aggressor, ready to fight when he finally confronted the foe. Yes, there was still the daily dose of physical jerks but now it was interspersed with walking in and out of gas chambers, with gas respirators clamped over his head. (Gas attacks were a new and deadly form of warfare first used by the Germans in January 1915, and the use of gas shells was by now a common occurrence on the Western Front.) Herbert was trained to manipulate sheets of iron and steel standing in narrow trenches as other soldiers poured liquid flame over him. He was instructed how to charge a trench and throw live bombs into it, bombs that would obliterate five men at a time. Officers, who incidentally had never used them in anger themselves, showed him how to throw Mills grenades – how and when to pull the pin, how to count to two, how to get the elevation right, how to accurately judge distances. And of course he was instructed on how to use the bayonet, that most fearsome of weapons, used only when the enemy soldier was in touching distance. The gentle man from Swaffham learnt how to rush a bale of straw, savagely yelling at the top of his voice, baring his teeth to subdue and cower the enemy. He was encouraged to "go for the chest" and never, never, to hold back. And he learnt to do it well because he was told over and over again that one day soon it might well be a matter of life and death.

Finally, he was taught to shoot. The standard equipment of the period was the Short Magazine Lee-Enfield (SMLE) rifle. Herbert had certainly never owned a gun and probably never used one. Shoots on the large Norfolk estates around Swaffham were common events and the young Herbert had often earned himself some extra coppers by being a beater. But he had never owned a gun of his own. He took to it readily and was, by all reports, a good marksman. But he never liked guns and in later life held them in contempt and would have nothing to do with them. But in 1916 his world was different and he quickly mastered the use of a rifle.

There was much more training to be done. It was amazingly comprehensive – how to erect a tented camp, how to protect your feet from getting trench foot, how to check your rifle and other equipment, how to dig a small foxhole or a large trench, how to use emergency rations, how to apply a field dressing – it went on and on until Herbert was well versed in what it would be like to be a soldier in the front line. At least he was versed in the theory. Like many of his colleagues, he was to find that, try as hard as the army did, the comprehensive training that he received went only part of the way to preparing him for the horrors of the real thing.

And of course Herbert was substantially older than most of the men with whom he trained. At nearly 35 years old, he could give as much as 17 years to those around him. To some no doubt, he was the older, perhaps wiser man in the group, a man for whom you had respect. To many he was a father figure, someone they could go to in an hour of need. He had that disposition. Even so he was desperate to "keep up" and would not want his older years to show. Even on 30-mile route marches, not uncommon at the time, he would give no concession to his older limbs. He might be the older man, but he was not going to let it be noticed.

After six months he had been transformed into a competent fully trained fighting man. The person that left Swaffham – gentle, parochial, family oriented – had become a more outward looking, more worldly, more aggressive combat soldier. During this training period, as far as we know, he never went back home. He was not granted home leave. Rose never went to Felixstowe. He therefore did not have contact with his family. Although they lived only two hours away on the train, they never saw one another. He missed them all painfully and they painfully missed him. He wrote letters home regularly although the content of the letters was somewhat matter of fact. Rose wrote to him frequently. Her letters in her small neat handwriting were very long. She regaled him with details about the children – their schooling, their health, and their pranks. She kept him abreast of news of the broader family and what was happening in Swaffham. She told him about herself, never complaining, always up and positive.

He sent home postcards. He started sending to his eldest son, Alf, cigarette cards that he collected from his mates. He himself was a pipe smoker, a habit he followed all his life, but he knew that Alf liked collecting cards and so he started sending them back home. He kept this up all through the war even when he was fighting in France. Many of the cards survive to this day and are part of a family collection (see Photo 17).

Family life at Ash Close continued without him. Rose took over the leadership of the household and assumed the jobs that had once been Herbert's. It was now her job to manage the family money. Every week she would go down to Swaffham post office to collect Herbert's soldier's pay. She grew astute at making the money stretch; she was always very good at that. All through the war, she never needed to take in laundry or get a part time job to make ends meet – she seemed able to get by. Of course, his soldier's money was "comfortable". It was a matter of policy by the Government that a soldier's pay should be "acceptable". The last thing that the authorities wanted was the wives of fighting men to be disgruntled and poverty stricken while their husbands fought and died in France. That was a source of discontent the war stricken country could well do without. Certainly Herbert's pay as a soldier was more than he had ever earned as a tailor. Rose was in fact a little better off after Herbert went to war. And there was one less mouth to feed.

She also had and was grateful for the support of her extended family. Unlike now, family units in 1916 were much more cohesive. Families lived in close proximity to each other; they socialised together and supported one another. Rose had both the extended family of the Drakes and the Barnes around her to help her out. Her sister Emma and her father lived nearly next door in Spinks Yard. Her second sister, Maud, was a few doors down Ash Close. Her kin were all around her. She had lived in Swaffham all her life – she had many friends and an almost bottomless pit of acquaintances.

She certainly needed help and support, especially in the early days. In 1914 she had lost her eldest brother, Arthur, who had died in Kings Lynn hospital of dropsy. In January 1916 while Herbert was square bashing and fatiguing in Felixstowe, he received news that Rose's mother had suddenly died. Alice

Drake was a gentle, loving woman and Rose adored her. She was heartbroken for a while. Such were the rigours of the army that Herbert was not allowed home leave and, as far as is known, did not attend his mother-in-law's funeral. But Rose could not afford to grieve for long. She had a family that depended on her. It was to be the first of a litany of personal losses that would strike this strong, indomitable woman in the next few years.

The children no longer had a father at home and would be effectively fatherless for the next five years. They would all grow up a little more quickly as a result. The Barnes children would form an incredibly close bond with their mother that would never be broken for the rest of their lives.

And of course Rose was not alone – there were hundreds of Roses in Swaffham alone, thousands in the county of Norfolk and hundreds of thousands in the country as a whole. It was a unique, unprecedented time in our history – there were very few young men in our towns, in our villages, and in our countryside. They had all left and the Roses of this world would keep the home fires burning as best they could. Rose Barnes was to do it pretty well.

During all this time, the stalemate on the Western Front in France had not been broken. Allied offensive enterprises which began in March 1915 continued unabated. In the words of Peter Barton in his book *The Somme*:

Actions were mainly prosecuted by the French with the British playing smaller supporting roles in battles at Neuve Chapelle, Aubers, Festubert and Loos. (All of which became household names because of the ever increasing casualty rate.) All failed. The main German offensive in 1915 in the Ypres salient came within a whisker of victory, but it too failed. A sombre lesson was being learnt – that even with the advantage of overwhelming numerical superiority, surprise and poison gas, the most primitive trench based defences manned by well trained and determined troops were a greater barrier than the most durable fortress cities had ever been.[5]

---

5   *The Somme* by Peter Barton published by Constable 2006.

The trenches got deeper and more sophisticated. "An ocean of British blood had been spent on small scale offensives for meagre territorial gain – battles with limited ambition and of short duration." The French were applying pressure for a British Offensive to relieve pressure on their own forces at Verdun. The high command of the French and British Armies decided that what was needed was a decisive push that would, once and for all, break the stalemate and deliver victory to the Allies. The British Army was to be tested on a grand offensive stage. With a million men of the new Fourth Army (largely formed from new volunteer battalions) in the vanguard, the offensive would take place in the summer of 1916 on the rolling hills of Picardy. It was to be called the Battle of the Somme.

The build up of men and equipment to support the "big push" began in January 1916. In April 1916, the 3rd Battalion, the Norfolk Regiment received orders to transfer as many able-bodied trained soldiers to France as they were capable of doing. Every man who could support the offensive would be needed.

On the morning of April 18, 267 men from the Norfolk Regiment were sent to France. Herbert Barnes was one of these. He had been in training for six months.

There is no evidence of how much warning he was given or how much time he had to prepare. He did not see Rose or the children before he departed; his goodbyes were short and were by letter only. He had never been out of the country before.

He and his 266 colleagues rose at dawn and packed their kit bags. They marched in full order once again back to the station at Felixstowe and boarded an overcrowded, grimy troop train. As it clattered its way to Folkestone, Herbert was apprehensive but also contemplative. What was in store for him? What would his fate be? How would he perform as a fighting soldier? Would he let his mates down? Would he do his duty? And, most poignantly, would he ever see Swaffham again? Would he ever see Rose and the children again?

He and thousands of other soldiers detrained at Folkestone. The port was a hive of activity. There were hundreds of boats, thousands of men, trains, the new fangled omnibuses, all carrying men and equipment. It was a stormy

April day. The wind on occasion reached gale force and there were heavy rain showers. The sea was heaving. He boarded the troop ship for the crossing to Boulogne in the early afternoon. The ship rolled and pitched. The faces of the men around him on the deck changed to a pallid hue as their stomachs reacted to the movement of the ship as she mounted the choppy waves. Men, violently sick, manned the rails to get some fresh air, others emptied their stomachs into the sea. There was the sour stench of seasickness. Was Herbert himself sick? We do not know. But on board that ship on April 18, 1916 men were as miserable as they could be. There was no escape from the heavy waves. Everyone must shudder and shiver until they reached the other side.

The white cliffs of England receded into the distance and the equally white but less inviting cliffs around Boulogne grew larger and larger. The sound of the thunderous rumble of the heavy guns was now not too far away. After two or three hours of utter misery, the ship dropped anchor. It was five o'clock in the afternoon.

Herbert Barnes had landed in France. He was going to war.

CHAPTER 4

A GENTLE INTRODUCTION TO WAR

APRIL–JUNE 1916

Herbert disembarked from the boat and marched in formation up the steep hill from the port to St Martin's camp. He was wide-eyed and alert, taking in all around him. He had never left England before and this was his first experience of a foreign land. The signs all around him, on the roads, on the shops, were in French with improvised notices in English dotted around for the benefit of the Tommies. The townspeople spoke a tongue that he did not understand. They paid no attention to him, or he to them. He was surrounded by the all pervasive sights and sounds of war.

Boulogne was one of the major ports being used to supply the war effort. As he climbed the hill up through the town and passed the old castle bastion, Herbert allowed himself a glance back at the harbour area. There he could see ships by the hundreds riding at anchor. Every inch of the quaysides was being used. He could see lines of trains waiting in the railway sidings and alongside the dock. The whole scene was covered in belching black smoke, billowing up and swirling around the breakwaters. Men were being landed in their thousands. Matériel was coming ashore by the hundreds of thousands of tons. Going the other way were more men being shipped out, back to England. These were wounded men with shattered limbs. These were men who had been gassed and could not see. These were men with grimy faces and tired eyes. Herbert saw it all as he marched through the town. He saw the hospital ships being loaded with their human cargo and he saw the ambulance trains with men laid out on stretchers on the platform of the station. Whatever expectations he might have had about France, about this foreign land, were quickly and abruptly dispelled

51

by the sights and sounds of war. It was the only French bonjour that he would ever know.

For Herbert and many, many others, the first night in France was spent at St Martin's camp, high on a hill overlooking Boulogne. It was his first experience of a hastily erected base for soldiers in transit. There were few permanent buildings. Accommodation was a forest of huge marquees and tents. His night was spent in an open dormitory under canvas with small cot beds with rough mattresses arranged in long lines for almost as far as the eye could see.

This was where thousands of disembarking soldiers stayed prior to being allocated and directed to their battalions. The soldier had no say in this process. The assignment was done on the bases of need – which battalion was short of men because of casualties incurred, or perhaps which battalion was in need because of some impending action of which the soldiers themselves were unaware.

The Norfolk Regiment had four battalions on the Western Front. These were the 1st, a regular army battalion, and three Kitchener (service) battalions, the 7th, the 8th and the 9th. All had seen action at different times; all had incurred casualties.[6]

The next day, on 19 April 1916, Herbert was posted to the 7th Battalion, the Norfolk Regiment. It was a part of the 35th Brigade which also consisted of the 7th Suffolks, the 9th Essex and the 5th Royal Berks. All were a part of the 12th (Eastern) Division.[7]

---

6   It is also of interest that the 2nd, 4th and 5th Battalions of the Norfolk Regiment were or had been in active service in the Middle East – in Gallipoli and Mesopotamia. Had the fates been different, Herbert could have found himself in Mesopotamia or Egypt. However, as we have seen, the need was closer to home. Men and matériel were pouring in to France prior to the Somme offensive.

7   A battalion was the scaffolding on which the British Army was built. It consisted of around 1,000 men, divided into four companies, denominated by a letter A to D. Each company was further subdivided into platoons who formed a closely knit group of men who lived together, fought together and often died together. It was within the platoon that lasting friendships and close interdependence were forged. A brigade, commanded by a brigadier general, was made up of four battalions of infantry (about 4,000 men). A division in 1916 was made up of three Brigades of infantry (12,000 men), three brigades of artillery, a howitzer brigade and a battery of heavy guns.

TED BARNES

The 7th (service) Battalion was the first of the Kitchener battalions raised by the Norfolk Regiment. It had been formed in August 1914 and had, at full strength, around 1,000 men. Of its four Companies, D Company and half of C Company were made up mainly of London men, who, in the press of work, had been enlisted in London and then sent immediately to Norwich, it would appear mainly for administration reasons. There were also men from Lancashire and the West Country. Only half the recruits were men from the towns and villages of Norfolk. Herbert was as pleased as he could be with his posting. In this strange new world, he could feel at home with men who had the same rustic drawl with which he himself spoke. He was assigned to B Company – he was with men who came largely from his own county.

The 7th Battalion had first gone to France in May 1915 and in September and October it had seen active service at the Battle of Loos where it had suffered very heavy casualties, with over 330 men killed, wounded or missing. In 1916 it moved to the trench system opposite the famous and almost impregnable Hohenzollern redoubt where it had helped to rebuff an intense German counter-attack, incurring another 29 casualties. At the time of Herbert's assignment, the 7th was in the front line trenches in an area called the Quarries near Loos. He was posted to join them immediately.

He left St Martin's camp, marched back to the town station at Boulogne and boarded a troop train for the short journey to the coal mining town of Béthune. This was the first of many journeys he would make on a troop train. The British Army had spent huge amounts of time, effort and money improving an already comprehensive French railway network. Every part of the front was now supported and accessible. While the front line trenches had become increasingly static, both sides in this terrible war had developed the ability to move men and equipment behind the lines with unprecedented speed and efficiency. While horses were still important, it was troop trains, hospital trains, and equipment trains that criss-crossed Western France and chugged their way from the embarkation ports to the front line. Herbert, in the next three years, was to undertake many, many long and uncomfortable journeys in open trucks, improvised wagons and the carriages of hospital trains. He would be carried along both standard and narrow gauge railways on wagons and carts pulled by steam engines and horses and men. He was to experience railways in every shape and form. The journey from Boulogne to Béthune was merely the first.

This troop train consisted of open wagons, probably about 30 of them (see Photo 15). The men stood up in the trucks as the train rattled along – there were few seats. Each man carried with him his kit bag which could provide an improvised seat if there was room. He held his rifle in his hand. As the train passed through St Omer and Lillers, Herbert's apprehension was growing and his fears of the unknown rigours of trench warfare were mounting in his mind.

He disembarked and with his fellow new recruits marched to join his battalion in the trench system. The noise of heavy guns was now much more than a distant rumble – it was a continuous and powerful pounding in the air. He was for the first time, but certainly not the last, "marching towards the sound of the guns" – something that he would have to do many times in the next few years.

It would appear that Herbert made his way straight from the train to the front line trenches at the "Quarry" area of the Loos front. He was not held in a forward area but immediately joined his new colleagues. It is not known which communication trench was used for Herbert to reach B Company but we can imagine his emotions as he made his way forward. When he first entered a trench system, Herbert would, with the best will in the world, have marvelled. It is the schoolboy's view that the First World War battlefield consisted of two trenches facing one another across 200 yards of no-man's-land. Reality was something quite different. A trench system consisted of a labyrinth of passageways, dugouts, shelters, bunk holes, latrines, observation posts, machine-gun posts, and first aid posts that stretched back sometimes as much as two miles from the front line and extended up to 50 feet below ground. Herbert was entering a subterranean world. Nothing could survive in daylight above ground level. Any movement would immediately attract deadly and concentrated machine-gun, sniper and artillery fire from the other side. Trenches were where men lived and worked. Trenches were home and offered what little safety was available.

In the Loos section of the front, the forward area consisted of an organised system of three lines of parallel trenches – a front line, a support line and a reserve line, all properly dug and extending one behind the other. Connecting them were equally deep and well dug communication trenches which were built in zigzags to limit the impact of blasts of exploding shells. Some were as much as eight feet deep. All had been boarded to enable soldiers to move without paddling in mud but the heavy rainfall of the previous few days meant they had become partially inundated. By the time Herbert arrived, the communication trenches were some 12 inches in mud above the boards. He had his introduction to that continuous enemy of the Tommy – mud and slime. Herbert was amazed at this new world that he was now to inhabit, an amazement that was put into words by a fellow soldier when he entered the trench system for the first time:

> *Yes the trenches, a veritable wonderland. From a road swept by shellfire and sharing the desolation much like the day after a flood, you enter the communication trenches and commence the most remarkable tour it is possible to imagine. Winding in and out, twisting and turning like around the edges of a jigsaw puzzle, you walk on and on through trench after trench and seem to be going miles and miles ahead when in reality you may have advanced only a few hundred yards. The dugouts you pass generally have some inscription over which signifies the purpose of their existence, the more flowery names, as Paradise Alley, etc, more often than not indicating that the cynic had been at work and that the life in that particular "abysmal depth" belies the name it bears, but dugouts and other sites on the way do not attract you so much as the noises that disturb the air. Very rarely are the trenches free from the intrusion of German explosives or from the music of ours that fly over in return and to the young campaigner sound rather ominous when every step you take seems to be landing him a few inches nearer an inevitable fate. You never know when a shell or the notorious trench mortars are going to fall above your head or the subtle bullets of a machine gun stray in your direction.*
>
> *(Private V. W. Garratt, 2/5th London Field Ambulance)*[8]

---

8   Letter from Pt V Garratt. *The Somme* by Peter Barton published by Constable 2006.

As Herbert went forward, there was a real danger of getting lost in this mole-like world, notwithstanding the fact that Herbert's sense of direction was always very good. To get to his battalion he followed the directions scrawled on temporary wooden signs that were erected to help the men find their way around. The name boards reflected both the humour and sometimes the origin of the Tommies that first dug them.

Herbert took more than an hour to make it through the labyrinth of communication trenches to the front line. He could not have been anything other than impressed by the deafening noise of sporadic artillery fire as he made his way forward. He had no time to get used to his new surroundings but his colleagues, all much younger than him, took him under their wing and did what they could to help him settle. It was a long tradition that the new man needed to be shown the ropes quickly and efficiently. He could see that the trench was about six feet deep and some three and a half feet wide at the top. A gently sloping parapet increased the height of the trench on the enemy side on which was furnished a fire step, about two feet high, which allowed the soldier standing on it to engage the enemy. He was shown that the fire step was the soldier's couch, bed-board, food-board, card table, workmen's bench and universal shelf – sometimes it was the only raised surface on which to set things down above water level. He was shown where the latrines were – a short trench cut back away from the enemy. He was taught how and when to eat, and how to man the fire step. He was shown where the dugouts were. He was told what to do and what not to do. He was told not to make too much noise or do anything at all that would attract enemy attention. The Tommies of B Company, 7th Battalion, the Norfolk Regiment would see the new man through his first few days in the front line.

Herbert did not have to wait long to experience the horrors that awaited him. At midday on his first full day in the front line trench his world was shattered by a huge explosion and showers of falling earth and mud. A tunnel had been dug by the British sappers below no-man's-land and filled with explosives. The blast created a new crater and a new trench had to be quickly dug to give men access to it. As the new trench was dug during the hours of darkness, several of the infantry from B Company were ordered to crawl out into no-man's-land and, lying flat down, provide cover and protective fire should the enemy detect the activity and mount an attack against the defenceless trench diggers. This might well have been Herbert's first exposure to hostile fire. If he was part of the detachment, he would have been placed in the line between two experienced Tommies who would have done their best to take care of him. The activity did indeed attract attention from the enemy 200 yards away in no-man's-land and a number of bombs exploded in the trench, killing an orderly and breaking an officer's leg. That same evening, as work on the tunnel continued, another nine men were hit by bombs. It was no more than "a normal day". There was no great offensive or defensive, no momentous attack just routine happenings that had cost the 7th Norfolk battalion eleven casualties and provided Herbert with his first experience of life on the Western Front.

At 5 am the next day another mine was exploded a few yards away from the Norfolk line. The explosion accidentally triggered a German mine. Rocks, earth and mud ballooned high into the air. Another tunnel was hastily started, inviting machine-gun fire and a German artillery bombardment. More casualties were incurred.

And during both days it rained almost incessantly. The Brigade Commander in his daily report simply describes the trenches as "excessively wet". It was a huge understatement. The trench in which Herbert stood became waterlogged, in effect not a trench but a ditch, where Herbert and his colleagues had to eat, sleep and live. Water crept up above the duckboards. Mud stuck to everything, to the feet, to the skin, to the clothing, to the food, to everything.

It was a very brief welcome to the Western Front. It was a million miles from the training ground at Felixstowe. In two short days, he had gone through most of the experiences that were a Tommy's lot. He had stood on his first firing step; he had cowered under his first aerial bombardment; he had seen his first dead and mangled bodies; he had gone for the first time out into no-man's-land, albeit in the dark; he had dug his first foxhole and helped construct his first trench; he had spent his first days and nights in the front line; and he had worked and slept in oozing mud. He had, in a short space of time, done it all – except go over the top. That would come later.

The next day was Herbert's third day in the front line trench. Two good things happened. The sun came out for the first time since his arrival in France. More importantly at 5 am the battalion was relieved and made their way back through the labyrinth of communication trenches to the village of Sailly-Labourse, two miles behind the front line. It was as if Herbert had been given a "gentle introduction" to the realities of trench warfare – a little snifter of what was to lie ahead of him – a dress rehearsal perhaps for the real thing.

The next day was a Sunday. Every Sunday all 1,000 men of the battalion, when not in the trenches, collected for divine service around midday either in the open, if the weather was good, or as in this case indoors in the Sailly recreation hall. The close proximity of prayer and devotion with the violence and killing of war has never seemed strange to the men of the British Army, and the Western Front was no exception. Herbert attended the service, all ranks did – and he was under orders now. He probably thought nothing of it, although he would have found it very different from the Baptist services he had attended in Swaffham. His devotions were immediately followed by his being sent out on a working party (250 men of the battalion were so detailed). That night the whole battalion were put through a practice gas attack alert, donning uncomfortable gas masks and presenting them for inspection. The Norfolks were about to spend time in reserve and very grateful they were.

But although they did not know it yet, "something was up". There was a sense of activity around them.

To the South, about 50 miles away, was the area to the west of Amiens, around the small town of Albert. It was an area of rolling chalk land that we now know as the Somme. The High Command was beginning the process of transferring the strength of the British Army to that section of the front. Everything that the 7th Norfolks did in the next five weeks was focused on that build-up. On only the fifth day after Herbert had disembarked at Boulogne, the 7th Norfolks, together with the 35th Brigade and all 20,000 men of the 12th Division were ordered to move to the Corps reserve area some 20 miles behind the Front. They marched the short distance to the railway at Nœux-les-Mines and "entrained" in open wagons just before midnight, chugged their way to Lillers where they marched again through the night to tented billets in the village of Cauchy. This was all flat agricultural land dotted with grimy coal mines which in normal times was full of smoke stacks, slag heaps and winding gear. These were not normal times. The front was only a few miles away and industrial production had been put on a war footing. French miners still worked the coal, not knowing when they descended the pits what would await them when they came back to the surface again. The countryside was full of the smoke and the dirt of an industrial landscape. Herbert thought that the green fields of Norfolk were a long way off.

On arrival at Cauchy, Herbert and the whole battalion was "washed" in the baths of an old coal mine. Trench life in 1916 was, even by the standards of the day, filthy in the extreme. Herbert's clothes were quickly riddled with lice and everything was covered in mud. A hot water shower was good for health and good for morale. Herbert stripped off and enjoyed the fun of a good scrub down with his pals. He had no shower at Swaffham, a good soak in a tin bath was his home routine on a Monday night. This now was a real hot shower. What's more, before he got back into his uniform, he was issued with a clean, freshly laundered shirt, perhaps not to the standard that Rose would have achieved, but very acceptable nevertheless. As long as Herbert was in the reserve area behind the lines, he would have a good wash and change of shirt every seven days.

For the next 11 days the 7th were in billets in Cauchy. The Battalion began training all over again. In beautiful spring weather, he and his mates were again put through their paces. The emphasis this time was on bombing along enemy trenches, scouting across no-man's-land and practising how to break through barbed wire. Apart from one day, when the whole brigade had to stand to, for fear that the Germans had launched a gas attack and would break through the front line (a fear that came to nothing), the training continued with high intensity. On one day, a visiting officer gave intense instruction on bayonet fighting. Herbert must have twigged that all this extra training was focused on "going over the top".

There was some relief. The church services continued on Sunday and the visits to the baths were a welcome respite. Herbert spent an evening watching the Divisional boxing finals. A Norfolk man had won his first bout but had been disqualified in his second fight for a "foul", the nature of which was not explained (the Battalion diaries deemed it expedient not to get into details). On Herbert's birthday, on the 6th May, he watched the Brigade's horse show in the grounds of Cauchy Château.[9] He also participated in competitions between platoons to see which could be the best platoon. He was not a boxer, neither was he a horseman but he was a football player and he joined in and excelled in the many friendly matches that were organised to keep the men busy.

Herbert regularly wrote home to Swaffham and he regularly received packages from Rose – little things that would help him in his daily life as a soldier. But at this time he also received from Rose a photograph which he was to keep with him for the next three years. The photograph was, of course, of Rose herself, looking pretty but tired. Around her were the children. Alfie, now nearly nine years old, was showing good promise at school. Phyllis, at seven, was even at this early age giving some indication of what a pretty young lady she was to become. Bertie had a mischievous boyish smile on his five-year-old face and little Teddy, not yet three, was standing stiffly to attention. Together, without their father around, the bonds that tied the family together had grown stronger. Rose with the help of her sister Emma and her father George was proving to be a very diligent mother. She read to all the children each night before they went to bed and they all sang songs together. No doubt a few prayers were said to keep Herbert safe.

If the men were not aware yet that "something was up" then they were given food for thought on 8 May when the 35th Brigade were on the move again, this time to billets at the village of Enguinegatte. It was not far, only eight miles from Cauchy, but it was significant because it was even further behind the front

---

9   Having noted the importance of railways for transportation, the horse was still a fundamental part of army logistics at this time when motorised vehicles were just appearing in any numbers. By 1917 the British Army had around 1 million animals, of which 460,000 horses and 82,000 mules were on the Western Front. Nearly everything that moved on the front was horse drawn.

line in the Special Manoeuvre Area. This was an area where mock trenches had been dug with fire steps and dugouts. A simulated no-man's-land was there for all to see, together with rolls of barbed wire and make-believe craters. This was as close to the real thing as it was possible to create. For 12 days, the battalion trained continuously but this time the training included mock attacks against machine-guns and artillery firing live ammunition. For the first time, Herbert went "over the top" leaving a trench to emerge into the exposed ground of no-man's-land, cutting through barbed wire, sheltering in bomb craters and charging enemy trenches. And always, the brigade attacks were rehearsed with the same formation – 7th Suffolks and 9th Essex in the front, 5th Royal Berks in support and the 7th Norfolks in reserve. Herbert never knew why the 35th Brigade always formed up in that way but, within a month, that choice of formation was to save his life, and condemn other men to an early death.

For 12 full and long days, the whole brigade played war games in conditions that were as close to the real thing as the high command could make them, with the exception, of course, that the bullets were not fired in anger and the artillery shells did not explode with venom. Even then it was not enough. They marched back to Cauchy and from there to a small village of Marle-les-Mines with another week of training – sniping, scouting, wiring and bombing. Herbert thought it would never end. Apart from two days in front line trenches he had been in training for eight months. He and the battalion were ready, ready for the big offensive that everybody knew was coming, ready to do the things they had all enlisted to do.

Then on 31 May 1916, Herbert's war came to a temporary but abrupt halt. It was not a shell, or a bullet or a bomb that put him into hospital for the first time. It was something much smaller but potentially equally deadly. It was a virus called influenza.

These days we talk casually about "getting the flu" but influenza epidemics have been the scourge of armies for generations. It could cut swathes through the men as effectively as any artillery bombardment or volley of rifle fire. More severe than trench fever, there was in 1916 no effective vaccine against influenza – that would not be forthcoming until 1933. Army generals knew it could reduce the effectiveness of an army in no time at all.[10] The wisdom of the time was to take the infected men out of their units as quickly as possible to prevent contagion and enhance recovery. In 1916 influenza was taken very seriously indeed.

Herbert reported to the battalion medical officer at the regimental aid post who confirmed that he was indeed sick and could not carry out his duty. He was passed on to the divisional field ambulance who confirmed that he could not be treated on the spot and was sent on to the casualty clearing station. There a decision was made that he needed to be evacuated to hospital to recover. He was very reluctant to admit to his sickness. Very conscious of his age, he did not want to "call in sick". He had no choice. As soon as he complained of a sore throat, headache and loss of appetite and became generally sluggish and clearly unable to keep up the gruelling pace, he was relieved of his duties, put on an ambulance train to travel the 120 miles to the Number 2 General Hospital at the embarkation port of Le Havre.

It was an experience that brought him face to face with the misery and maiming of trench warfare. His travelling companions on the hospital train included every sort of injury, from walking wounded to stretcher cases on the brink of death, all on their way to hospital, many on their way back home to England. Some would not survive; many would never fight again in the trenches. Herbert might have even felt a little embarrassed that his injury was no more than influenza – but in 1916 that too could kill. For the hours of his journey, he was glimpsing all too painfully a part of his future.

The Number 2 General Hospital was one of the huge Stationary Hospitals dotted around north eastern France. They were manned by men of the Royal

---

10 The most severe outbreak of influenza was to attack the fighting strengths of all participants in the First World War in the spring of 1918 when a pandemic of the disease swept through Europe. The symptoms could be very harsh indeed leading to bronchial pneumonia, heliotrope cyanosis and septicaemia (blood poisoning). Between October and November 1918, there were 45,000 flu admissions to British casualty clearing stations of which around 6 percent or 2584 died. The German and French casualties from flu were probably much higher. It is therefore likely that deaths on the Western Front during this two month time period were approaching 10,000.

Army Medical Corps and were generally located near the coast where rail communications were good and access to England swift. Number 2 was by 1916 a huge facility and was the place where decisions were made to send wounded soldiers back home to England or patch them up and return them to the Front. When Herbert arrived, it was a forest of huts, marquees and tents that covered many acres on the outskirts of the town.

Of the 30 men that appear on the admission roles on the same day as Herbert, only two others had influenza. Another four had shellshock (a condition not yet fully understood) while 14 had minor wounds such as sprained ankles or broken wrists. Five had diseases associated with the hard life in the trenches such as boils and piles. Of all of them, Herbert was the oldest and had been in France the shortest amount of time. Only five boarded hospital ships for England, the rest recovered and were returned to their units.

On arrival, Herbert went through a procedure that he was to experience in a far more dramatic way later in the war. His uniform was taken off him and burnt – it was almost certainly lice infested and was considered a liability in a hospital. He was dressed in the light blue "hospital uniform" which he would wear for the rest of his stay. He was looked after not only with the Royal Army Medical Corps but also the nursing staff of the Queen Alexandra's Imperial Military Nursing Service (QAIMNS).

Herbert's brush with influenza, while severe enough to take him out of service, was never life threatening. Under the continuous care of the nurses with regular washing, clean sheets and high hygiene levels he recovered rapidly. He probably thought his recovery far too rapid as he had a much more comfortable life with influenza than he would ever have with his battalion. His stay at Le Havre was to last only two weeks. He was able to explore the town a little and he sent postcards back home to Rose to let her know how he was doing. But on 14th June, he was declared fit and he boarded a troop train and made the journey back to his unit which was by this time at a mining village in France called Marles-les-Mines.

The Battalion to which he returned was, by this time, in a high state of readiness. While he had been away, it had continued practising attacks to and from mocked up trenches. The regiment had doubled its number of Lewis guns and been fully made up to battle ready strength, receiving over 180 new recruits. Herbert was no longer the Johnny-come-lately in his platoon.

On the day after Herbert arrived back to join his colleagues, the 12th Division, nearly 14,000 men, were ordered to move south. The Norfolks marched to the little village station of Fouquereuil to be ready to leave at midnight on the 16th June. The men were not told of their destination. They spent the day cleaning up their billets, getting rid of surplus stores and at 11 pm in darkness and in fine weather they moved out. Herbert, fit and well and completely recovered, marched the four miles in the dark gloom of night to the station. He, of course, did not know it, but he was now a part of the massive build up of forces 50 miles to the south around Amiens. The British Army was on the move and such a large movement of troops could only take place at night to avoid detection by Germany observation aircraft. Herbert spent the whole uncomfortable night on the train, unaware as to where he was going and what he was going to do. At 9.40 am they disembarked at Longeau station, one mile south-east of Amiens. They marched through the streets of the old beautiful city. It had suffered some bomb and artillery damage but the medieval cathedral still stood proud and tall. They stopped for breakfast in the early afternoon. The brigade commander became irritated that it took two hours for all of them to feed and he hurried them on. They marched northwards, halted again for dinner, and at 8.15 pm arrived at the billets and camps at the village of Vignacourt, eight miles north of Amiens. It had taken only 10 hours to make the move. Herbert slept well that night.

For the next nine days, Herbert found himself engaged in a full scale rehearsal of a major battle. Once again the infantry men of the 7th Norfolks practised attacks in simulated trenches, attacks over no-man's-land but this time in full battle dress with all the equipment that a Tommy needed to be an effective fighting man.[11] With fixed bayonets they swarmed across the open ground,

---

11   Much has been written about the equipment that Tommies carried into battle. Field Service Regulations listed around 60 pounds of items per man, a number that included the boots and clothes that he stood up in. In an attack, large packs were not carried by the front line troops. That

jumped into simulated enemy trenches, bombed their way down communication trenches. They ate in the open under simulated enemy fire. They replicated as exactly as was possible the trenches and mines that they would face in their next great offensive. The whole of the 35th Brigade were involved together with their machine-guns, stretcher-bearers and artillery support. The villages of Vignacourt, Fremont and Flesselle became a mock battle ground. The 7th Norfolks were always positioned in reserve. That was to be their job.

By this time, everybody knew that "something was up". They all knew that "a big push" was about to happen and Herbert now knew that he would be a part of it. Nearly all the Tommies wrote home to their loved ones and Herbert did the same. His letters at this time have not survived but his thoughts would have been back in Ash Close in Swaffham with Rose and Alfie and Phyllis and Little Bert and Teddy. He wondered if he was going to make it through but he would have been stalwart and optimistic – that was his way.

On the night of Saturday 24th he was billeted in the village. It was evening and the men were resting following another day of manoeuvres. Suddenly the peace of the evening was shattered by the roar of heavy guns firing at the German lines along a 25 mile front. Four hundred and fifty-five heavy guns, the greatest concentration of allied artillery ever assembled, and over 1,000 lighter guns all opened up. The guns blazed and boomed from the valleys and hills at the front 10 miles away. A carefully planned programme of artillery barrage had begun. The sky was lit up with tracers and the rumble of shells exploding in the distance. The men of the 7th Battalion had never seen anything like it.

The preliminary bombardment had commenced. The Battle of the Somme had begun.

---

said, Herbert would have had at a minimum his rifle, an entrenching tool, two gas helmets, wire cutters, 170 rounds of ammunition, and two grenades. As he was in a battalion held in reserve, when going forward he might also be carrying sandbags and extra equipment to turn round and secure a trench once it had been taken.

CHAPTER 5

THE BATTLE OF THE SOMME

A VISIT TO MASH VALLEY – JULY 1916

The Battle of the Somme was a milestone event in the First World War. It was a cataclysmic event in the history of the British Army. It was equally cataclysmic for Herbert Barnes. He saw action in three of the important stages of the battle. Firstly, he fought in the area known to British soldiers as Mash Valley[12] during the opening few days from 1 to 6 July, days when the British Army suffered unprecedented casualties. He fought in the second phase of the battle, the long grinding war of attrition where the two sides battled it out for control of woods and strongpoints. Herbert was to be in the hell hole called Delville Wood – or Devil's Wood as he would always refer to it. Then, towards the end of the battle he was to fight and suffer around the stronghold of Thiepval and the taking of the stronghold of the Schwaben Redoubt – now a household name because of the location of the imposing memorial designed by Sir Edwin Lutyens to commemorate the fallen that have no known graves.

During the 1,364 days that Herbert was a soldier, the Battle of the Somme provided him with the most vivid, the most disturbing, and the most horrendous memories of his time as a fighting man. For the rest of his life, the images of what he saw and more importantly of what he did, would stay with him. They would on occasions haunt him and at other times fill him with gratitude and give him cause for thanks. His experiences would show him the depths to which man's inhumanity to man could stoop and would also provide him

---

12   "Mash Valley" was the valley north of La Boisselle, so called by reference to the southern "Sausage Valley", which was named after the sausage-shaped German observation balloon that was flown there.

with glittering examples of goodwill and mercy. In later life, on the very few occasions that he made reference to his time in the trenches, nearly all of them referred to things that had happened during the three months of the Battle of the Somme.

The Somme was the first major all-out offensive that the British Army launched in the First World War. Up until this time, attacks on the German trenches, although costly, had been on a somewhat smaller scale. It was also the first major offensive where cooperation with the French Army positioned immediately to the south reached new and more sophisticated levels. Although the original plan had called for the British, as junior partners, to launch only a secondary or diversionary attack, by the time negotiations between Generals Joffre and Haig had been concluded, the British had got their way to launch a major joint offensive where the two armies came together on the rolling chalklands to the north and south of the river Somme. The objective was to relieve pressure on the dangerously stretched French positions around Verdun much further to the south, to draw in German resources in men and matériel and, with a short sharp punch, to smash through the enemy's lines. From the time of the final decision, the build-up of men and matériel, of which Herbert had been a part, had been massive and unprecedented in size and complexity. Some battalions had been training for offensive warfare since December 1915.

The British sector stretched for 23 miles and was cut approximately in half by the old Roman road that ran in a dead straight line from the small town of Albert to Bapaume.

The Somme Battlefront - July 1916 with the proposed lines of attack

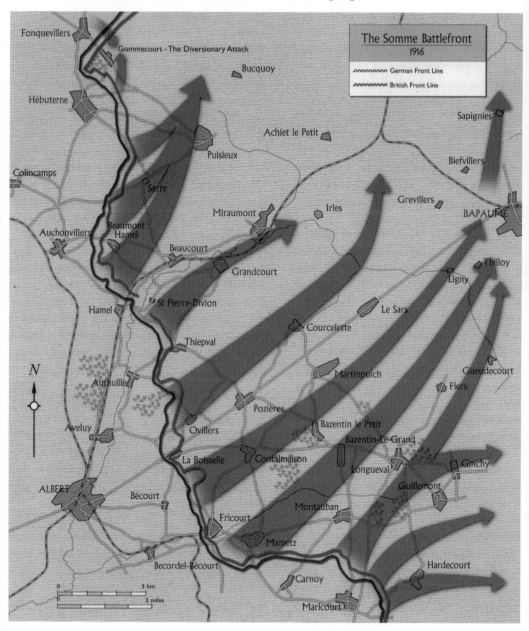

Map taken from Peter Barton's book "*The Somme*"
published by Constable in 2006.

The road passed through the front lines and through no-man's-land at the village of La Boisselle. To the north of La Boisselle, the two sides confronted one another on a front that ran approximately north to south through small villages that were to become household names throughout the British Empire – Ovillers, Thiepval, Hamel, Beaumont Hamel, Serre and Gommecourt. In many of these villages the Germans held the high ground overlooking the valley of the River Ancre, a tributary of the Somme. In nearly this entire sector they overlooked the forward British trenches.

To the south of La Boisselle, the front line ran more in an east to west direction through or close to villages that would also gain notoriety in the days to come. Fricourt, Mametz, and Montauban were also to take their place in British history books. Here the battlefield geography was equally as favourable to the British as to the Germans.

All the way along the front, the German trench system was well constructed and had been long established. It had been built in 1915 as a defensive line and had been dug deep into the chalk subsoil. Since its first construction, it had been systematically developed and strengthened. The system was up to two miles wide and consisted of three parallel lines of deep trenches, festooned with shelters, dugouts, redoubts, machine-gun nests and funk holes. Underground shelters were up to 50 feet below the surface and many had been constructed in thick concrete. Periodically, along the line, impregnable strongpoints called redoubts had been constructed of thick concrete that could withstand artillery bombardment. The Germans could protect the whole area by bringing artillery to bear into those areas of no-man's-land that came under attack. The only way to assault such a line was by a full frontal attack by infantry across no-man's-land, hopefully having first of all pulverised the opposition by an artillery barrage. The frontal attack was to be preceded by a carefully regulated, meticulously planned, five day long artillery bombardment that eventually became seven days long. It was to be the biggest bombardment in the history of warfare up to that time and was designed to destroy the front line German trenches, cut the defensive wire in front of them, wipe out the defenders so that the infantry men could easily assault and take the German trench system.

It was this bombardment that interrupted and disturbed Herbert's morning at Vignacourt on the 24th June. It heralded to him and to many thousands of men stretched along the 23 mile front that this time "something was really up".

———————

Back in Swaffham, Rose knew nothing of the impending attack. She did not read a newspaper every day but she had access to the *Eastern Daily Press* and she saw the *Norwich Mercury* regularly. During 1915 and the first half of 1916 the reporting of the war was not so heavily censored. However, reports that were published abounded with good news. Every day, it seemed, the British Army were winning victories – more ground had been taken. More Germans had been taken prisoner. Things were always going well. She received regular letters from Herbert at the front written in his neat and precise handwriting but the control of the battalion censor meant that there was no news of any consequence.

Herbert was sending to his eldest son, Alfie, a regular flow of cigarette cards, and Alfie's collection was growing. He was getting to the point that he had two of some of the cards which enabled him to play "swopsy" with his school friends to try and complete sets. Alfie had just had his ninth birthday and was doing well at school. Rose knew that he was a bright lad and as the eldest boy, she was thinking ahead about his education and how best to harness his future potential. Every bit as bright was young Phyllis, coming up to six years old. She too was showing a lot of promise. It was clear that Rose's creative flair and love of literature and music was being passed onto the children. With their father away, Rose would read to her children before they went to bed, either under the glow of candlelight or of a more powerful paraffin lamp. On occasions she would sing to them in a sweet melodic soprano voice. They would all sing together, especially the chorus. The children would remember those evenings at Ash Close for the rest of their lives.

For Rose, bringing up four children without her husband around was never easy. She seemed to be working from dawn to dusk – there was always something to do, food to prepare, clothes to mend, shoes to sole. It helped a little that she was financially slightly better off than she had been when Herbert was at home. His pay as a soldier, which she picked up every week at the post office, went further than his meagre wages as a tailor. As far as we know, Rose never had to work to make extra money. She seemed to make ends meet. Family life continued without Herbert, although of course he was sorely missed.

Young Bert, when he was in his seventies, would later recall:

The war took its toll in Ash Close and I still have vivid memories of incidents that never seem to fade. I was never aware of the full implications and the human tragedy and suffering, as children we accepted it as a way of life, often finding thrills and excitement where our elders found grief. My father sent home lots of cigarette cards and beautiful silk pictures. There were postcards with a line leading from the bottom left hand corner to the top right hand corner where a German Zeppelin was depicted. A match was put to the bottom of the line which slowly burned until the Zeppelin was reached, which then exploded with a little bang. We had boards placed over the outside of the windows as blackouts as Zeppelins frequently flew over. Two men occasionally came round to check them. I was always frightened of them and would hide until they had gone. There were no shelters from the raids, people stood in little groups outside. Mother once woke us all up and took us out to watch the search lights playing on the Zeppelins. For a time, Canadian troops were stationed on the Campingland. We would follow them around at the Fair in the marketplace until they gave us a piece of their coconuts. I remember pushing an old pram to the coal yard at the station to get coal bricks made chiefly from coal dust and some kind of cement. We would gather conkers from the horse chestnut trees around the recreation ground and take them to the town hall to be used for the war effort.

Rose was proving to be a dependable rock to the rest of the family. In early 1916 she had lost her mother to cancer. Herbert was not even allowed home to attend the funeral. Rose's sister Emma had moved in next door to look after her father. She was grateful for the support that was around her. Emma and Rose were not only sisters, they were bosom pals. Rose knew she could depend on her for help whenever she needed it and Emma became a second mother to all the children.

———◆◆———

The beginning of the preliminary bombardment told Herbert, the 7th Norfolks, the 35th Brigade and the whole of the 12th Division, indeed the one and a half million men of the Fourth Army that the long awaited attack was now imminent. On the morning of the 27th June, the 7th Norfolks had reveillied early and at 5.45 am they and the whole of the brigade set off on what was to be a series of approach marches. The marches brought them day by day closer to the front line trenches in preparation for the attack.

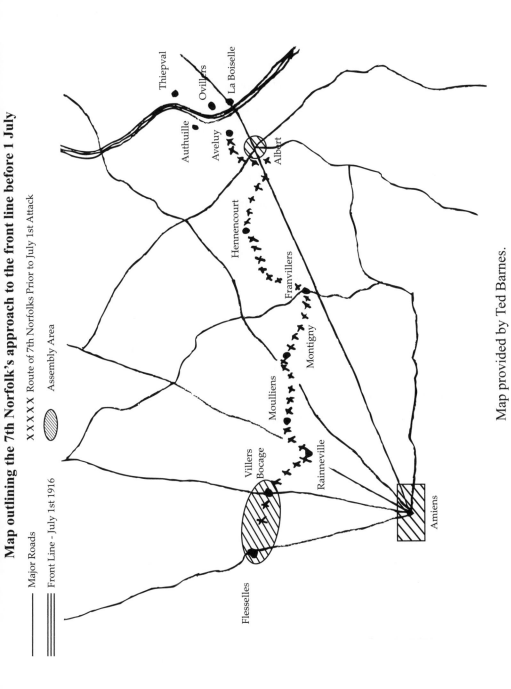

Map outlining the 7th Norfolk's approach to the front line before 1 July

—— Major Roads

≡ Front Line - July 1st 1916

XXXXX Route of 7th Norfolks Prior to July 1st Attack

⬭ Assembly Area

Thiepval

Ovillers

La Boiselle

Authuille

Aveluy

Albert

Hennencourt

Franvillers

Montigny

Moulliens

Rainneville

Villers Bocage

Flesselles

Amiens

Map provided by Ted Barnes.

They marched with all their equipment (all 60 pounds of it) through the villages of Flesselle and Villers-Bocage[13] and arrived at Rainneville just as the sun was setting. They marched in formation through country lanes that passed through small agricultural communities with churches, farms and houses, deserted and partly damage by the German heavy guns. They were not alone. Battalion after battalion were alongside them, also beginning their inexorable journey to the front line. Herbert was marching to the sound of the guns for a second time. All of the time the heavy guns around them were rumbling away, spitting out shells that whistled through the sky above their heads. The next day, the 28th, they were due to move on further to Franvillers, only four miles behind the front line trenches. The major attack was planned for the 29th. It was getting close.

In a methodically planned, detailed build-up to the biggest frontal assault in the history of war, no-one, not even the army high command, can order the weather. On 28 June it rained, pretty much all day. Two centimetres of rain washed over the battlefield. The area was deluged. Herbert, even in his greatcoat, was soaked through to the skin as were all the men along the line. Shelter was hard to find. Trenches filled with water, roads became quagmires and men and horses struggled to move the heavy guns. The commander of the 7th Norfolks, Lt Colonel F. E. Walters, wrote in the Battalion Diary, with typical English understatement:

> ... *today it rained a good deal and at 3pm the order was received that no troops were to move today – this is due apparently to the wetness of the ground which in the event of an advance would prevent the movement of the heavy guns. Today, which should have been "Y" Day is nothing particular and "Y" Day has been postponed indefinitely.*

The attack had not been postponed indefinitely, but it had been postponed. One and a half million men were held in their current positions, neither moving

---

13 This is Villers-Bocage in the Somme département, not the village of the same name in Normandy which was famously the scene of heavy fighting in 1944.

forward nor moving back, worrying, waiting for General Haig to decide their destiny. Herbert and the 7th Norfolks spent the whole of 28 and 29 June waiting in defensive positions in the woods. As far as is known, they did not have the luxury of shelter from the constant rain. They were very wet, ankle deep in gooey chalk slime. And all the time, the bombardment of shells whistled and whined overhead, incessantly, day and night. The bombardment was continuing, rain or no rain. Surely nothing on the German side could still be alive. Surely the enemy was being annihilated. Herbert might even have felt some sympathy for the common German soldier caught beneath such an onslaught.

On the evening of the 30th the Battalion was on the move yet again. General Haig had ordered that the attack would be postponed for only two days and was now planned for 7.30 on the morning of the 1st July. The build-up, held for two whole days, kicked into action again. The 7th Norfolks marched at night, in pitch darkness, from Rainneville through the villages of Molliens and Montigny and bivouacked for the night at Franvillers. In other circumstances, Herbert would have found this a very enjoyable country walk through rolling chalk downlands and pretty Picardy villages. It would have reminded him of north-west Norfolk where he had spent many an enjoyable afternoon with Rose and the children. But these were not "other circumstances". The continuous thunder of the guns and the knowledge of what lay ahead of them increased the level of apprehension minute by minute.

On the morning of 1 July the last approach march was completed. They had covered between five and eight miles each day. Herbert found himself at Hénencourt Wood in trenches and dugouts surrounded by trees. The trenches in which they took shelter are still visible today. They were now only four miles from the front and well within range of the German heavy guns. The wood provided some protection from exploding shells and incendiaries that could now fall down on them at any time. All along the skyline ahead of them was the Thiepval Ridge. It was quite visible to Herbert albeit covered in smoke from exploding artillery. The frontal attack was about to begin.

What happened next in Herbert's war goes a long way to demonstrate that to the Tommy, the First World War was very much a lottery. The role that each battalion was called to play, the orders they received, where attacks were to take place and who was to take part in them, largely determined whether or not any one individual became a casualty. It was the major factor in who lived and who died. Survival had very little to do with courage and nothing to do with the content of a man's character.

The 12th Division had been earmarked to be in the second wave of attacks. On either side of the village of La Boisselle both north and south of the long straight Albert to Bapaume road, the 24,000 men of the 8th and 34th Divisions were ordered to attack on 1 July and overrun the German front.

**The trench system at Mash Valley showing the ground occupied by the
7th Battalion the Norfolk Regiment on 3 July 1916**

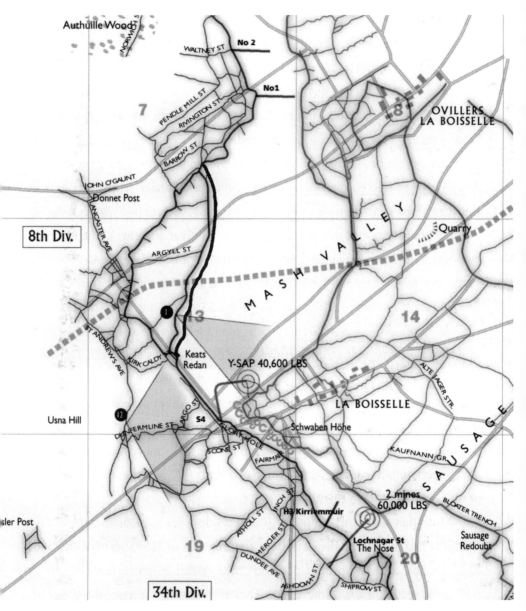

Map taken from Peter Barton's book "*The Somme*"
published by Constable in 2006.

The 12th Division would provide the second wave of assaults on 2 July and they would swarm forward over the land taken by the previous day's attack and advance as far as the village of Martinpuich, a full three miles behind the German front line. Victory would be complete. The 7th Norfolks were to be part of the second wave. Their big day was to be the 2nd July.

Of course, it never happened that way. At 7.30 on the 1st July, the bombardment, now seven days old, lifted to concentrate on the second line of German trenches. Tunnels that had been driven beneath the enemy lines and filled with explosives were blown up, sending plumes of dirt spiralling into the air. The earth shook. The whistles blew and thousands of men went over the top. They swarmed into no-man's-land for a direct frontal attack on the deeply dug trenches of the German front line. While the bombardment had wreaked havoc to the German trenches, it had not come close to pulverising them. The German defenders, having been underground and isolated for nearly a week, emerged dazed but intact, manned their machine-guns, and the attackers were mown down in their thousands. In places along the 23 mile front, the British Army recorded glorious successes. In the area around La Boisselle and Ovillers ahead of where Herbert and the 7th Norfolks were dug in, it was a disaster. The men of the 8th Division were decimated, suffering high casualties as they attempted to get across 800 yards of no-man's-land in Mash Valley (see Photo 18). It is now a matter of history that on 1 July 1916 the British Army suffered the worst day in its history. It was the highest number of casualties ever recorded in one day – nearly 60,000 casualties of which nearly 25,000 were dead or would die of their wounds.

While this drama of slaughter was unfolding in front of them, the 7th Norfolks had left the relative safety of the trenches of Hénencourt Wood and had marched to take up their positions near Albert in preparation for their part in the second wave of the attack. They were, as they moved, the target of occasional artillery fire but incurred no casualties. As Herbert marched forward with his battalion and got to the crest of the hill that overlooked La Boisselle, much of the battlefield was laid out ahead of him, covered in a pool of smoke and punctuated by continuous explosions of artillery shells and the chatter of machine-guns. The noise was deafening and the scene in front of him resembled a living hell. The opposite side of the valley was strewn with bodies of fallen men who had gallantly tried to get across between 100 and 700 yards of no-man's-land.

It became obvious that the 8th and 34th Divisions ahead were being held up, and that they stood no chance of getting through and holding the front line trench system. In the mid-morning, as the 7th were still moving forward the order went out to cancel the second wave of attacks. Such is the lottery of life and death. Such are the things on which Herbert's safety depended. The march forward was stopped and the Norfolks were diverted north of Albert. They marched to the west of the town under light artillery fire and found relative safety, bivouacked on the western slope of the embankment of the Albert-Hamel railway line. The Berks, Essex and Suffolks were sent forward to the reserve trenches but the Norfolks were told to dig in on the steep slope of the railway line. Amazingly they did not arrive at the embankment until around 3.30 am on July 2. On this most momentous of days in the history of the British Army, they had been on the move for nearly 24 hours – while thousands of men ahead of them lay dead or wounded. They had been lucky but extreme fatigue was their only reward.

The railway embankment behind which they took shelter is still there to this day (see Photo 16). Although only one mile from the front line, the embankment faced west and provided huge protection from the constant shelling coming from the east that now pervaded the whole front line area. Lying flat against its slope, Herbert and his colleagues took out their short shovels and feverishly dug out foxholes. The 30 foot flank of the embankment became in no time at all a veritable rabbit warren as men vigorously scraped out small burrows that offered them protection from whistling shrapnel. The 7th Norfolks had found a relatively safe place for the night. And that's where Herbert would stay for much of the next day.

He had been lucky. He and the 7th Norfolks had survived the most dreadful of days. But it was far from over. As the 8th and the 34th Divisions had failed to make a breakthrough on the 1st July, it was decided that the 12th Division would now have to try on the 3rd of July. The 35th Brigade was to be a part of the attempt. They were to take the German front line in Mash Valley, over exactly the same ground as the 8th Division had been unsuccessful the day before. Once again the order of attack would have critical repercussions on which units were to sustain casualties. The Berkshires would be in front on the right, the Suffolks in front on the left, the Essex in support and the Norfolks in reserve. It was the same formation that had been used so many times in the mock simulations during rehearsals behind the lines. Unlike on the 1st July, this was to be a night time attack over ground still covered with the bodies of the dead from the previous two days together with wounded and dying men who had not been able to get back to their own trenches.

At 11.15 at night, the Norfolks arose from the safety of the embankment and moved forward to link up with the rest of the Battalion. They were all to move to the forward area. The men of Berkshire and Suffolk went first, closely followed by the men of Essex and then the Norfolks. The first few yards were uphill and over open ground. At first fortune smiled on them. It was a dark and misty night and their movement was hidden from the enemy. However as they reached the crest of the hill, they soon attracted artillery fire. Bombs and shells were exploding all around them. At last they reached the relative protection of the communication trenches. What they now ran into had never been written into any of the training manuals back in England. Whole stretches of the communication trench were impassable. The confusion was indescribable. Men of the 35th were trying to get forward against a stream of troops coming back out of the line. Stretcher-bearers with casualties were mixed with walking wounded and exhausted soldiers streaming back. What is more, the trench was cluttered with the dead and dying of the previous day's fighting. To make matters worse, many sections of the trench had been destroyed by heavy artillery fire and had collapsed. Herbert saw for the first time in close up the stark horror of the previous day's disaster. As Herbert moved forward, he had to pick his way over the bodies of the dead and the dying. He found that all normal movement through the trenches was stopped by the congestion of human traffic. And all the time artillery shells were exploding in and on these passageways of human suffering. The German guns knew exactly the range of the communication trenches – they had had months to fix their positions. Some of the Norfolks, exasperated by the traffic jam, climbed out of the communication trench to try to reach the front line over open ground, thus exposing themselves to murderous machine-gun fire from the German lines. The 7th Norfolks lost some 14 men killed and 70 men wounded merely in the act of getting forward to the front line trench. According to the Battalion Diary, it took the battalion nearly three hours to move less than a mile to get to the position overlooking Mash Valley.[14]

Herbert was one of the men who made it through unscathed. He was one of the fortunate ones. Once again, the lottery of life and death was to smile on him. The order of battle indicated that the Berkshires and Suffolks would go over the top first, followed by the Essex and then by the Norfolks. The Norfolks were only to go over the parapet when they received a special order from brigade headquarters and when it was clear that the other battalions had made it across no-man's-land. At 3.15 am, on a dark, misty night, the whistles blew again and the men of the Berkshires and Suffolks, and then the Essex, went over the top and swept down into Mash Valley. Although this time the men moved forward in the half gloom, the result was a repeat disaster of the previous day. The bombardment had once again failed to nullify the German trenches and the extensive area of no-man's-land was lit up by Verey flares and swept from three directions by German machine-guns and pounded by artillery. The result was the decimation of the attacking infantrymen. It is amazing that many did make it over to the German front line trench, but not in sufficient numbers to hold onto the ground that they had taken. They were quickly bombed out. The attack had failed and by 4.15 it was clear to all that it had failed. No-man's-land was littered with the dead and dying of two failed attacks. Lying out there were over 1,500 men, dead or wounded, to add to the 2,000 men from the previous engagement. Mash Valley had become a killing field.

---

14   The communication trenches in this sector of the front had Scottish names, given to them by Scottish battalions earlier in the war. The three main communication trenches where the above took place were Dunfermline Street, Kirkcaldy Street, and Argyll Street. It is likely that Herbert advanced up Argyll Street to get to the front line.

While the carnage took place a few yards from them, as wounded soldiers crawled back into the trench from no-man's-land, as the cries of the dying rang in their ears, the 7th Norfolks stood in the front line trench and waited. In full battledress, they prepared themselves for their turn to go. Herbert composed himself, thought of Swaffham, thought of Rose and the children; thought of playing football in the park at Kings Lynn. The ladders were in place, rifles had been checked, grenades counted and prayers said. Just as Herbert had focused his mind, cleared his thoughts, overcome his fear – just as he was about to go over the top for the very first time, the attack was called off. The Norfolks were in support – but there was nothing left out there to support. The Norfolks would not go over the parapet – there was no point.

Even in the darkness, the scene was one of chaos. Fit men were struggling back to the safety of the trench while the wounded that could move were crawling back as best they could. The cries and moans of the men caught out in no-man's-land could be clearly heard by the Norfolks in the front line trench. And as day broke the devastation of the events of the last 36 hours was all around.

The scene is recorded by a photograph taken on 3 of July by an observation camera (see Photo 19). In the foreground is the British front line trench. The German front line trench winds it way across the view 800 yards away. The ground between is potted and scarred by craters, ripped open by mines and artillery shells. The ground is strewn with hundreds of bodies of the dead and wounded. It is very much the view that Herbert had as he and his colleagues manned the parapet of the trench.

But it was not over yet. The Norfolks had another job to do. There were very real concerns about a German counter-attack as the British front line was now exposed and vulnerable. The rest of the 35th Brigade had been decimated. The 800 or so remaining men of the 7th Norfolks were ordered to fan out along the front line trench to prepare for a counter-attack. They took over the whole of the Brigade line from Dorset Road to Barrow Road. For a while, they had to ignore the plaintive cries of dying men in order to secure the line. They stretched out over more than 1,000 yards. The defending line was very thin indeed but fortunately no attack came. The Germans were in no condition to take advantage of the situation. Herbert, as a member of B Company, was one of the men asked to defend the trench and for most of that day he and his colleagues were standing on the firing step of the trench with their eyes glued onto no-man's-land at Mash Valley and the rubble of the village of Ovillers, preparing for a possible German onslaught.

The ordeal was not over. The Germans now unleashed a very heavy artillery bombardment which targeted the trench. For the next 36 hours periodic heavy shelling deterred any further attack. Indeed the commanding officer of the Norfolks, Lt Col F. E. Walters, was hit and injured although he did not have to immediately withdraw. An observation post took a direct hit with inevitable casualties. Herbert survived the bombardment too, even though it must have been as intense as any he experienced for the whole of the war.

On the night of the 3rd and 4th July, men of the Norfolks were also engaged in a bloody task that was fraught with danger. They ventured into no-man's-land in the darkness to locate and bring back wounded men, some of whom had been left exposed to the elements since the 1st July. In the eerie half light of the night, Herbert and his colleagues "froze still" when lit up by the glow of flares which periodically lit up the sky. They crawled through the shell craters keeping close to the ground and calling quietly to wounded comrades desperate not to give away their positions and invite an incoming artillery shell or a sniper's bullet. Bodies were scattered all over the ground and in the half light it was difficult to establish the living from the dead. Such was the confusion of those nights that the Battalion medical officer Captain R. B. Lucas accidentally wandered into the enemy trench, was taken prisoner and never seen again.

Then the thunderstorm came. Rain came down in stair-rods. A deluge covered the whole area. Two centimetres of rain fell in a few hours. Lightning flashed and thunder rumbled over the sky, mixed with the noise of shells and guns. The trenches again filled with water and Herbert and his colleagues were standing in inches of slimy white mud. No-man's-land became a quagmire. The wounded in shell holes now faced the threat of drowning. The horror of Herbert's visit to Mash Valley was now complete.

The Norfolks held the line until the 6 July. While they manned the front, scouring no-man's-land for enemy activity, they also were asked to construct 200 yards of new front line trenches to connect their position to newly taken ground around La Boisselle. This meagre piece of churned up land was the only territorial gain that the Tommies had to show in this part of the front for five days of combat and thousands of casualties. The infantrymen had always been the workhorses of the British Army. Approaching exhaustion, without sleep, and still grieving their dead comrades, Herbert and his colleagues set about digging into the chalky soil to drive a trench south westward across what was until recently no-man's-land. The flurry of activity attracted the attention of the enemy guns yet again and the work was repeatedly interrupted by exploding incendiaries. It was very different from the digging that Herbert so enjoyed back home on his allotment in Swaffham. One shell dropped on the trench bay of the headquarters of D Company killing a lieutenant and wounding two others.[15] The shellfire was intense.

On that day, the high command made a strategic decision that was again to have a dramatic impact on Herbert and his war. The repeated attacks around La Boisselle and to the north had all failed to achieve their objectives and the cost in human life and matériel had been huge. No more attacks would be made for the time being. The Norfolks, indeed the whole of the battered brigade, was withdrawn and fell back to intermediate line trenches at Bazincourt to recover and reorganise. As Herbert staggered back through the communication trenches, he knew that the casualties in his battalion had been high. Thirty-two of Herbert's colleagues had been killed or were missing and would not return or would die of their wounds. Ninety-one had been wounded. The five days at Mash Valley had cost the 7th Norfolks nearly 15 percent of their strength. Herbert had survived. He had slept little in the last five days. He was near the end of his tether. He had witnessed five of the bloodiest days in the history of the British Army. He was still in one piece. He was one of the lucky ones.

---

15 Lieutenant Green was killed and Lieutenants Allen and O`Donnell critically wounded.

The Battalion however was battered and bruised – indeed the whole of the 35th Brigade was no longer an effective fighting unit. It needed, and would get, rest and recuperation. It would take quite some time to build it back into a fighting unit. It needed new recruits to replace its losses. The men needed time behind the lines. Herbert himself needed rest and some sleep. He needed a change of clothes and a square meal. He needed time to get over Mash Valley.

He was destined not to get that time. Having returned to Bouzincourt, three miles behind the front line, he was informed, on the 6 July that he and over 100 other survivors of Mash Valley were to be immediately transferred from the 7th Battalion to the 8th Battalion of the Norfolk Regiment. There was more fighting to be done. He was on his way to a different but none less deadly part of the Somme battlefield.

There was to be no rest.

CHAPTER 6

THE BATTLE OF THE SOMME

A WALK IN "DEVIL'S" WOOD – JULY 1916

Herbert's transfer to the 8th (Service) Battalion of the Norfolk Regiment was a direct result of that battalion needing to replace casualties incurred in the first few days of the Battle of the Somme.

It also reflected a major strategic decision made by General Haig, Commander-in-Chief of the British Expeditionary Force and General Rawlinson, Commander of the Fourth Army, on how the Battle of the Somme was to develop. Herbert, of course, was not aware of that. All he knew was that just when he thought a well earned rest was to come his way, he was ordered to march to Grove Town Camp, a few miles to the South East of the ruined town of Albert. He was to join his new Battalion. He was not alone. Over 100 men were transferred with him. Men who had fought so valiantly at Mash Valley were leaving the 7th Battalion and being drafted into the 8th.

In the first five days of the battle, the attacks along 13 miles of front in and north of the pivotal village of La Boisselle had resulted in fearful casualties and almost no territorial gains. The week long preparatory barrage had failed to destroy the deeply entrenched German defensive line. On the few occasions that the men had penetrated the forward trenches, it had not been in sufficient numbers to consolidate any gains. Local successes quickly turned into failures as German counterattacks bombed out the Tommies who had occupied their trenches. By 6th July, the attacks had been called off. The British and German front lines were, with a few exceptions, much the same as they had been at 7.30 am on the morning of the 1st July.

To the South and West of La Boisselle, the story was very different

The position of the British front on 14 July 1916 showing the position of Delville Wood in relation to the advancing British Army

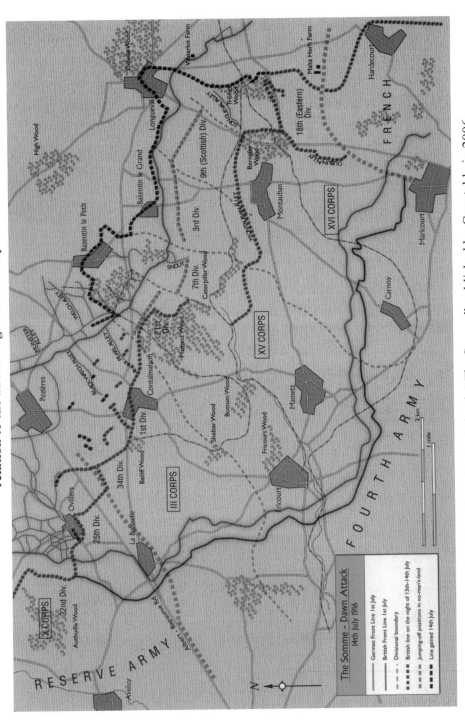

Map taken from Peter Barton's book *"The Somme"* published by Constable in 2006.

From 1 July onwards, significant advances had been made by the British Army as they pushed eastwards and northwards. The villages of La Boisselle, Fricourt, Mametz and Montauban had all been taken. Progress had been made. The French army, immediately to the east, had also moved forward.

History is still debating why these gains had been achieved from La Boisselle to Maricourt and so little progress had been made in the North between La Boisselle and Gommecourt. Geography certainly played a part – the German trenches did not overlook no-man's-land to the same degree. Also the artillery bombardment appeared to be more effective, with greater use on this part of the front of delayed fuses in artillery shells, which pulverised the German front line trenches to a greater degree. The digging of deep mines and saps under the enemy front line was more effective and used to greater advantage. Indeed many have argued that the division commanders in this part of the front were more effective in their management of the battle. They are credited with having developed better communications with their front line troops. They were encouraged to use their own initiative to react to the developing battle as they saw it. Whatever the reasons, the advances in the first few days of July on the south-eastern segment of the front had been considerable.

It was for these reasons that the High Command made the decision to abort the attacks in and north of La Boisselle and to concentrate their resources in the area where some success had already been achieved. This change of strategy had a direct impact on Private Herbert Bogey Barnes in sparing him from going over the top at Mash Valley and also bringing about his transfer to the 8th Battalion.

The 8th Battalion, the Norfolk Regiment was part of the 18th Eastern Division commanded by Major General F. Ivor Maxse. The 18th Division was to gain a reputation for thorough planning, effective training, creative innovation and considerable success as the war progressed. This reputation started as a result of their exploits on the opening day of the Battle of the Somme and was to grow through subsequent actions. The Division was made up of three brigades, the 53rd, the 54th and the 55th. The 53rd, commanded by the popular Brigadier General Higginson, was made up of the 8th Norfolks, 10th Essex, 6th Royal

Berks and the 8th Suffolk Regiments. It was thus mainly an Eastern Counties brigade with a high number of men who came from the farms and villages in the rural areas of East Anglia.

The 8th Norfolks had been fully employed in the first wave of attacks on 1 July in the area of Montauban and had achieved all of their major objectives. The 8th's first big battle had, however, cost it dearly. Eleven officers had been killed or wounded and of other ranks 103 had lost their lives and 219 had been wounded. A further 13 men were missing. Out of a strength of nearly 1,000 men, 345 had become casualties according to the Battalion War Diary. (War Diary casualty numbers are notably inaccurate but are used here for consistency's sake.) Although the Norfolks received congratulations from General Maxse himself, it had been a very heavy price to pay.

However, the 53rd Brigade, as well as the 54th and 55th Brigades, was to be fully involved in the second phase of the Battle of the Somme and it was urgent that their fighting strength be repaired. On the 6th July, an order was issued to draft 10 officers and 240 men from the 1st, 7th, and 10th battalions of the Norfolk Regiment to the 8th Battalion, Norfolk Regiment. Herbert was one of these men, again illustrating how the overall strategy for the conduct of the war had an all-pervasive impact on every individual soldier, whoever and wherever he might be.

The march to Grove Town camp from near the village of Bouzincourt was a short journey of a few miles but was nevertheless an ordeal for Herbert. He was dog tired and close to exhaustion. The route taken, skirting the southern side of Albert and through the small village of Méaulte, was never out of the range of the German heavy guns. The country roads were clogged with the traffic of war. It has been estimated that it takes seven men behind the front to keep one man at the front. A view of the valley near the village of Fricourt near where Herbert marched on that day (see Photo 20) shows very graphically a mass of men, horses, wagons, guns and early forms of motorised transport, all working to keep the men at the front supplied. Millions of tons of food, water, munitions and other matériel were being carried over every stretch of available road, track or footpath. Through it all Herbert marched with his colleagues to join his new battalion.

He arrived at Grove Town Camp sometime between the 9th and 13th of July. The camp was situated just off the Albert to Bray road and was some five miles behind the front. The whole of the 53rd Brigade was there, resting and recuperating. The name Grove Town was a gross misnomer as there was no town in the vicinity, neither was there anything that resembled a grove. The place was no more than a railway stop on a temporary loop that connected to the Albert-Amiens line. Apart from sidings, there was not much by way of geographical features. The area was used for camps and for the entraining and detraining of troops and equipment going to and from the front. The men had christened it "the City of Dumps" and as Herbert and the Norfolks marched to it, it was living up to its description. The flat plateau, worn bare of grass and void of trees, was a wide open space filled with equipment, tents, and marquees for thousands of men. Alongside there were barbed wire enclosures in which were incarcerated tired and frightened German prisoners. There were also "dumps" behind a large marquee for equipment and personal belongings of the dead that were "no longer needed", something Herbert would rather not have seen.[16]

In the midst of this morass of metal and men, and after the ordeal of death and destruction in Mash Valley, Herbert was to have a huge piece of good fortune. Amazingly, in this most unlikely of places, the Barnes brothers were to have a little family reunion. Firstly Herbert's younger brother Jack was also in the 8th Norfolks and had been since the middle of 1915. He was with his battalion in Grove Town Camp. He had survived the actions of 1915 and, more significantly, had come through the carnage of the previous two weeks. He, too, was exhausted from his experiences but was fit and well. His hair had greyed a little and his moustache looked a little unkempt. Nevertheless Herbert was very excited at the prospect of seeing his brother again.

---

16 The area now is the site of a War Graves Commission Cemetery standing on a windswept hill top. The neatly arranged white crosses standing in closely mown grass surrounded by tall green trees swaying gently in the breeze provide a peaceful setting, very different to the war-torn sight that greeted Herbert on his arrival here in July 1916.

It did not end there, however. Another battalion in the 53rd Brigade was the 8th Suffolks of which Herbert's elder brother, Alf, was a part. Herbert quickly learnt that the 8th Suffolks were in the same camp and he knew that before too long he would be able to meet up with brother Alfred as well. He had not seen Alf since he enlisted at the outset of the war in August 1914 and he did not know whether he had survived the slaughter of the previous few days. But survive he had. Indeed he had come through nearly two years of war still in one piece and still healthy and well. Herbert was reunited with both his brothers.

It was a poignant moment. Alfred, two years older than Herbert, had been not only his older brother but also his playmate. Jack, a little younger, had always been his bosom pal. They all looked very much like one another. All sported moustaches and spoke in a broad mid-Norfolk accent. Alfred had never lost his in spite of his years in India. They had played football together, been a part of the same Swaffham team. They had got up to all sorts of mischief in the streets of Kings Lynn and Swaffham. They had been as close as brothers could be. To meet up again in France, surrounded by the trappings of a brutal and bloody war, must have seemed a far cry from their peaceful and happy family life back in Norfolk.

There is no record of what was said or of how long they talked but they would have made the very best of the meeting. They would have shaken hands of course. In 1916 men did not hug one another. They were all pipe smokers so they would no doubt have pulled out their baccy tins, filled their pipes and had a quiet smoke. Perhaps they caught up on family news from back home, news received in letters from Rose or from Alf's wife Florrie. There would have been some jokes, of course, there always were. Alf had a wonderful sense of humour and a very quick wit and Jack knew a story or two. Herbert's long and hearty chuckle would have resonated around the camp. A twinkle returned to their eyes for a short time. Perhaps they also exchanged news on the other brother, young George, who was further up north in the trenches at Loos fighting in the Gloucesters. They might even have had a hand of crib. Herbert would have noted with some satisfaction the three stripes on Alf's arm and would have felt a little twinge of pride that his brother had made it to sergeant. Then they would have shaken hands again, wished one another good luck and gone back to their Battalions. The emotions would have been intense but always under control. For the next two months, the three brothers, now all in the 53rd Brigade, would never be too far away from one another.[17]

For the whole of the 53rd Brigade the training at Grove Town Camp was relentless. For the first few days, Herbert was fully engaged in integrating into his new Battalion. The Battalion, with its new recruits, had to be reorganised. Men who up until now had not known one another, had to forge a close relationship in order to get the 8th Norfolks back to the fighting force that they had been before they had been so cruelly decimated on the 1st of July.

In the meantime, the British Army had become involved in what had now become a war of attrition. The first initial punch having failed to deliver a knockout blow, the Battle of the Somme became a long, murderous grind to gain the upper hand. In this, the second phase of the Somme offensive, much of the action was centred on a number of woods that were viciously fought over.[18]

The woods were of strategic importance for a whole host of reasons not least as they afforded the soldiers holding them some protection against artillery bombardment. These woods, which took such a toll on British and German lives, have become household names, even 90 years after the conflict was over – Mametz Wood, Bernafay Wood, Trone Wood, High Wood and perhaps, most notably, Delville Wood which Herbert would always refer to as "Devil's Wood". The men who fought in these woods would always remember them, even when other aspects of the war had faded. A private in the Lincoln Regiment who wrote:

Devils Wood is another sight I could tell you something about but it is too horrible to mention and I shall not forget it to my last day. It is impossible for me to try and describe to you what these woods looked like after a battle. There

---

17   It is a matter of regret that it is not known in which Company of the 8th Norfolks Jack served – his papers have not survived. Herbert was to join D company. The assumption that Jack was in a different company is based on anecdotal evidence only.
18   Refer again to the illustration on page 87.

are hundreds of things I could tell you which 9 people out of 10 would say are all lies. It is only we who have seen them who can believe it. But ask anybody who was in the battle of Delville Wood and see what they will tell you. Murder is not the word for it. These are places where hundreds of men have said their prayers who had never said them before. I was wet to the skin, no overcoat, no water sheet. I had about 3 inches of clay clinging to my clothes and it was cold. I was in an open dug-out and do you know what I did – I sat down in the mud and cried.

Private D J Sweeny, 1st Lincolnshire Regiment.[19]

All this aptly describes the experiences of many soldiers, including Herbert Barnes. Of all the actions in which he took part, it was the death and destruction that he witnessed in Delville Wood that stayed with him, haunted him, and disturbed him, even when he was an elderly man in his 70s. It seemed for him and for many others to epitomise the wanton destruction of war and the futile and wasteful loss of human life that went with it.

Indeed, from the start, the involvement of the 53rd Brigade and the 8th Norfolks in Delville Wood was bedevilled by strategic indecision. The sequence of events is complicated but suffice it to say that on the 14th July, the 9th Scottish Division launched an attack on Delville Wood. On the same day, at 6.30 in the morning, the reorganised 8th Norfolks and the 53rd Brigade moved from Grove Town Camp to bivouac first in Billon Valley and subsequently in shelters in Trigger Valley. On 18 July, four days later, they moved to Talus Boisé just east of the ruined village of Carnoy. They had temporarily left the 18th Division and had been "loaned" to the 9th Division to help carry out attacks after Delville Wood had been taken. Had they known, the men would have made some wry jokes about the word "loaned". However the attacks on Delville Wood had not gone well and at 7.30 pm on the 18th July, 18th Divisional Headquarters had received an urgent and critical message from 9th Division: "send a brigade

---

19 Letter from Pt D J Sweeney. 1st Lincs – *The Somme* by Peter Barton published by Constable 2006.

immediately to support the South Africans of the 9th Scottish Division (in Delville Wood)". The Brigade chosen was the 53rd.

At this time, the wood was a salient in the front line turning at right angles and protruding into German territory. This enabled it to be bombarded in three directions by German guns and made it very vulnerable to counter-attack. It was, however, considered critical that the wood was held at all cost. For three long, bloody days the South Africans of the 9th Division had held the wood against fearful odds, first of all capturing the whole wood, and then having to retreat under fierce counter-attacks, moving forward again only to retreat under heavy bombardment. They had taken horrific casualties and were in urgent need of relief.[20] The wood had become a mass of twisted roots, truncated trees, a labyrinth of shallow trenches filled with the bodies of dead soldiers from both sides and the cries of wounded trying to seek out safety. It had become a hell hole (see Photo 23).

It is very little comfort to the men involved that the attack of the 53rd on Delville Wood should not have taken place at all. Three days earlier General Rawlinson had decided that "the time for isolated attacks had now finished and an organised attack along a broad front was now necessary". Indeed this broad front attack had originally been planned for the 17th but could not be organised until the 23rd. But in spite of this overall strategy, for some reason, isolated attacks continued in Delville Wood all through this period when it had already been decided that they were largely futile and unlikely to succeed. The action of the 53rd Brigade was a part of these unexplained isolated attacks.

At 8 am on July 18, the Germans had opened a tremendous bombardment on Delville Wood with guns of all calibres. By 2 pm in the afternoon, the shelling increased in fury, a prelude to a massive attack by picked troops of the 7th and 8th Divisions, Magdeburg Corps. The South African Brigade was once again forced to concede ground. By early evening they were maintaining a desperate hold on only the south-west corner of the wood.

---

20   Out of 121 Officers and 3,032 other ranks in the South African Brigade, only 29 officers and 751 men survived.

Herbert and the 8th Norfolks were blissfully unaware of this bigger picture. At 1.30 in the morning of the July 19, an order was received to move out of the disused trenches at Talus Boisé. It was an overcast night and in the dark gloom, visibility was poor. The men moved forward to collect in a shallow valley north of the captured village of Montauban. The approach to Delville Wood was to be up a sunken road in this shallow valley until it emerged at the shattered remains of Longueval, the pile of rubble that used to be the village at the south-west corner of the wood (see photo 21). The safer route, up through a deep communication trench, was not taken as it was heavily congested and in some cases blocked by stretcher-bearers, wounded men and the wreckage of five days of fighting in the wood. Just as at Mash Valley, Herbert was to find that the most protected route to the front line was impassable due to the death and destruction of the battle going on ahead of him. The Norfolks were to lead the way, followed by the other battalions of the Brigade. On arriving at Longueval, the Norfolks were to turn right, enter the trench system which led to an orchard and there they would deploy and enter the wood.

A map of Delville Wood showing the trench system through which the 7th Battalion the Norfolk Regiment advanced on the 19 July 1916

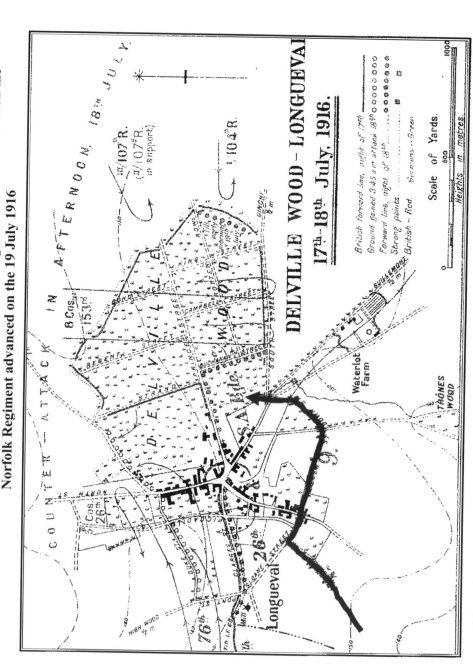

Map take from Nigel Cave's book "Delville Wood". Published by Pen & Sword Books Limited in 1999 and reprinted in 2003.

By 4.30, just as the dawn was beginning to break, the Norfolks had collected in the valley and the commanding officer, Lt Col Ferguson, indicated that the men would be ready to begin their attack by 6.15. He reckoned without two factors. As Herbert and the Norfolks moved forward up the valley, they were protected from artillery fire, but emerging from the valley closer to the village in the early morning daylight they were in the open and became vulnerable to artillery fire from High Wood to the north which was in German hands. They began taking casualties. Other battalions of the Brigade coming up behind, particularly the Berkshires, were hard hit, taking nearly 50 casualties. This was an inauspicious start to the attack but it was to get worse. When the first two companies of the Norfolks reached the wood, one of them, B Company, was unable to deploy as it had come under heavy machine-gun fire. Adjustments had to be made and B Company backfilled the trench behind A Company. While this drama was unfolding Herbert and D Company were static in the access trench waiting for events to unfold. As the official history of the Norfolk regiment unemotionally states "this delayed the deployment and no attack was possible before 7.15am". The men, of course, by this time had already been up for many hours.

The orders for the attack were both simplistic and ambitious and reflected the extreme seriousness of the moment. The South Africans, on the previous day, had been forced back. They held only the south-west corner of the wood. The Norfolks were to attack eastwards and to clear the whole of the southern sector of the wood, putting down strongpoints along Princes Street as they went. These strongpoints were to face north to protect the advancing troops and prevent counter-attacks. The rest of the brigade, the 10th Essex, the 6th Royal Berks and the 8th Suffolks (Brother Alf's Battalion) would then attack northwards and clear the whole of the north of the wood. Delville Wood would be in British hands by the end of the day.

It is to the lasting credit of the Norfolks that they achieved much of what was asked of them. The challenges they faced were legion. The attack was starting at least an hour late. The men were new to the Wood (indeed none of the Brigade had trained in fighting through woodland shattered by shellfire) and did not know the ground. They were moving forward without the protection of a covering barrage and as they moved forward they were subject to both machine-gun and artillery attack from the German positions north of Princes Street and even a few positions south of it. They were bedevilled by communication problems between platoon, company, battalion and headquarters – indeed Brigadier General Higginson was back in his cellar headquarters at a loss to know how the battle was progressing. In spite of all these problems, remarkable and heroic progress was made.

The Norfolks' attacks started at 7.15 am. B Company on the right made very good progress and took much of Campbell Street. But A Company on the left, exposed as they were to the German lines, were badly mauled by machine-gun fire and had to be supported by C Company. Casualties were becoming alarmingly heavy. Nevertheless the men against all odds continued to advance and by 11.30 the forward companies on the right had reached King Street. The forward platoons were then held up by their own barrage that was trained on the area ahead of them but as soon as it lifted, they dashed forward and by 12.00 noon had taken the south east edge of the wood. A Company on the left were then able to move forward but again took heavy casualties from machine-gun fire coming from north of Princes Street. Yet they continued to advance as C Company and some of D Company laid down strongpoints behind them to ward off counter-attacks. Throughout the advance, the opposition was fierce. Individual German machine-gun nests had to be cleared, often with heavy casualties. Machine-guns from the north of Princes Street wreaked havoc and often could not be silenced as the British bombardment was focused on that part of the wood. Fighting was at very close quarters indeed as the men used bombs, rifles and bayonets to clear a way forward. It was a heroic effort with success achieved at huge cost.

By 12.40, Colonel Ferguson could report to Brigade Headquarters:

My right company has pushed forward to the east edge of the wood and is consolidating its position as ordered. My left company last reported in touch with the right company on a line running north to south 80 yards from the east edge of the wood. A platoon of the support company entered Princes Street without interference from enemy and is holding centre portion of Princes Street. Portion of wood south of Princes Street now reported clear.

He can almost be heard to be saying in a loud voice – job done – so there.

It had been an outstanding effort and was undoubtedly the 8th Norfolks' finest hour. They would fight many more actions and achieve other successes but nothing would ever compare with their attack on Delville Wood for sheer courage and persistence. Against incredible odds and in the most difficult conditions they had done everything that was asked of them. At 1.30 pm the other three battalions of the brigade were now able to be sent forward to attempt to take the northern part of the wood, while the Norfolks dug in and made strongpoints all around the part of the wood they had captured.

Herbert's exact position in the attack is not clear. He was a member of D Company who were both in support and followed up behind the attacking A and B Companies. If this was the case, he was spared some of the heaviest face to face combat but was certainly fully involved in laying down the strongpoints along Princes Street as the attack moved forward. These strongpoints were then subjected to counter-attack from German infantry which involved bayonet and pistol charges. The strongpoints were also subject to very heavy artillery bombardment as the Germans tried to dislodge the Norfolks from the ground they had taken. Sniper fire was also directed at the strongpoints as men tried desperately to hold their ground and dig down to get some protection in the tangled undergrowth, lying in shallow, water filled holes amongst the roots and ruined trees. It could be that Herbert was in the support platoon that first got into the Princes Street trench and held it against counter-attacks. There is no way of knowing. What is certain is that, as many Tommies who were there said "the devil alone could survive in Devil's Wood".

Although the Norfolks had "done their job" the attack of the other battalions in the northern part of Delville Wood could make little progress, and everybody had to "dig themselves in" and hold their ground. For the next two days, the 53rd Brigade held onto the captured portions of the Wood against a tremendous bombardment, persistent fire from snipers and periodic local counter-attacks. As casualties piled up, a stalemate was reached with the Germans continuing to hold the northern part and the 53rd Brigade the southern part.

For the second time in three weeks, the 8th Norfolks had suffered fearful casualties. The War Diary records that it had three officers dead and eight wounded. Of the men, 78 were killed and 174 wounded. Another 36 men were missing. A total of 299 men had been casualties, nearly a third of the whole battalion (see photo 22). For a second time in a few days, the 8th Norfolks had been battered and bruised and their strength decimated.

In the midst of all this mayhem, Herbert had somehow survived – unhurt and uninjured. He had been, for the first time, in hand to hand fighting at close quarters. He had used his bayonet. He had shot at the enemy at close range. He had killed other men. The gentle man from a Norfolk country town had done what a few months previously would have been inconceivable and unbelievable. He had not only witnessed the carnage and slaughter, the heroism and bravery, the dirt and the filth, he had been a part of it and played his role in it.

The events of Devil's Wood never left him. The effects were long lasting and he buried them deep inside himself. However, on the very few occasions in later life that he recalled the war, his memories were invariably of "Devil's Wood". He would relive the "bombs going off all around me – they kept going off – they wouldn't stop". He would remember the killing and his part in it – "I saw the Germans and I shot them".

More poignantly, he told to one of his granddaughters the story of how a German soldier had saved his life. He recounted how he was helpless on the ground, unable to defend himself, when a German came upon him "he could have shot me, he could have done it quite easily, but he didn't – he looked at me, he looked me up and down and moved away again. Only he will know his reasons". Even in the hell of Delville Wood where man's inhumanity to man plumbed depths beyond comprehension, Herbert held onto the memory that told him that there was some goodness everywhere and in everybody. It is perhaps the mark of his character that he would choose to remember the saving of life, rather than the taking of it. It was perhaps his way of coming to grips with the hell hole that was Delville Wood.

Devil's Wood is now a peaceful place. Trees have regrown and the grass is carefully tended by those that look after the South African War Memorial which gleams white amongst the green foliage. The rides cut between the trees that once were the lines of the trenches now provide opportunity for people to take country walks. Princes Street, which the Norfolks fought so valiantly to hold, is now a beautiful tree-lined path. In spring, birds sing high in the trees. The bracken on the ground is lit by the shafts of sunlight that glint through the canopy above. There is now quiet in the places where Herbert Barnes and the men of the 8th Battalion, the Norfolk Regiment paid their visit to the Devil's Wood.

On the night of 21/22 July, the battered and smashed battalion was relieved. Another isolated attack had failed to achieve its objectives but Delville Wood was still partially in British hands. The survivors made their way back down the communication trench that had been denied them on their way forward and in time they returned to Grove Town Camp. They were a mixture of tired men, exhausted but unharmed; of walking wounded on improvised crutches limping along as best they could; of German prisoners, frightened but relieved to be alive; of stretcher-bearers getting their bloody loads back to the casualty clearing station. They left Devil's Wood behind them and it would be many more long and bloody days before the British would take control of it. Indeed, some of the wood was still in German hands throughout August.

The conclusion on Delville Wood must be left to the much respected commander of the 53rd Brigade, General Bernard Higginson, who was quite aware of the futility of the endeavour and risked court martial by writing a bitter report in which he compared the operation at Delville Wood with his brigade's success on 1 July which he noted:

... was characterised by careful attention to all details of the attack, artillery preparation and wire cutting and co-operation of the artillery with the infantry in the attack. The Delville Wood operation by contrast was characterised

by; insufficient time for careful consideration of plans; insufficient time for artillery preparation; difficulty with communication of battalions; lack of co-operation between artillery and infantry; difficulty of obtaining accurate information about the situation; lack of co-operation with neighbouring units and (perhaps more damningly) the fact the attack was not launched until 45 minutes after the artillery bombardment had ceased.

He concludes that "the failure of these attacks was not due to in any way to the lack of determination on the part of the troops".

This could be of little consolation to Herbert. The results of all the strategic indecision were to provide him with a terrible experience he would never forget and would cost the 8th Norfolks 299 men dead and wounded (see Photo 22).

What is more, as he marched back to Grove Town Camp, he did not know if his two brothers were among the living, the wounded or the dead.

CHAPTER 7

THE BATTLE OF THE SOMME

FOR KING AND COUNTRY – THIEPVAL
JULY–SEPTEMBER 1916

Herbert and the exhausted survivors of the Norfolks returned to Grove Town Camp.

After the hell of Delville Wood, Herbert still found the camp a welcome relief. As bleak as the place was, it was nevertheless a haven of peacefulness compared with the cauldron he had just left. However, he was not to be there for very long. The 8th Norfolks were no longer an effective fighting unit. They desperately needed a period of recuperation and reorganisation behind the lines and out of the range of the German heavy guns. In fact, the whole of the 53rd Brigade needed a break and soon. If Herbert thought that after the ordeal of Delville Wood rest was to be immediate, he was to be disappointed. He would soon be on the move again.

However, his anxiety about his brothers would not let him rest. He immediately set about finding out what had happened to them. Like him, they had both been in the thick of the fighting. Within hours, he was able to ascertain that Alf had also miraculously survived the carnage of Delville Wood. The 8th Suffolks had been one of the battalions that had attempted to capture the northern part of the wood, north of Princes Street, after the Norfolks had cleared the southern section. They had been unable to move forward very far and had quickly lost the little ground they had gained. They had been beaten back, bombarded, and suffered heavy casualties. They had to dig in for two days and repulse determined German counter-attacks. Alf had been in the thick

103

of it, only a few yards from his younger brother. He had pulled through. He was still in one piece.

Jack was less fortunate. Somewhere during the attack by the 8th Norfolks in the southern part of the wood, he had been hit by shrapnel from an artillery shell. His right leg from knee to upper thigh had been badly mangled. He had bled profusely but compared with many of his colleagues he had been lucky. He had been quickly evacuated back down the communication trench and had reached the casualty clearing station in time for the surgeons to save his leg and his life. He had "a blighty", a wound severe enough to give him a ticket back to England. He was in heavy pain and some distress but he would survive. He would never play football again and he would from that day on for the rest of his life be an "invalid". By the time Herbert got back to Grove Town Camp, Jack was on a stretcher on his way to a Channel port and back to England. Herbert would not see him again in France.[21]

Even given the hectic schedule of the 51st Brigade, there can be little doubt that Alf and Herbert met up again at Grove Town. They might well have recounted to one another their own harrowing experiences over the last few days. They would, neither one of them, talk much about them in subsequent years. They might have been distressed but secretly relieved that Jack, battered as he was, was on his way home to the safety of the home country. We know that they both wrote short letters home to their wives that said little more than that they were "going on fine". It would have been a sober meeting as they caught up on which of their pals had made it and which ones had not. This was a terrible war.

To recuperate and reorganise, the battalion was sent that self same day back north to Northern France, indeed all the way back to Flanders. There was to be no immediate rest. Having been relieved from the trenches in Delville Wood at 1 am, the war weary men of B, C and D Companies arrived back at Grove

---

21 As shall be seen as Herbert's story unfolds, this was not the end of Jack's war. He would never go to France again but after recovering in a War Hospital in England, he was posted to the 3rd Battalion, the Norfolk Regiment and saw out his war in Felixstowe as part of the training battalion. Herbert's and Jack's paths would cross a number of times before the war was over. Jack would not be invalided out of the army until 1919, three years after his wound at Delville Wood.

Town Camp at 6.30 am. A Company were to arrive a day later. They waited over seven hours for a train. There was no shelter at the station. Indeed there was not even a platform. Fortunately, although it was an overcast day, there was no rain. The men wandered around the camp taking in the sights and sounds of the place. Some slept, some played cards, and others just lay down and stared into the distance, alone with their thoughts.

They boarded the train and the first part of the journey (30 miles) took 12 hours to complete as the troop train negotiated its way eastwards past Amiens. The offensive was still in full swing and railways were congested with men and matériel going to and from the front. They eventually arrived at Longpré-les-Corps-Saints, a small town much further down the Somme Valley. It was intact and undamaged, out of range of enemy guns, and for the first time in four weeks Herbert was again in touch with a civilised world. For two days the Norfolks were put up in hastily arranged billets waiting for their transport to catch them up. Then at 6 pm in the evening of 26 July they were entrained again. For most of that night, they clattered 50 miles through the French countryside starting, stopping and starting again, until at 3.30 in the morning while it was still dark they disembarked in a small village of Arques near St Omer. The men gathered on the platform at the station where they were hastily served hot tea, sandwiches and a piece of cake. And still there was no rest. At 8 am the same morning, they route-marched five miles to the village of Blaringhem. They had been on the move for a very long time since leaving Delville Wood. The next day saw another route march of three miles followed by a further seven miles the next day. At last they had arrived at Godewaersvelde, which Herbert found impossible to either spell or pronounce.[22] They had finally arrived at the camp where they could begin to recover.

---

22 Herbert always referred to it as simply "Gods" although it bore little resemblance to anybody's concept of heaven.

Rose knew very little about Herbert's tribulations and the children knew nothing at all. Of course, the local newspapers were reporting that a new co-ordinated offensive was taking place north and south of the Somme River but its scale had not been fully outlined. The Eastern Daily Press, which Rose saw nearly every day, carried a day by day account of the progress of the attack. The accounts nearly always used glowing words like success and advance, with copious details of territory captured and German soldiers taken prisoner. There was, of course, no mention yet of the thousands of deaths of July 1 and the growing casualty list of the first four weeks of the battle. That would come later. The *Norfolk Mercury* also found its way into Ash Close. It had started to publish lists of the dead and wounded from Norfolk, Suffolk and the surrounding counties and continued to do so for the remainder of the war. But since July 1 there had been silence on that subject.

Rose might not have known which part of the front Herbert was fighting. The frequent letters had been brief, asking after the children and telling Rose that Herbert was "going on fine". There was of course, no mention of Mash Valley or Delville Wood. There was no point. The Censor would deem such information sensitive and likely to compromise the war effort and he would strike it all out. However, Rose was an intelligent lady and would have known in her heart that her husband, along with thousands of other husbands, was involved in the new offensive and was now exposed to extreme peril. She lived in deadly fear of the dreaded telegram from the war office. Swaffham was a small town and news travelled fast. Charlie Horsley, a Lance Corporal, whose parents lived along the Lynn Road, had been killed on the 10th July. George Long who also lived with his wife on Lynn Road was killed three days later. Bob Rasbary had died on the opening day of the offensive as had Ernie Angell. Both were in the 8th Norfolks, both were well known to Herbert – and to Rose too. Swaffham was a small community. There were others. Bert Brightwell, whose parents lived in Theatre Street, would not be coming home either. Rose's cousin by marriage, Bert Negus, who had lived in Ely, had met his end on the 20th July. Rose did her best to keep the worry away from the children but with the best will in the world, Alf and Phyllis could not help but be aware that their father was in dire danger. The letters from Herbert and Alf about their own safety and the news of the wound to Jack were a huge relief to all the family.

Life in the small Norfolk town went on as best it could. Rose was more than fully occupied from dawn to dusk keeping the children fed and clothed, helped by her father and sister, Emma, who popped in from next door regularly. Their diet was supplemented by the plentiful produce from the allotment. The children spent almost as much time in their Grandfather's house as they did in their own. They also played outside during the long summer evenings and as young Bert was later to recall "we were very lucky as we had two yards – one at the front and one at the back – it made us feel a little special". Rose did find time to go to the Baptist church. She was a regular member of the chapel choir and her melodious soprano voice rang out around the small house in Ash Close as she went about her many chores.[23] She had also become involved in helping at the Chapel in the many charity events set up to provide the men at the front with some small extra treats and comforts. She had nothing to give of course other than what she sent to Herbert but she was a very capable organiser and could give a little of her time.

It was at this time that Rose started to nurture a little dream of her own. Alf, who was now nine years old, and Phyllis, now seven, were both showing promise at school. She watched them as they ran off together in the morning a few hundred yards to their school along the White Cross Road. She was aware that the many evenings that she spent with them, reading, reciting poetry, singing and talking was having a very positive effect. She, a poor working class lady, living in a humble two-up-two-down cottage began to wonder whether it might be possible for Alf the eldest and the boy, to aspire to go to Hammond School, the Grammar school in the town. Of course, it was almost unheard of. This was 1916 and the Grammar school was reserved for the sons of the well-to-do and very rarely opened its doors to those of a different class. Anyway, Rose knew it would cost money – a lot of money and that was something that Rose did not have. But Alf was clearly a bright boy and maybe there were scholarships or

---

23 The choir would later perform a fully fledged version of Handel's Messiah which Rose would recall in later life with huge pleasure and satisfaction.

bursaries that could be found. She was not an ambitious woman but she began to develop an ambition for her son – an ambition for his education. She would ask some questions in the town. She would make some enquiries and see what could be done. Who could say what might be possible in these unusual times?

Whatever her dreams, they were rudely shattered on the 22nd July, the self same day that Herbert and the 8th Norfolks were in Grove Town recovering from their ordeal in Delville Wood. The dreaded telegram was received, but not at Ash Close. Herbert's father, now living with his second wife and family at Wells-next-the-Sea was advised by the War Office that George, the youngest of the five brothers, was missing in action in France. The news was devastating and brought home to the whole family the tragedy of this war. George was only 23 years old and engaged to be married to a local girl called Gertrude. At the outbreak of the war he had enthusiastically enlisted in the 1st Battalion the Norfolk Regiment and had subsequently been transferred to the 2nd Gloucesters. He had been amongst the first to be shipped to France, arriving on August 17 1914, only a few days after the declaration of war. In a letter home, written a few days later to his eldest sister, Mary, he spelt out in typical Tommy fashion what it was like to be whisked away to the front (see Appendix Five).

Dear Mary

I suppose when you see the writing on the envelope you will soon conclude where I have got to. Well of course I can not tell you where I am but this I will tell you, mind you, keep it secret. I am "somewhere in France" and not very fond of it either but at the same time I am not downhearted and live in hopes of better times later on. We are within sound of guns and it seems rather creepy but I shall no doubt get use to it in time. We are billeted in barns with a number of rats for company but I sleep outside at night as I fancy there are other live things about besides rats. And I expect to have enough of them when I get in the trenches. My word it was quick work. Though I volunteered on the Friday we heard nothing further until last Wednesday week. We moved off to Tidworth and were attached to the 2/6 Gloucesters and we left Tidworth last Tuesday and well here I am and are likely to remain I suppose perhaps for ever but I keep a stout heart and trust to luck. I had no chance to go home nor yet see Gert before I came away. It has been all rush since I left N Walsham. There are about 100 of the old 6th in the battalion and we are all together.

He had seen much action but had survived through 1914 and 1915. He seemed unaware of what was happening to his brothers and seemed not to have had too much news at all. He had written again to Mary in July 1916:

Your kind letter & cigs duly received & I hardly know how to thank you enough. It has quite cheered me up & I am afraid I was getting a trifle downhearted as yours is the first letter I have received since I have been out here & I have written a good many & one or two before yours but of course some of them may have gone astray but I certainly thought I should have one from Gert but I wrote her again yesterday week so perhaps I shall soon hear from her. I believe there was a bit of a muddle with the letters when we first came out but I think everything is alright now. I did not know Herbert was over here. Perhaps you will send me his address when you write again and I will write to him, also Alfs if you have it. Was Alf wounded do you know or was it sickness? You are indeed right about the weather dear it has been & is wicked. We have had a spell in the trenches & it was rotten. Raining nearly all the time & as you know we are up all night and it was miserable really in the rain. Oh did I tell you I had all my hair clipped off all over. You would hardly know me now I expect. One thing dear I have seen the serious side of the war now & I should never have done so in N Walsham. I don't in the least regret having volunteered although perhaps I have compared doings out here to what I should have been doing in N.Walsham especially when I turned in my dugout wet through at about 4 am in the morning. It is a bit different to a feather bed I assure you. But I have the consolation of knowing that I am doing my little bit now dear.

In July 1916 he had not even been in the Somme offensive at all but had been holding a relatively quiet part of the front 60 miles to the north near Loos.

A few days before he was killed, he had written a very matter of fact letter home, again to his sister, not knowing that he had so little life left to live:

> *My Dear Sister,*
>
> *Many thanks for your letters and cigs received yesterday morning. It is very good of you indeed to send them as English fags are so scarce. Fancy you not knowing my writing but there we have no desks here to write on and have to do the best we can. Yes dear I have received several letters since last writing you and a huge parcel from Aunt Jane at Ely and as it came to me in the trenches it was lovely. There were some eggs and my chum and I had eggs and bacon in the trenches hardly creditable is it. Yes dear do write every week as it is very often impossible for me to get off the letters after I have written them as I may be on duty or not near where letters are collected and then it is no good until next day. I tell you what I do want, dear, and that is an indelible pencil. I cannot get one out here and ordinary black pencil is no cop for addressing envelopes as it rubs off so easily. I hope Ernest is better. (Ernest was Mary's husband.) It is not at all unlikely my meeting Aunt Nellies boy as I have met Percy Hunter who was with Herbert at Swaffham and he and I went to school there together. He is in the same division as I. We hear a good deal about peace but I can not see it coming off yet but I truly believe we have got the Hun whacked. I am feeling quite jolly today dear as I have just had such a lovely letter from Gert. Well give my love to Ernie and kiss the children for me and thank you once again for cigs with fondest love and kisses from*
>
> *Your Loving Bro*
>
> *George*
>
> *PS We have been in rest billets the last ten days at a decent sized place and saw " Charlie Chaplin" last night.*

Less than two weeks later, poor George was dead. He and two of his colleagues had been hit by an artillery shell while out in no-man's-land on a working party. His mortal remains were never found and he became one of the thousands of soldiers remembered on the Loos war memorial who have no known graves. The family now had its second casualty – it would not be the last. The Somme offensive was beginning to impact families up and down the country in a way that war had never done before. Alfred George Barnes, a mere engine driver living in Wells, was hit hard by the news. It is not surprising. They were a close family and he had had one son killed, another seriously injured, and two more surviving by the skin of their teeth.

Rose wrote to Herbert and told him the news. It is likely that Herbert searched out his brother Alf who was also at Godewaersvelde when the news came through. The two brothers sadly recalled the young boisterous George with his bright disposition and impish character. They remembered the day he was born – they were over 12 years older than him. They recalled his growing up in Swaffham; the ball games they played; the times they bullied him a little and the times they protected him from being bullied by others. Most of all, they felt for their father because George, although he was the youngest, was also the brightest with perhaps the most potential and the greatest hopes. It was not to be. A light had gone out. This was indeed a dreadful war.

Herbert and the Norfolks, following their arrival in Flanders, continued to move from billet to billet. They stayed in the village of Estaires, then in Les Haies Basses, and four days later near Bailleul. Herbert was seeing more of northern France than he had bargained for. The battalion was reorganised following their heavy losses. New recruits from England were drafted in to make up the numbers and the men had an opportunity to take it easy for a while, away from the dangers of the front line. The routine that Herbert got to know when he first arrived in France – church on Sundays, bath days once a week, regular laundering of his uniform, recreational activity interspersed with renewed training, route marches and periods of rest – took over his life again. Herbert was learning that, although the short periods of intense action in the front line exposed him and his mates to the most deadly peril and had the greatest long-lasting impact on him, by far the biggest proportion of the time was spent behind the lines.[24]

However, on 14 August the Battalion was woken up earlier than usual in order to march the two miles to Bailleul. Every element of the battalion and its men were particularly spick and span that morning. No stone had been left unturned. Uniforms were neatly creased, boots sparkled, and guns glittered. Even as the battalion marched through a showery sky, nothing could be allowed to take away from the fact that they looked a fine group of fighting soldiers. They arrived at Bailleul and lined up on an immense parade ground together with other units of the 18th Division. King George V arrived. He inspected the battalion in the early afternoon under a grey sky and light rain. The King had made a habit of making frequent visits to France to show his face and to support his soldiers. It was considered an essential part of keeping morale high amongst the fighting troops. He had arrived on 10 August in order to visit his Generals and inspect many of his units. On Thursday 14 August it was the turn of the 8th Norfolks.

Herbert stood to attention in the rain. In spite of all the hardships, it was a moment of pride for him. He had never seen the King before. He had been brought up close to Sandringham House, the Royal family's country home, but he had never been in the House. His father told the story of how he had once driven the Royal train from Kings Lynn to Wolferton, the station closest to Sandringham House. One day, his father was asked to stand to attention on the platform and the King presented to him a gold watch chain on which hung a medal. Each link on the chain was embossed with the initials G R and from it hung the medal with George V's face stamped on it. A stop watch was essential to a railwayman and Herbert's father had attached to the chain a fine American Waltham Pocket Watch engraved with his name. His father still had the medal and carried it with pride on a hook on his belt.[25]

---

24 During the whole of Herbert's military service in France, nine days out of 10 would be spent in comparative safety, mostly in training, often within the sound of guns but never really threatened. This ratio of front line action to time spent behind the lines is fairly typical of all the Tommies. It was during this time that the friendships that were the essential and fulfilling part of army life were developed and fostered.

25 The chain, medal and watch still exists in the family. It has been passed down from eldest

The King, sitting on a magnificent horse on one end of the parade ground, reviewed the troops. As Herbert marched past and saluted his monarch, he felt a stirring that belied the continuous anxiety of his situation. He would remember the moment for the rest of his life.[26]

The King saw more than just a parade. The Battalion put on a small demonstration for his benefit of a replica of the attack of the 1st of July. It was a mock battle. A Company acted as the German defenders while B and C Companies played the role of the attackers. There is no record of what D Company did but it is likely that Herbert went over the top yet again but this time nobody got killed or injured. Herbert must have hoped that the King was suitably impressed as it could not have been much fun for the men who had lost so many pals in the real attack.[27]

Herbert and the Norfolks spent the following 12 days in the Bailleul area. The training was intense, as the new recruits integrated into the battalion and the whole range of trench warfare activities as rehearsed time and time again. The Battalion needed to get back up to be the effective fighting force it had once been. As the month of August turned into September, the Battalion moved by train further south to the area around the town of Diéval where training and route marching began all over again. Herbert was sick of it, bored with the repetition and with the immense physical exertion as he worked hard to keep up with his younger colleagues. However the objective was achieved. The 8th Norfolks became fighting fit again. They became efficient, well trained and ready to handle once again whatever this terrible war would throw at them.

He wrote home regularly, mostly to Rose, but also some little notes to Alf and Phyllis. His letters were brief, unemotional and not very newsy. He said

---

son to eldest son and is now being held for eight year old James Edward Barnes, great, great, great grandson of the train driver.

26   In 1952 when the news of the death of Queen Mary was broadcast over the radio, the author happened to be sitting with his Grandfather who casually mentioned in a low voice that he had once "met the King". Nobody paid very much attention to his comment and it was not until during the research for this book that it was realised to what he was referring.

27   There is no reference in the Brigade or Battalion War Diaries to a parade before the King although the re-enactment is mentioned. It took place at Mont de Lille near Godewaersvelde. The parade is described in this narrative only because Herbert once made reference to it.

very little about how he felt. He made a point of collecting more cigarette cards from his mates, packing them up and sending them back to Swaffham. He knew his young sons would thank him for it. He did not know what the future would hold and he saw no point in thinking much about it. He had been in France for less than six months but a kind of resignation had set in. He missed Rose and the children but it was best not to think about that either.

While the 8th Norfolks were reorganising and recuperating the battle of the Somme to the south had turned into a bloody conflict of attrition. Casualties on both sides were reaching proportions unprecedented in the history of warfare. Not even in the American Civil War or the Franco-Prussian War of 1870 had there been anything like this. By the middle of September over half a million men on both sides had been killed or wounded.

The British had continued to slowly grind their way forward to the south and to the east. The villages of Ovillers, Contalmaison, Pozières, Bazentin-le-Petit and Bazentin-le-Grand had all been captured – but with horrifying casualties. The pivot of the British front line now revolved around the fortress village of Thiepval, the same Thiepval that had been attacked way back on 1 July but had resisted then, and continued to resist now. All attempts to take it had failed. Standing on high ground overlooking the Ancre Valley and protected by the defensive strongpoints of the Schwaben Redoubt, Stuff Redoubt and Goat Redoubt it had taken on a reputation of being impregnable.

In the third week of September, Generals Rawlinson and Gough took the view that any further progress by the forward British units was being compromised and could not be made, as long as Thiepval and the Schwaben Redoubt remained in German hands. Prior and Wilson, in their excellent book *The Somme* take up the story:

> It was decided that on 26 September an attack would be launched by four assault divisions along a 6,000 yard front – the objective, to take Thiepval and all the strong points protecting it. The most difficult task would fall to the 18th Division which had played such a conspicuous part in early operations on the Somme. Since then it had been "resting" further north, now it would be

brought south and given the intimidating task of capturing Thiepval and the Schwaben Redoubt, strong points that had taken such a fearful toll on 1 July and which had not been successfully attacked since.[28]

That general strategic decision was to have a dramatic effect on the next year of the life of Herbert Barnes.

In response to these grand strategic decisions, the 18th Division including the 8th Norfolks and the 53rd Brigade started their return journey back to the Somme battlefield on 8 September. The journey south from the relative safety of Artois to the front line trenches on the Somme was carried out, a few miles at a time, and largely on foot. From 1 to 8 September, Herbert was billeted at the small village of Béthonsart, not far from Bailleul and some 12 miles to the west of the front line. There then began a series of route marches southwards. On the 9th the Norfolks covered 15 miles to Rebreuve, the next day another seven miles to Halloy Camp and yet another six miles the next day, to Léalvillers. Each day they were marching by 8.30 in the morning and arriving at the destination at close to midday. There was no doubt as to what lay ahead of them. Close to Léalvillers village they began four days of intensive training at Clairfaye Farm. The farm was situated on high ground slightly protected by a shell-ravaged copse.[29]

On the 17th the Norfolks moved to Acheux camp and then to the village of Bouzincourt – and then the next day back to Forceville camp. They were now very close to the front line. What were all these small route marches for? The reason for this activity was less than clear to Herbert or, for that matter, to the Battalion commander. He did not know that it reflected some indecision by the High Command as to exactly where the planned attack on Thiepval ridge was to take place. All Herbert knew was that he and his mates were moving from place to place for no apparent reason, and all this time within earshot of the rumblings of the heavy guns from the front. One can hear him complaining in his Norfolk accent beneath his breath "we wan t Swafum t' do a days trarshin for narthin" –

---

28 *The Somme* by Robin Prior and Trevor Wilson published by Yale University Press 2006.
29 Nowadays, the farm is best viewed from the peace of the Varennes War Cemetery.

which, loosely translated means "we went to Swaffham to thrash corn but were not paid". In short, someone was wasting our time.[30]

At Acheux camp, Herbert and his colleagues saw something they had never seen before. They looked on it with a degree of incredulity. They saw a new contraption that went under the name of "tank" (see Photo 24). In the co-ordinated attacks in early September for the first time in the history of warfare, tanks were employed. As these huge mechanised monsters rumbled their way to the front, the impact on the soldiers was a mixture of excitement and suspicion:

> *Then, all of a sudden, I heard a strange noise, accompanied by shouts and cheers, and saw the most extraordinary vehicles approaching, with men sitting on them cheering. They were a kind of armoured car on caterpillars and each towed a sort of perambulator behind it. They are said to be the new assault wagons called tanks. I don't know if any Germans knew about them, but the secret had been very well kept on our side. None of us had any idea of their existence.*
>
> *J Glubb, 7th Field Company RE.[31]*

The impact of these strange new weapons was yet to be tested but as far as Herbert was concerned, he was only too happy to see any new initiative that might distract attention away from the infantry.

---

30 It became evident later that the 53rd Brigade was planned to move up to the front line to relieve troops of another division on September 18 but the order was rescinded at the last moment.

31 Letter from J Glubb - 7th Field Company Royal Engineers – *The Somme* by Peter Barton published by Constable 2006.

Photo 17 – Cigarette cards sent by Herbert from the front: A selection of the organic cards sent here from France by Herbert to his 2 sons Alfred and Bert.

Photo 18 – Mash Valley on July 1 1916: A view of Mash Valley, now and also as it looked in July 1916. Photo by Peter Barton.

Photo 19 – Mash Valley 3 July: *A dramatic view of Mash Valley taken on July 3 1916. Herbert Barnes and the 8th Battalion Norfolk Regiment were occupying the trench in the foreground when this photograph was taken.*

Photo 20 – The valley at Fricourt: *The hectic activity near the village of Fricourt. A few days before this photograph was taken, this was part of no-mans-land. Herbert marched close to this valley when he transferred to the 8th Battalion the Norfolk Regiment.*

Photo 21 – Longueval village in ruins: *The devastated village of Longueval in July 1916. Herbert and his colleagues moved through this area on their way to Delville Wood.*

Photo 22 – The Cemetery at Delville Wood: *The makeshift cemetery at Delville Wood and its modern equivalent where some of Herbert's colleagues are interred.*

Photo 23 – Delville Wood, before and after: *Deville Wood – then and now. The camera is in approximately the same position in both photographs.*

Photo 24 – Mark IV tank, Acheux September 1916: *A Mark IV Tank being used for the first time. Similar to the one that Herbert first saw in the village of Forceville in September 1916.*

Photo 25 – Ancre River at Autuille: *The Temporary bridge over the river Aisne at Autuile and the dug-outs on its west bank. Herbert crossed this bridge when going up to the front at Autuile Wood in September 1916.*

Photo 26 – Evacuation light railway Anthuille Wood – September 1916: *The horse drawn railway cart similar to the one on which an injured Herbert was evacuated from Authuille Wood in September 1916.*

Photo 27 – Ruined Chateau at Thiepval – September 1916: *This rubble is all that remains of the Thiepval Chateau where Herbert's brother, Alfred Barnes, was seriously wounded in September 1916. It is now the site of the Thiepval War Memorial.*

Photo 28 – Main entrance Horton War Hospital – October 1916: *The main entrance to the Horton County of London War Hospital where Herbert was admitted October 1916.*

Photo 29 – Ward O, Horton War Hospital – December 1916: *Ward O of the County of London War Hospital at Horton taken at Christmas 1916, Herbert was a patient there.*

Photo 30 – Horton War Hospital – November 1916: *Another view of the Horton War Hospital taken from across the park. Ward O is towards the left immediately behind the man forking the hay.*

Photo 31 – Herbert and the men of Ward O, Horton – November 1916: *A postcard sent home to Rose showing the patients of Ward O at the Horton War Hospital in December 1916. Herbert is on the left, circled.*

Photo 32 – Avenue of Elms Ligneureuil: *The famous Avenue of Elms at Lignereuil down which Herbert and the Norfolks, along with thousands of others marched on their way to the Arras Battlefields.*

The small village of Forceville was four miles west of the imposing Thiepval ridge. It was one of the recognised centres for units arriving to take part in the Somme battles. Within the range of the German heavy guns, the village itself, its church, its houses and its principal buildings had been flattened. It was no more than a pile of rubble. A few of the barns on the village outskirts were still intact and the cellars of the ruined houses provided protection against artillery bombardment. As Herbert marched into what remained of the village, he could not help but notice, over to the right behind where the church had once stood, that it was also the location for a dressing station for both stretcher cases and "walking wounded". Several receiving sheds had been erected; some had been subsequently destroyed by artillery fire. Between 300 and 400 men were waiting on stretchers to be attended. There was a regular flow of stretcher-bearers and wounded men arriving from the front. It was not a very uplifting sight for men to see as they marched to battle. What Herbert felt as he settled into his bivouac can only be imagined. That feeling of resignation had returned.

The Norfolks stayed at Forceville camp for seven long stressful days. Occasionally artillery fire fell in the area from the German heavy guns. By this time they knew its exact location and aerial observation had told them that it was a collecting place for troops bound for the front line. This made it a "hot" place to be. More disturbing for Herbert was the almost constant rumbling of guns and the crackle of machine-gun fire coming from just over the ridge to the east, only four miles away, across the Ancre River. From Forceville camp, the uninterrupted silhouette of the high ground of Thiepval Ridge was highly visible. It was so clear that he could almost touch it. He could see the burst of artillery shells as they gouged great holes in the ground.

On Sunday the whole battalion went to the battalion church service. It was not in the village church itself – this had been flattened weeks before – but in the open ground, exposed to the elements. Everyone was hoping that no artillery fire was focused in their direction. Herbert was not given to prayer but there was probably not a man in the battalion who did not ask to be kept safe over the next few days.

Towards the latter part of the wait at Forceville they began a specific and focused piece of training; four days of intensive training. Carefully constructed on the desolate hill was a recently constructed, intricate system of dummy trenches, marked out with plough and spade. The markings represented in every detail the German trenches at the Schwaben Redoubt system that would be the target of the upcoming offence. The training area was however quite small so that a brigade field day could not be held. Battalions went through their manoeuvres one at a time. Each battalion of the 53rd Brigade repeatedly practised their attacking routines in this simulated battleground. Unfortunately not far away were a walking wounded collecting station and an advance dressing station – its huts and marquees providing hospital and medical arrangements for the almost constant supply of wounded men coming from the front only four miles away. Herbert therefore had every day a constant reminder of what he was about to confront.

The 25 September dawned a bright sunny day. There was hardly a cloud in the sky and the temperature was to soar to over 70 degrees. The order came that the whole of the 53rd Brigade was to advance to the front line. Once again Herbert was marching toward the sound of the guns. In full fighting battle order, they crossed the slow flowing Ancre River by a hastily erected pontoon bridge that served as a river crossing in place of the stone bridge that had been blown up months ago (see Photo 25).

The east bank of the river was festooned with funk holes and bivouacs and occupied by hundreds of men seeking what protection they could. The Norfolks did not stop however. They entered the labyrinth of trenches, working their way up the valley side until they reached the sanctuary of Authuille Wood.

Detailed map of Autuille Wood and its surroundings showing Herbert's evacuation route after his first wound - 29 September 1916

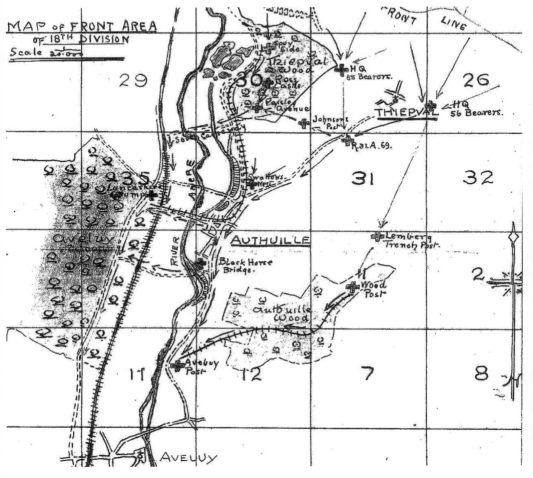

Map provided by Mr Dick Rayner.

In the middle of the wood was Wood Post which had been chosen to be the battalion headquarters. Brigade headquarters was positioned a little further back. The front line trench in open ground just in front of the wood would be the jumping off point for the attack the next day.

Herbert was used to woods. Authuille Wood, was, like Delville Wood before it, a tangled mess of shattered trunks, twisted roots and shallow winding trenches. It did not come close to resembling the green, leafy glades that Herbert knew so well in the chalk hills of Norfolk. In spite of all that, it was protection – protection from the now almost constant whistling of flying shells and the zap of sniper bullets. This protection allowed the sappers and engineers to build a light railway line that ran along a trench through the middle of the wood (see Photo 26). The ingenuity of such a construction in a violent war zone almost beggared belief. A small wagon could run along the iron tracks or be pulled by a horse allowing the speedy evacuation of the wounded back to the regimental first aid posts. Herbert marvelled at the inventions of a modern war. Little did he know that that self same railway track was to be very important to him in the next few days.

The night of the 25th was spent in the trenches in the wood. All the Battalion knew that the next morning was to see them again involved in a fearsome battle. The 8th Suffolks were in the same wood, waiting, trying to sleep, and trying hard not to think too hard about the next day. The brothers did not meet as far as is known. The Battalion, the 8th Norfolks and the 8th Suffolks were in full battle order. This was no time for fraternisation.

The next two days had such an all-pervasive impact on Herbert's war that it is necessary to draw back a few moments from the anxiety of the men at Wood Post in order to describe the general picture of the attack.

Map of the British Army's attack on Thiepval and the Schwaben Redoubt showing the line of advance of the 8th Battalion the Norfolk Regiment on 26 September 1916

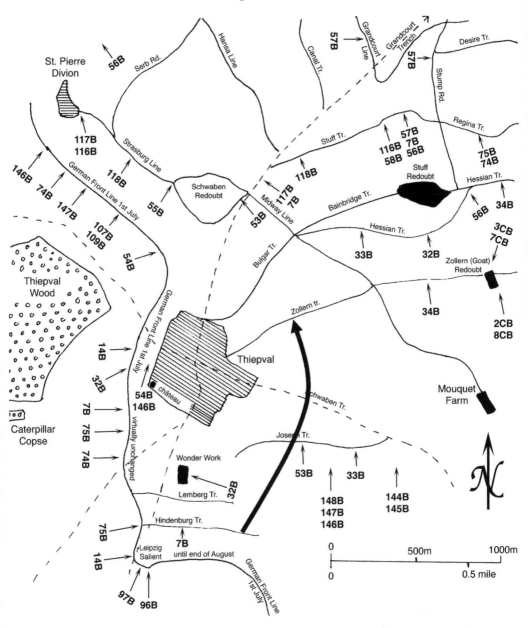

Map taken from Barry Cuttel's book "*148 days on the Somme*"

published by GMS Enterprises in 2000.

General Maxse was under no illusions as to the difficulty of the task that confronted the men of his division. The first objective had to be the village of Thiepval itself. Above ground, hardly one stone stood upon another. The village, its chateau, its church and its buildings had all been obliterated (see Photo 27). However, below ground were some 144 cellars and some or all housed German machine-gun units and hundreds of men. A creeping barrage would help carry the attackers to the village itself, but once in the village the Tommies would have to clear out each cellar, one at a time. It would mean hand to hand fighting.

If and when Thiepval had been subdued, attention could then be turned to the Schwaben Redoubt. General Maxse knew how difficult this challenge was too. Situated on the reverse side of the ridge, a full 1,000 yards further on from the village, the redoubt was only partially in view to the attacking forces. It was the most formidable of all the second line German defences. It was protected by a double line of deep trenches with concrete dugouts. Underneath the trench defences lay a complex of tunnels large enough for hospital facilities and a telephone exchange. The dugouts were deep, impervious to shellfire and protected from artillery attack.

Maxse's approach to the attack was methodical and thorough. Waves of attacking infantry would go over the top and assault the enemy. Each attacking battalion was to be reinforced by a company of "moppers up" from other units who were to clear the large number of dugouts known to honeycomb the whole area. Gas shells were to be used. Two tanks were detailed to assist in the assault.

Herbert and his colleagues did their best to snatch some sleep. He felt great fear and apprehension as to what would happen the next day and it prevented all but the most fitful of sleep. Brigade Commander Major General Higginson moved among his men during the night – encouraging, motivating, reassuring. The attack on Thiepval was to start at 12.35 pm the next day, 26 September, in full daylight.

When the detailed orders were received, Herbert felt a mixture of relief tinged with heavy concern about his brother. The attack on Thiepval was to be led by the 8th Suffolks – Alf's battalion – and the 10th Essex. Of Herbert's own battalion, some of C Company and a platoon of B Company were to support the battalions in mopping up and clearing out the many cellars and dugouts in the village, but Herbert and D Company were in reserve and would not be involved in the initial attack. They would spend all day close to the battalion headquarters in trenches in the wood. The word quickly went round the battalion. Once again, fortune had smiled on Herbert but he was only too aware that the 8th Suffolks and his beloved brother Alf would be the first to go over the top.

Private S. T. Fuller of the 8th Suffolk Regiment takes up the story:

> *It was a lovely day, bright and warm. Our guns were fairly quiet all morning only an occasional shell going over. A very big howitzer was firing into Thiepval and huge splinters from the shells kept buzzing over our trench which being a newly dug one was very good cover. We were informed that the barrage would commence at 12.35pm and we were not to fix our bayonets until then in the case the enemy saw them glitter in the sun and rumbled us. The rum was issued. A few minutes before that the order was passed along the trench "fix your bayonet's". Then, at what was, according to our watch ½ minute or more to 12.05pm, four 18 pounder guns fired. I found it difficult not to keep "ducking".[32]*

At precisely 12.35, 4,000 men of the 8th Suffolks and 10th Essex of the 53rd Brigade, and the 12th Middlesex and 11th Fusiliers of the 54th Brigade emerged from the trenches in front of Authuille Wood to attack the village. The assault was grim from the start:

> *The trenches and dugouts in this area were too numerous for the bombardment to have dealt with them all effectively. As the fighting progressed across the ruins the battle developed into an incoherent welter of hand to hand combats. Snipers were encountered in every shell hole, machine-gun fire was continuous and every inch of ground had to be fought for.[33]*

---

32 Letter from Pt S T Fuller – 8th Suffolks - *The Somme* by Peter Barton published by Constable 2006.

33 *The Somme* by Robin Prior and Trevor Wilson published by Yale University Press 2006.

Alfred Negus Barnes was hit by a sniper's bullet in the early afternoon, while advancing over the ground just south of the village. The bullet entered his right shoulder, passed through and smashed into his left arm. By a miracle, it did not hurt or sever any vital organs, neither did it enter the main part of his body. He could only have been crouching or running forward at the time when the German sniper brought him down. He crumpled to the ground bleeding profusely. Back in Authuille Wood, Herbert had no idea that Alf, his mate, his brother, his second father, was lying wounded, perhaps dying, only a few hundred yards away.

Herbert himself and D Company were on the move. As soon as the frontal attack had left the British front line, D Company moved forward and occupied the trenches that they had just vacated. They stood on the firing step. There they stayed for the next three and a half hours. Over the parapet of the trench, Herbert could see the attack of the 8th Suffolks as it developed over no-man's-land. The ground, a mangled mess of shell holes, was being swept by machine-gun fire and artillery shells. Alf was out there.

By mid afternoon all but the north east section of the village had been taken but casualties among the first wave were very heavy. Some battalions were nearly expended and reserve units had been decimated as well. Many had become disorientated. A few men of the Norfolks who had been "mopping up" had also become casualties but far higher casualties were incurred back in the forward trench, mostly from shell shock. However Maxse had learned a lot since 1 July and he knew that the attack on the Schwaben Redoubt could not begin until the whole of Thiepval had been subdued. Therefore on the 27th he called a halt to the general advance and asked a company of the Bedford regiment to clear the rest of the village which they did, winning a VC in the process.

At around 4.00 pm Herbert and D Company moved forward yet again. Firstly they went to Joseph Trench and then to one of the assembly trenches. They were moving up with the battalion commanding officer. General Maxse and Brigadier Higginson were practising what had been so clearly learnt on 1 July – commanding officers must be close enough to the action to keep their fingers on the pulse of what was happening but not so close as to become casualties themselves. Colonel Ferguson moved up to the old German front line trench. This movement forward attracted the attention of German gunners and D Company was subject to a fierce bombardment. Herbert was being shelled again. "Bombs falling all round us," he was later to recall. Casualties were incurred again but Herbert was not one of them – his luck was holding out.

D Company spent that night in the first assembly trench. There was very little opportunity for sleep, the bombardment of the German positions was as intense as ever and tracers lit up the sky and flares periodically turned night into day. And all night the enemy returned the fire.

The attack on the formidable Schwaben Redoubt could now proceed. There was no longer a danger of flanking machine-gun fire from Thiepval village. Wednesday 28 September would at last see a full frontal attack on the German positions which had resisted all assaults since 1st July. Indeed, as Herbert was to discover, the ground around the redoubt still held the decayed remains of soldiers killed in the attack three months before.

The order of battle contained foreboding news for Herbert. The daylight attack was to be led by the 7th Queens and the 8th Suffolks. D Company of the 8th Norfolks would be mopping up. Mopping up was a very dangerous business. The German trenches had deep dugouts and 60 yard intervals all along the line. Each dugout had been built with two entrances and could accommodate between 10 and 20 men. Each one had to be cleared out, one at a time. That was the moppers-up job. For the final assault on the redoubt, Herbert was going to be very much involved.

The attack began at 1.00 pm. The ground was a mud-bath due to a considerable fall of overnight rain. Shell holes had filled with water. Two thousand men swarmed over the mud and filth of no-man's-land behind a moving barrage which was soon lost. An hour later the fire was still so heavy that both battalions remained pinned down. Eventually showing high levels of personal bravery, the Queens bombed their way from machine-gun nest to machine-gun nest and forced their way into the southern face of the Redoubt.

D Company, Herbert amongst them, moved forward. Their job was to clear away any German resistance that had not been quelled by the first wave. This was not easy. Every trench, every dugout, every shelter might contain German soldiers, some ready to surrender, some ready to fight. The deeper dugouts housed up to 50 men. Any movement across the open ground exposed the Tommies to attack from snipers and artillery shells coming from those parts of the Schwaben redoubt still held by the Germans. D Company continued to move forward. They got into Zollern trench that ran westward from Thiepval village. They cleared it of any German resistance. They moved to the next trench – Bulgar trench – and cleared that too and began to move forward again getting ever closer to the defensive works that surrounded the Schwaben Redoubt. Snipers were active. They were picking off the men from D Company as they moved forward from shell hole to shell hole.

As daylight gave out, D Company were positioned furthest forward of all the Norfolks. The Schwaben Redoubt was only about a hundred yards away. The whole attacking army dug in for the night. D Company found themselves in Martin Lane. The trench was of course "back to front" as it had until earlier in the day been occupied by the Germans. The dead of the day's battle littered the area. The trench itself was full of dead soldiers. The firing step faced the wrong way. The Norfolks quickly made the trench defendable against a counter-attack from the north-west, an attack which never came. What did come, however, was a merciless bombardment. All through a long and sleepless night the whole area was swept with artillery fire. Casualties were incurred but Herbert was not among them.

The next morning, 29 September, the assault on the redoubt continued as fiercely as on the preceding day. However the Norfolks had done their job, and, with the exception of B Company who were detailed to carry dead for burial, the battalion was ordered to withdraw back to their starting position of two days before. It looked as if Herbert had survived another major engagement and would make it back to safety yet again.

It was not to be. Herbert's luck ran out. Around midday, at about the time that the withdrawal was taking place, he was hit by a sniper's bullet which almost certainly came from the Schwaben Redoubt. The bullet hit him in the lower neck, entered from the front and exited through his upper back. He collapsed to the ground. He was unconscious. He was bleeding profusely. It was a mortal wound. His war was over. He would almost certainly die. He would never see Swaffham again. He would never see Rose and his children again.

CHAPTER 8

HERBERT GETS A "BLIGHTY"

SEPTEMBER 1916–FEBRUARY 1917

Herbert lay on the ground, bleeding profusely from the neck wound. Light rain was falling. The scarred, bare ground was becoming a quagmire. Shell holes were filling with water and becoming death pits. He felt nothing. He was quite unconscious and bleeding to death. Up ahead of him, the battle for the Schwaben Redoubt was raging. The 8th Norfolks, at least the survivors, were being withdrawn. Their job was done. But Herbert would not be going with them. He lay prostrate in Blighty Valley.

Herbert Bogey Barnes' good fortune came rushing to his aid yet again. The same good luck that had brought him through the traumas of Mash Valley and the carnage of Delville Wood stayed by his side at this, his greatest hour of need.

A number of things combined to keep him alive. The sniper's bullet, although it had passed clean through his lower neck, had miraculously not severed any vital organs. Perhaps the sniper's aim had been a little unsteady. Perhaps the range was too long for complete accuracy. Perhaps he had moved as the bullet whistled towards him. Whatever the reason, the critical organs had not been hit. However his neck was a mess. The flesh had been ripped apart and a large bloody entrance hole gouged out in the front and an equally bloody exit wound at the back. His casualty report would later describe his wound as "very serious".

His good fortune did not stop there. Because the Norfolks were mopping up – indeed were about to withdraw from the front line area – help was immediately at hand. His was not that hell that often was the lot of wounded men – in no-man's-land, part of a failed attack, lying in ground swept by enemy fire. The trenches up ahead had already been taken from the enemy albeit at a bloody cost. His mates saw him go down. They quickly got to him. They applied field dressings to the wound and were able to go part of the way to stop the life-threatening loss of blood. Moreover, stretcher-bearers from the 8th Norfolks and from the Royal Army Medical Corps were close by and ready to give assistance. Like many others before him, Herbert owed his life to his comrades who came quickly to his aid.

The army had learnt a lot since the slaughter of 1st July. They knew what to expect in terms of casualties during and after a major attack and they had made many improvements to the manner in which wounded men were got back to the relative safety of their own lines. The first source of assistance to the wounded soldier on the battlefield was indeed the stretcher-bearers of his own battalion and also those provided by the RAMC. These unsung heroes did unbelievably effective work attending the injured while the battle raged all around them. They went to the aid of wounded men even though they in the process exposed themselves to sniper and artillery attacks. Having got to the downed man and given him assistance, their second job was to get him back to the Advanced Dressing Stations where some basic medical attention could be given.

The improvements in evacuating procedure extended all the way from the combat zones right back to the war hospitals in Great Britain. From Regimental First Aid posts a few yards behind the front line through the Advance Dressing Stations to the Main Dressing Stations, the wounded soldier moved as quickly as circumstances allowed and at each stage an assessment was made of the seriousness of his situation and whether he could be patched up and returned to his unit or needed to be sent further behind the lines for more intensive treatment.

If that was the case, the man would be transported by all manner of means, including motorised field ambulance, to a Casualty Clearing Station which was always sited on a railway line. The ambulance trains then transported the man to a Stationary General Hospital (stationary because they were permanently sited) along the English Channel coast. (The number of Casualty Clearing

Stations and Ambulance Trains had been increased on the basis of lessons learnt since July 1.) If it was warranted, the wounded Tommy would then be put on a hospital ship to cross the Channel and then by train to a war hospital somewhere in the British Isles. Needless to say each stage along the way could be critical – lives were at stake. Deaths occurred. Indeed a War Cemetery now marks the location of many of these stations. Herbert was to be thankful that by 1916 it had become a very efficient operation and very streamlined for its time.

The Battle Orders for the attack on the Schwaben Redoubt on the day that Herbert was shot show 56 stretcher-bearers were operating from the advanced dressing station to the north of Thiepval village and 55 bearers were operating to the west of Thiepval Wood. There was also an advance dressing station at a place called Crucifix Corner only a few yards from where Herbert went down. The battle orders also dictated that "stretcher cases will proceed and evacuate to Aveley Post via Wood Post". We have no way of knowing exactly which route from the battlefield the wounded Herbert took. By piecing together the evidence and using intelligent guesswork it is possible to speculate what might well have happened (*see* page 127). What is certain is that within 72 hours of being gunned down, Herbert was lying in a hospital bed in England.

On being hit, Herbert was initially attended by colleagues who did their best to stop the flow of blood and apply a rudimentary field dressing. Stretcher-bearers from the RAMC were quickly on the scene and carried him to the nearest trench (probably Bulgar trench) or shell hole to get protection from enemy fire. He was then taken on a stretcher to the Advance Dressing Station at Lemberg Trench Post a few yards north of Authuille Wood where he was attended by qualified doctors and surgeons. He was quickly passed on to the Advanced Dressing Station at Wood Post itself. (He covered on the stretcher almost exactly the same ground in Blighty Valley that he had advanced through two days before.) All this time, his life was in danger. Whatever diagnosis the medics could make about the severity of the neck wound would only have been as good as the battle circumstances would allow. Speed was of the essence and speed is exactly what Herbert got.

He was in all likelihood carried on his stretcher on one of the wagons of the light railway line that he himself had seen a few days earlier. It ran from Wood Post through the middle of Authuille Wood to Aveluy Post. Protected from enemy fire at the bottom of a trench, it descended down the valley side. The wagons that ran along the line were pulled by horses up the hill and were allowed to descend by force of gravity down the hill. It was quick but extremely uncomfortable. If Herbert was conscious, he would have been in extreme pain. Perhaps he had been given a morphine shot. Whatever his circumstance, it seems somehow apt that this son of a railwayman was evacuated from the battlefield on a railway wagon pulled by a horse.

He was then transported to the Number 11 Casualty Clearing Station in the small village of Gézaincourt, this time by motorised ambulance. Gézaincourt was described by one soldier as a "pretty village, with apple orchards growing over the rolling chalk downs". Herbert was not in the least bit interested in apple trees. He was quickly "processed" through the clearing station which was being inundated with casualties. Immediately ahead of him was a man from West Yorkshire called Carney who had lost part of his scalp and had a bloody dressing over his head. He would later die. Behind him was a Private Carron from the Bedfordshire Regiment who had lost one of his legs and after him was Private Belloy from the Royal Engineers who had been shot. There were men from the 8th Suffolks, three in all, within a few minutes of Herbert. None of them was his brother. (It would be some time before Herbert heard what had happened to Alf.) There was a continuous stream of seriously wounded men coming from the battle up on Thiepval ridge. No. 11 Casualty Clearing Station attended to over 1,000 men that day.

Herbert was allocated to Ambulance Train Number 30 that was going to the Number 13 General Hospital at Boulogne, the same port that he had docked at when he first arrived in France. The records do not show how much time he spent at the Casualty Clearing Station but it could not have been long. It was quickly decided that he was too badly hurt to consider patching him up and sending him back to the front. He was loaded into the train the same evening of the day that he had been wounded.

Ambulance trains by 1916 had become a little more sophisticated than in the early days of the war when they consisted of goods vans with racks built to support stretchers. Herbert's transport was made up of rolling stock from the London and North Western Railway. It had accommodation for 306 stretcher cases and 56 sitting cases. They normally had 16 coaches each one identified by a letter to facilitate marshalling. They were equipped with kitchens and a pharmacy car set up for treating emergencies. There was even a rudimentary form of steam heating coming from the engine. Both gas and electric lighting were available. Each train carried over 3,000 gallons of water. Herbert was put into coach B, C, D or E. These were the ward coaches, each with 36 beds arranged in three tiers, eighteen at each side. Each coach had toilet and washing facilities at either end, although they would have been of little use to Herbert. The beds were arranged at right angles to the direction of travel and were made of wire which supported an ordinary mattress with a blanket thrown over it. It is likely, given the severity of his wound, that Herbert was laid on the mattress on his stretcher.

Nurses from the Casualty Clearing Station made him as comfortable as possible. The normal procedure was for them to bustle around an hour before the train departed to settle the men as best they could. Once the train left Gézaincourt, however, the men could get little respite until the train reached its destination. Doctors and nurses travelled in another car and access to the men while the train was moving was limited. Regulations said that "the train should travel at not more than 12 miles per hour in order not to shake up the men too much". But regulations also said that the "patients will sleep, they have left the battlefield behind them, they have had their wounds dressed and all tension is at an end".

Herbert found the reality very different. The train moved through the night; it was a caravan of human misery. He lay in the dark in a very confined space with 35 other wounded men for the whole of that night. Some were unconscious while others were fighting to stay alive. A storm was raging with gale force winds and torrential rain. The carriages probably leaked a little. He might have slept. He might have been drugged to take away some of the pain. He might have drifted in and out of consciousness. He was unable to move much because of the concern for his neck. The clanking of the wheels, the jolting as the train stopped and started, the swaying of the carriages, all contributed to make this unlike any other train journey he had ever experienced.

The train journey ended in the early hours of the next morning. He arrived at the sidings and was taken by ambulance car to the General Hospital at Boulogne which, like all the other General Hospitals run by the Royal Army Medical Corps, consisted of hastily erected marquees, wooden huts and very few permanent buildings. This was more like a proper hospital. There were over 3,000 men being treated at the time Herbert arrived. For the next 24 hours Herbert stayed at the hospital. The records do not show and he never related what happened during his time there. Whether he needed surgery is not known. Certainly his wound was cleaned and the dressing changed. Procedures took place to minimise the risk of serious infection. He was fortunate that there was no bullet or shrapnel to dig out of him. It is not known if he suffered from shock trauma, a common occurrence after a gunshot wound. He was made as comfortable as possible. A judgement must also have been made that he was well enough to travel. The next day, Monday 2 October, he was loaded onto a hospital ship. He was going back to England.

The SS St David was one of the many hospital ships that plied back and forth across the Channel, taking the wounded men back home. Before the war, it had been a cross-Channel ferry and had taken tourists across to France. The Victorian and Edwardian middle and upper classes had taken to "doing the European Grand Tour" and enjoying holidays on the European Continent. The cross-Channel ferries of those days had been built to a high specification, to pamper wealthy passengers during happier times. Now, all the cabins and saloons had been converted to take stretcher cases as well as walking wounded. It could only take 180 patients at a crossing but there were almost certainly many more than that on board when Herbert left France. It was not unusual for there to be upwards of 500 at any one time. Herbert, still on his stretcher, was laid down on one of the public areas. It was a wet and misty day but, fortunately, there was very little wind (the storm of two days ago had blown itself out) and

Herbert had a gentle crossing that lasted no more than three hours. He was in pain and in much discomfort, but he was going home. As the boat pulled into Dover, Herbert must have realised that he was going to survive. Perhaps, after all, he would see Swaffham again. Perhaps it would not be too long before he saw Rose and Alf and Phyllis and Bert and Teddy. Perhaps he would never go back to France. Perhaps, perhaps …

———◆◆◆———

It is not known how or when Rose heard the news that Herbert was seriously wounded. Perhaps it was by telegram; perhaps by letter. In many cases wives heard that their husbands were missing, which plunged them into a period of terrible doubt. The horror of just not knowing was a dreadful pain all of itself. Rose knew that Herbert had survived. Nor is it known what she told the children or when she told them. She would have handled it all in her quiet, competent, compassionate way. Alf and Phyllis would have fully understood. Bert would have had a lot of pride in his Dad and no doubt would not have been slow in bragging a little to his friends at school. Teddy was too young to understand anything at all. Wounded, of course, did not mean safe. As good as medical facilities were for their time, infection was commonplace and post-wound traumas could carry men off at any time. So while Rose felt huge elation that her husband had been wounded and not killed, she would also carry with her the anxiety and apprehension about him. How bad was the wound? Was he seriously crippled? Would it get him in the end? What did the future hold?

She was not alone of course. On 4 October the *Norwich Mercury* carried listings of the sons of Norfolk and Suffolk who had become casualties in the recent battle. The list was immense and must have sent shockwaves through the local communities. It covered two complete columns of the broadsheet newspaper and listed over 300 names. From Wisbech in the west to Yarmouth in the east and from Cromer in the north to Ipswich in the south, the names kept coming and coming.

And there were, of course, men from Swaffham on the list. Corporal H. Clark had been wounded, as had two brothers E. and J. Saunders, both within a few days of one another. Both had survived. P. Wilson from Lynn Road was also listed. The list was woefully incomplete. For some reason, not fully explained, Herbert's name never did appear among the list of wounded on 4 October or in any of the subsequent editions. His name got lost in the roll call of thousands. Swaffham, all the county towns of Norfolk, and every village in the county had been impacted. Men had been lost, brothers killed, sons wounded and crippled, friends gassed. Everybody, whoever they were, knew of someone who had been killed, wounded or was missing. For the first time in the history of our country, a single military action had left a scar on every community. Rose was not the only one.

On arrival at Dover, Herbert was transferred to another ambulance train. Where would he be taken? He knew he was heading to a war hospital. But which one? With his record of good fortune, perhaps he would go to the war hospital in Norwich, where he could be close to his family. Perhaps he could see Rose before too long.

It was not to be. On that same Monday 2 October, his train pulled into Epsom Station in Surrey. It had made its way up from Dover and pulled into the sidings alongside the main line owned by the London and South Western Railway. The hospital that Herbert was destined for stood on the high ground overlooking the Surrey market town. Connecting it to the main line was a normal gauge light railway – the Horton Light Railway – which had been built to haul men and matériel up the hill to aid the construction of the hospital. The two light locomotives used on the line belched out smoke and steam as they struggled up the steep gradient. However a few months before Herbert's arrival, it had been decided that the line was "unsafe to carry wounded soldiers" and the transfer was now carried out in Ford motorised ambulances. Herbert was carefully taken from the train on his stretcher and placed in the vehicle with other men whose wounds prevented them from walking.

The ambulance trains carrying wounded men were now arriving at Epsom station every few days. In the early part of 1916 when they pulled into the West Street sidings, they were met by local people who welcomed the men and offered them refreshments and cigarettes. As 1916 wore on, and the numbers increased, the sight of shattered men with broken bones had become a routine and attracted less attention. It was not that the townspeople did not care anymore. It was more that they could not afford to distress themselves over what had become an everyday event. For that reason, the transfer of wounded men from train to ambulance was quickly carried out, without fuss.

Herbert might well have noticed something else that was quite new to him. The drivers of the ambulances were nearly all women. Before he enlisted in 1915, back in Swaffham, the driving of these new fangled motorised vehicles was the preserve of the menfolk of the town – and the richer menfolk at that. Things had changed since he'd been away and young women both in nurses' and military uniform had taken over these sorts of tasks.

Herbert was driven out of the town, up Christchurch Road into Horton Lane and through the main gates of the City of London War Hospital built in the grounds of the old Horton Manor (see Photo 28). He was entering a new world. He had never been in a proper hospital before. He had never had the need to go to hospital in Norwich or King's Lynn or anywhere else for that matter. The hospitals at Le Havre and at Boulogne were marquees and prefabricated buildings. The Horton War Hospital was a massive establishment. It was the real thing.

It was not so much a hospital as five hospitals rolled into one. It had been recently built at the behest of the newly formed London County Council to look after the mentally sick of the metropolis. It was a purpose-built mental asylum. Building had started in 1899 and had been completed in 1907. The Victorians, who never did things by half, had decided to construct five mental hospitals together on the same integrated site. The location chosen was the beautiful parkland of Horton Manor high above the Surrey countryside near to Epsom Downs. At the time Epsom was separated from the built-up areas of London and provided comfort to middle class sensibilities that the institution was far enough away not to cause any problems. It was at the time the largest cluster of mental hospitals in the world, covering more than two square miles of ground. It accommodated over 2,000 patients.

At the onset of war, the ever increasing demand to look after wounded men placed intense pressure on the medical facilities in the UK. Any institution that could be a hospital was commandeered by the War Office. In 1915 the huge facility at Epsom was taken over and the 2,143 patients were rather summarily transferred to other asylums elsewhere, causing intense overcrowding and considerable hardship. Over 2,200 beds were quickly filled with soldiers coming from the Western Front. At the time that Herbert came through the front gates there were over 2,500 soldiers already there. Doctor J. C. Lord was the man in overall charge of the Mental Hospital and when it was converted to a war hospital, he was swiftly given the honorary title of Lt Colonel in the Royal Army Medical Corps and stayed in charge. The staff was made up of hundreds of doctors, nurses, gardeners and a myriad of other workers. The London War Hospital at Epsom was like a small town.

The hospital consisted of some 33 wards. Each ward housed between 30 and 80 beds, lined up in regular order in the cavernous rooms. An unusual design feature was that all the wards were connected by a crescent shaped covered corridor that allowed rapid movement from ward to ward. Inside the crescent was a Great Hall which could accommodate 1,200 soldiers at one sitting. There was a laundry, and a massive kitchen. There was also a mortuary. Within the complex was a large chapel and looming over the whole site was a 200 foot tower with an observation stand on the top. The hospital administration was housed in the old Horton Manor House. Herbert had never seen anything quite like this in his life before.

Surrounding the buildings and between them was the mature parkland of the Horton Manor Estate. Huge oak and ash trees towered over well-tended gardens with pagodas, seats and ornamental walks. The place had been designed to soothe the pain of disturbed minds. The shade of the trees and the scent of the flowers were designed to be a comfort for the inmates. The Nursing Times reporting at the time that Herbert arrived captured the emotions that he must have felt: "A stronger contrast between the confined air of the trenches, the ceaseless roar of the guns, the shriek of the shells and soft-centred breeze and the restfulness of the gardens of the County of London War Hospital, it would be impossible to imagine."

The soldiers simply called it "a poor man's stately home".

On arrival at the hospital, Herbert changed his clothes. He was dressed in the very distinctive blue pyjamas which identified each one of the soldiers as casualties. It was also suspected that this "uniform" was to stop the more mobile of the patients sneaking off to the town for a drink. Herbert was assigned to Ward O on the upper storey of the south-east side of the hospital (see Photo 29). There were about 30 beds in the ward, laid out in three rows side by side. The bedsteads were made of durable black wrought iron giving them a very solid and somewhat uninviting look. The mattresses were, by 1916 standards, full and deep and the light coloured blankets were of high quality. Herbert had not been in a proper bed since he left Felixstowe six months before. At one side of the ward were large sash windows that extended all the way to the ceiling, letting in lots of light and giving the large room a very airy feel. Herbert had again "struck lucky". When he was well enough to walk around, he found his ward overlooked the parkland and had an extensive view of the Surrey countryside beyond.

It quickly became evident that although severely wounded Herbert was going to survive. Although his neck and upper shoulder were seriously damaged, everything else was intact. He had also not picked up any serious infections to the wound while lying in the battlefield or on his journey back home. The Royal Army Medical Corps had done its job well. However, the bullet had wreaked havoc with the muscles and tissues of his lower neck and shoulder. His recovery would take some time and there was a good chance that he would never be able to fight again. He had sustained a "true blighty".

For the first few weeks, Herbert was confined to his bed, looked after by the nurses and orderlies of the Royal Army Medical Corps. As the days passed and he began to make progress, he was taken in a wheelchair into the gardens that surrounded the hospital. Photographs taken at the time show many soldiers in wheelchairs or lying on blankets under the trees. In some cases and if the weather allowed, beds were carried outside so that the more serious cases could take in the early autumn air. In spite of the discomfort of his wound, Herbert loved his time at Horton. The contrast with the hell of the Somme battlefield, the comfort of his own bed, the attention of the nurses and the peace and serenity of the parkland were not lost on him. And he was relishing the joy of being alive.

As November turned into December, the weather became colder and the leaves dropped off the trees. Recreational activity was available indoors every day. The Great Hall, which at one time housed billiard tables and was reserved for officers, was converted to become the centre for musical concerts, plays and occasionally a sing-along where the men let rip with rousing patriotic songs to the accompaniment of a piano. Herbert was never a great singer – he had always left that sort of thing to Rose – but he heartily joined the fun. In spite of the overcrowding – by December 1916 there were 3,000 soldiers in the hospital – there were still recreation rooms for dominoes, shove-ha'penny and a whole host of card games. Herbert was in his element again, showing his expertise in cribbage and dominoes. He could teach the younger men a trick or two. When he was fit enough, he participated in the hastily arranged football matches played outside in the park. He watched the sports events that the local community laid on to entertain the soldiers. Most of all, he enjoyed the long strolls in the autumn air around the park or just sitting in the gardens chatting. Towards the end of the stay he walked down the hill to visit the market town of Epsom and must have been struck with the similarities to Swaffham. There was a spacious market place with its impressive clock tower just like the one back home.

As Christmas approached, the battlefields of France seemed a long, long way away, recalled only by the constant inflow of newly wounded men. He wrote home a lot and Rose wrote long letters to him. He sent postcards to her with pictures of the hospital all of which survive to this day (see Photo 29). In November he wrote, "This is one side of the hospital. I'm writing another letter tomorrow. Love to all the little ones and yourself."

The postcard sent by Herbert to his wife Rose from the Horton War Hospital in November 1916 while he was recovering from his first wound

Postcard taken from the Ted Barnes collection.

Certainly his very factual way of writing had not changed much.

The patients of Ward O had a group photograph taken of themselves which was made into postcards (see Photo 31). It shows 26 men accompanied by two nurses. Six of the men are sitting down, one in a wheelchair and all carrying walking sticks. The rest are standing, one of them on crutches. Herbert is standing very upright at the back. His neck is bandaged and he looks as if he might be wearing a neck support but otherwise he looks well. His moustache is neatly trimmed and his hair is beginning to recede. He sent the picture to Rose and wrote, "I hope you like this picture of the boys." Then, as always, he quickly remembers his children: "I hope all is well with the children, I have sent you a letter. I am going on very well. With love from Herbert." He sent the same postcard to his sister Mary, the same Mary who had been in receipt of brother George's last letters. She was by this time married and the mother of two children and had moved to Edinburgh with her husband in connection with his work.[34] "I am sending a photo we had taken in the grounds of the hospital," he wrote. "I expect you will find me. I hope you are all quite well. I am glad to say I am going on well at present. I shall be out soon. I wish you all a merry Christmas and lots of love to all."

Herbert spent Christmas 1916 at Horton. It was one of the few times in his life that he was to be parted from his family during the festive season (the other was 1915 when he was in France). There is no evidence that Rose came to Epsom, even though the authorities had built a hostel in the grounds for the wives of wounded soldiers. Rose and the children spent their Christmas at Ash Close with her father, her sister and other members of the extended family. This was a very hard time for Herbert. Christmas had always been a special time for him, a time for family, and he vowed that if he was lucky enough to come through this war he would do his utmost to ensure that Christmas would once again be a happy family festivity.

The men made the best of it. Streamers were hung around the ceiling of Ward O and a few greeting cards were strung up along one end. Plants that looked a bit like Christmas trees were placed in pots at the end of some of the beds and some improvised red ribbon was tied around them. A photograph was taken and converted into a postcard to send to families back home. Everybody did their best to make it a happy time but the war was still raging in France and the ambulance trains were still arriving nearly every day down at Epsom at the West Street sidings.

Herbert spent another six weeks at Epsom. As his wound improved he became mobile again. He took to taking long rambles over the Epsom Downs. He had a look at the famous Epsom Racecourse, not, of course, in use for the duration of the war. The soldiers taking strolls in their "blue uniforms" were a common sight in the locality. Herbert, for perhaps the first time in his life, mixed with men not just from other parts of England but from all over the world – soldiers from Australia, South Africa and Canada, from India – faraway places that he had only ever read about in books.

---

34 One of these children, a little girl called Connie, was to play a big part in the later life of Herbert's family.

GRANDDAD'S WAR

On 17 February 1917, four and a half months after being shot in the neck, Herbert was declared fit and fully recovered. He was deemed able to rejoin the Norfolk Regiment and he was posted back to the 3rd Battalion in Felixstowe. He was not granted any home leave. He did not go home to Swaffham. He never saw Rose and he didn't see his children. He was bitterly disappointed, and extremely dejected. After all he had endured, surely a short period of home leave was not too much to ask. The army thought otherwise. Herbert went straight from hospital to the barracks at Felixstowe. If he thought at any time during his ordeal that his war was over, that he would never go back to France, that he would never be asked to fight again, that he had done his bit for King and Country, he was to get a big surprise. The Army were preparing for another big push. Within six weeks of leaving hospital, he was going to be back in the front line trenches in France – King and Country were calling once again!

CHAPTER 9

THE BATTLE OF ARRAS – MUD AND BLOOD IN ARTOIS

FEBRUARY–MAY 1917

On the 17 February 1917 Herbert returned to the 3rd (Training) Battalion of the Norfolk Regiment. It was a Saturday morning. It was cold and overcast as he made his way across London to Liverpool Street station to catch the Felixstowe train. Fifteen months had passed since he had first arrived there as a fresh recruit. He was going back almost as a veteran. Many of the officers and men that he had known all that time ago were still there. He recognised some of their faces. However, many were new. They were men like him who had been in the front line and tasted the reality of trench warfare and had been wounded too severely to be sent back over the Channel. They were nevertheless fit enough to play a role in training new recruits. Their experiences were improving and making more relevant methods used in all the training battalions around the country. They knew something about real trench warfare, as did Herbert himself.

By this time, he knew he was going back to France. The bullet wound, which but for a matter of half an inch would have killed him, had left no lasting damage. Indeed, a scar where it had entered and another where it had exited, together with some stiffness in the arm and neck was all he had to show for his ordeal. He was approaching his 36th birthday. The British Army needed him.

Although he was well, he was far from fighting fit. Lying on his back in the hospital at Epsom "did not a soldier make". He had put on weight. He had become a little sluggish. For the next six weeks he went through, once again, the intense, repetitive physical training programme very much as he had done as a new recruit. It was time once again for the numbing routine of route

151

marches, physical jerks and strength-building exercises. He was taught all over again how to shoot, how to bomb, and how to use the bayonet as if he'd never done it before, as if he knew nothing. He also helped in the back-breaking work of keeping in good repair protective trenches that were being put into place all around the coastline of Suffolk – just in case the Boche got it into their heads to launch an invasion of these islands. It made little difference that that possibility was receding by the day. It was now submarine warfare that was the main threat to the industrial output of the country. Herbert got fit again, fighting fit, as he knew he needed to be. He had to keep up with all those young new recruits who surrounded him, some now only half his age.

In Felixstowe, he stayed in billets in the side streets of Walton once again, the part of the town in which the 3rd Norfolks were located. It might have even been the same billets as before. He was frustrated, resentful and bitterly disappointed that he could not and did not see Rose or the children. They were all less than three hours away by train and in an age when train travel was reducing distances dramatically, a visit back to Swaffham would not have been difficult. However, no home leave was granted and Rose did not go to Felixstowe. The 80 miles that separated them was not breached but it is not clear why. The army was in a hurry. A major new offensive was being planned. Every man was needed. Herbert was very upset but in his stoic Norfolk manner would never show it. What was the point?

April 1 had always been a day of fun in the Barnes family. Before 12 am it was the custom to play harmless pranks on your friends and family. It was alright to catch them out with some little trick and call them, when all was revealed, "an April Fool". Herbert used to play such jokes himself, accompanied by that contagious chuckle that reverberated through his moustache and lit up his eyes. It was all harmless fun. However, April 1 1917, a Sunday, was anything but harmless. The joke was certainly on him and he did not consider it very funny at all because it was the day he returned to France for the second time. The next 30 days were to be the most intense, the most dramatic and most rapidly moving of Herbert's whole time as a soldier.

Of course, he had done the journey before and knew what to expect. This was not now a journey into the unknown as it had been almost exactly a year before. This was a repeat performance and he knew exactly what was ahead of him – the discomfort, the deprivations, the fear and possibly death. He was determined and at the same time resigned. What would be would be. He would do his duty.

By coincidence he took the same route, leaving Felixstowe early in the morning, travelling to Folkestone and taking a troop ship to Boulogne. This time the sea was smooth and the crossing calm. He and the hundreds of other men making their way were able to stand on the deck taking the sea air. Herbert almost certainly smoked his pipe and chatted to his comrades. He thought of home. They were the last peaceful moments he would have for some time.

On arrival at St Martin's camp in Boulogne, the same St Martin's camp that he had passed through a year before, he learnt that he was to rejoin the 7th Battalion of the Norfolk Regiment. To him this was good news indeed. He had left the 7th after the action at Mash Valley and had made many good friends in the battalion. The purists might argue that the 7th was never a true Norfolk battalion as in 1917 nearly half the men came from outside the county. However many of the men were from Norfolk itself. They came from similar backgrounds and they were men with whom he could identify. He felt comfortable even though they were nearly all much younger than him.

The 7th had had a rough time since he was last with them. In the latter stages of the Battle of the Somme they had been heavily involved in action around the villages of Pozières and Flers and around Bernafay Wood. They had acquitted themselves well but in the process had lost over 130 men killed (87 of whom were from Norfolk) and around 350 wounded. Since October 1916 they had left the Somme and had made their way 40 miles to the north, to the cathedral city of Arras. They had been there for nearly five and a half months and although they had been in the front line for short periods, they had not been involved in any major actions. They had been able to recuperate, reorganise and regroup. New recruits had come in to get the fighting strength back to nearly 1,000 men.

The last few weeks had been relatively uneventful but all that was about to change.

Herbert stayed his first night back in France at St Martins Camp but then the next day on Tuesday 2 April he boarded yet another troop train to yet another destination, the small market town of St Pol 15 miles to the west of Arras. From there he marched the six miles to the village of Lignereuil where he joined his battalion. Unlike his first arrival in France, there was to be no extensive training period, no getting-to-know-you time, and no period of adjustment. Within a few days of arriving he was to be pitched into the front line trenches. A major offensive which history now calls the Battle of Arras was about to start.

——•◆•——

The Battle of Arras has often been described as the forgotten battle of the First World War. The Somme in 1916 is well remembered, maybe because of the shocking casualty rates of July 1. Passchendaele and Third Ypres in the autumn of 1917 feature even more strongly in the national conscience because of the horror of the dreadful fighting conditions. Both are readily associated with the suffering and deprivations of the First World War. The Battle of Arras is less well known, and until recently, less written about. Yet the battle itself was fought just as fiercely. The casualty rates were just as heavy. They ran into the hundreds of thousands. The impact on the German army was just as severe and the memories of the British men who fought there were just as vivid. While Vimy Ridge is a household name in Canada, British people are less aware of names such as Monchy-le-Preux, Tilloy, or Feuchy. But Herbert was to get to know them well. He would never forget the manic days when he was caught up in this Artois fight.

The Battle of the Somme had petered out in November 1916. The British had gained a mere seven miles of territory at a cost of over half a million casualties. The decisive breakthrough had eluded them. The French however had successfully resisted German attacks further south. At Verdun they had turned the tables. General Nivelle, commonly dubbed the victor of Verdun, came to the French high command in December 1916. Confident, brash and aggressive, he pressurised the British to launch a 1917 spring offensive to relieve the pressure further south. It was agreed that the British Army would attack along a 21 mile front north and south of the capital of Artois, the strategically important city of Arras. What had started out as a diversionary attack became, in the planning, a full blooded broad offensive. The 12th Division, of which the 7th Norfolks were a part, was to play a central role.

The British High Command had four months to plan the offensive. The German front was less than 1,000 metres to the east of the city centre

Map of the front line trenches to the East of Arras in April 1917

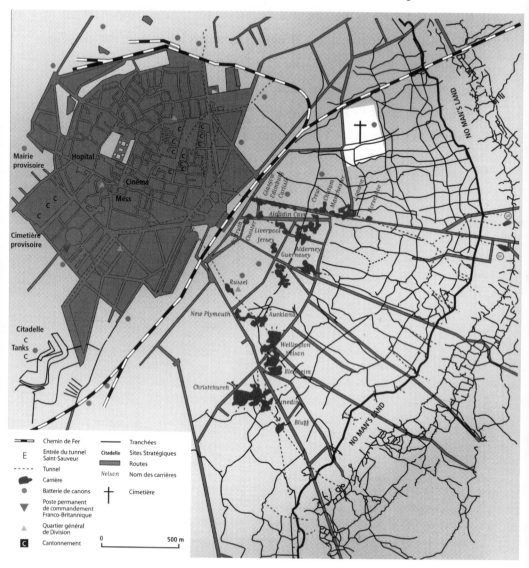

Map taken from the book *"Somewhere on the Western Front"*
by Girardet, Jacques and Duclos published by Editions de George in 2003.

Arras was subjected to daily bombardments and was a city in ruins. The old cathedral was largely destroyed with the remnants of its tower tilting hideously over the rubble (see Photo 33). The central railway station was no more than a pile of bricks and the railhead for incoming troops had had to be moved five miles to the west. Conditions were so bad in Arras that the soldiers quickly gave the town a nickname which was closely related to its English phonetic pronunciation and which is unrepeatable here.

One of the High Command's main worries was that of moving forward large numbers of troops without alerting the enemy. In order to avoid the heavy loss of life that had taken place on the Somme, British staff headquarters mapped out an ambitious plan. A vast underground network of tunnels, including medieval chalk quarries, would allow the troops to appear by surprise only a few metres from the German front line. New Zealand sappers, reinforced by other units, systematically excavated cellars and sewers in the city, linking them together and then connecting them to the caves and underground chalk caverns. An underground world was created with sleeping quarters, medical units, latrines, kitchens, and pipes and wells for water supply. Conditions in the underground world were uncomfortable. The air was damp and foul, sleeping quarters incredibly crowded and sanitary conditions very unhygienic. But the men did not care. The caves offered great security and protection from bombardment. Before they went up to the front they could get some sleep without the noise of German "wiz bangs" or the fear of being blown up as they slept. Nobody was complaining. By the eve of the battle, the caverns could shelter 24,400 men (see Photo 35). Thirteen thousand were beneath the town squares, 2,000 in the St Sauveur Tunnel under and around the Cambrai Road and 9,400 in the Ronville Tunnel under and around the Bapaume Road.

The attack, scheduled to begin on 8 April (it was subsequently delayed until 9 April), was to take place along a 21 mile front involving 26 British infantry divisions and three cavalry divisions. It would be preceded by a preliminary bombardment and subsequently supported by unprecedented levels of artillery. Tanks would again support the infantry. Objectives were clearly defined. A black line drawn on a map was the first objective. A blue line further east was the second objective. The final objective was "the brown line". The capture of each line was set to a precise timetable. In the planning, as little as possible was left to chance. On the ground things would be very different.

———————◆——————

Herbert arrived at Lignereuil tired from his journey. He was there for less than three days and all the time the weather was very bad. It was bitterly cold and snowstorms were frequent. The village itself had a large chateau that had been completely taken over by the British. Alongside the impressive chateau stood a very large barn and other outbuildings that had also been commandeered for use by soldiers. They were using the whole complex as a command post. Leading from the chateau was a long avenue of magnificent elm trees that stretched off westwards into the distance. They lined both sides of the road that pointed to Arras and the battlefield.[35] Many of the soldiers remembered well that avenue. It was a well-worn route for men and equipment going to and from the front (see Photo 32).

Herbert spent two nights in the large barn. According to a South African infantry man who stayed in it a few nights before, "it was free of rats but very dirty and extremely lousy as there were no hot baths available in the village". Herbert participated in some of the pre-attack training with his new battalion but missed most of it because of his late arrival. He also missed the church service that had been held the previous Sunday asking for God's protection during the upcoming assault.

In the early morning of 5 April the battalion headed down the long line of elm trees. They marched to Agnez-lès-Duisans, a village only three miles from Arras itself. This village was a popular billet for the soldiers as it had a most beautiful permanent bathing pool, rising from the numerous springs coming out of the chalky soil. The pool was clear, cold and deep, set among meadows and trees. However there was no time for the 7th to enjoy such luxury. After only one night came the order to move onto Arras itself.

---

35 This magnificent area was never touched by shellfire throughout the war and still stands proud and beautiful to this day.

On the evening of the 6th at about 7 pm, the first companies left the relative comfort of Agnez to march to Arras. Some 150 men were left behind to catch up the next day. The march was very difficult even for the fittest men. Although they were dressed in full combat gear, they did not have the protection of their greatcoats. As the Battalion Diary stated, "all packs and leather jerkins and fur lined coats were handed in and stored in the Divisional dump". It turned out to be a very bad move indeed because the temperature plummeted and snowstorms started again. The men became uncomfortably cold.

On arrival at the western outskirts of the rubble that was once Arras, Herbert's world changed yet again. The Battalion descended steep steps into an underground labyrinth of caves, caverns, cellars and tunnels. The whole Battalion of nearly 1,000 men joined the underground army beneath the bombed-out city. The Norfolks were accommodated in the cellars beneath the museum in the west of the city. They had settled into their underground billets by 10 in the evening, cold, wet and complaining heavily of their lot. Herbert had been in France for less than a week.

No-one expected to be underground for long. A major offensive was planned to start on 8 April and all the men knew it. A ferocious bombardment of the German lines had already started. The men had been briefed at Agnez-lès-Duisans and had studied a layout model of the German trenches mapped out on the ground. They all knew what was coming. April 7 happened to be Good Friday, the first day of the Holy Easter weekend but that had not prevented the Allied High Command from deciding that it was the optimum date to send thousands of men over the top in the biggest offensive of 1917 so far. However, plans have a way of being disrupted.

The Norfolks, the whole of the 35th Brigade, in fact all of the 12th Division were scheduled to spend only one night underground. But on the 7th, the snow fell yet again. A late winter depression sucked in bitterly cold air from the east and the battlefield was blanketed in white, wet, fluffy snow. On the 8th, the snow turned to sleet – a wet, cold, damp fall that turned no-man's-land into slimy mud and water-filled shell holes. The attack was postponed for 24 hours to await better weather conditions.

Herbert and the Norfolks were stuck in the cellars beneath the museum. They had entered the system in full battle order – helmets, guns, bayonets, medical kits, grenades, backpacks – in fact all the equipment that is required of a front line infantryman. However the Battalion Diary again noted, rather ruefully, that "only one blanket per man was taken to Arras and the cookers had been left behind at Agnez". It was cold down there and very crowded. The air was stale and putrid and the ground damp.

For three nights the Norfolks bedded down in the cellars. They slept on wooden trestle bunks, three deep, placed in long lines. Their equipment was hung on hooks on the side of the wooden supports or stored on the stone floors. Rudimentary latrines had been placed inside the tunnels. In fact, everything needed to house and supply an army was provided. Light railways ran the length of some of the tunnels and electric lights lit the main avenues and caverns, powered by makeshift generators. Some of the tunnels had telephone wires. There was running water, rubbish collections and a medical centre with a fully equipped operating theatre. Through the winter of 1916 as the town of Arras above was destroyed by German artillery fire so the underground city had grown. Now it would come into its own. In the days before the assault over 20,000 men were underground.

The men decorated the walls with drawings using crayons and pencils. The more gifted ones would create a drawing of their girlfriend or wife. Some cut their names into the brickwork or etched out a message to their loved ones. They wrote poetry. They talked. Some of them wrote to their families back home. They all knew that although they were safe in their underground prison, a major offensive was only hours away. Herbert almost certainly wrote home to Rose but the letter, if it was ever sent, has been lost.

In that tense 72 hours, two significant events happened. On the morning of the 7th the battalion commander Colonel Walters reconnoitred the route that the battalion would take to get to the front line trenches. They carried out a dummy run. They checked the underground route from the museum via the cellars and sewers to the St Sauveur underground system and from there to the assembly positions that were to be used for the attack. The next day, on Easter Sunday, the men collected in a large chalk quarry to attend a Sunday service. Wooden tables were hastily erected to serve as altars, set up in the middle of the stone floors (see Photo 36). The army chaplains gave thanks to God and asked him to keep everybody safe over the next few days. Herbert went to the service. Tomorrow the Battle of Arras would begin.

Zero hour had been set for 5.30 am on 9 April – Easter Monday. At 2.00 am, Herbert and his colleagues stirred from a broken sleep and at three o'clock on the dot soldiers moved from the cellar in full battle dress. They had 2,000 metres of tunnel to pass through to get to the front line. They set off. The noise of thousands of boots moving in unison reverberated off the walls. The shadows of every man thrown onto the sides of the tunnels by the dim lighting created a ghostly effect that added to Herbert's natural apprehension. He noticed that the tunnel had signposts all along it, arrows painted onto the brickwork with the names of major caverns going off to the left and to the right. He marched down "Kings Avenue" which connected all of the caverns like a modern day motorway carving its way through the countryside. They passed through Glasgow, Carlisle and Crewe.

The Underground labyrinth beneath Arras showing the line of advance of the 7th Battalion the Norfolk Regiment on Easter Monday 1917

Map taken from the book *"Somewhere on the Western Front"* by Girardet, Jacques and Duclos published by Editions de George in 2003.

Above them the cacophony of the artillery bombardment rent the air. They could not hear any of it. In the half-light, they saw Chatham, Manchester and London. They kept going until they emerged into the bright daylight, into the air splitting noise of an all out attack on the enemy trenches. They were in Horseshoe Trench, still relatively protected. Here the trenches divided into four separate route ways that went to different parts of the front line, leading to the assembly trenches that would be their jumping off point. The 1,000 men of the 7th Norfolks took less than one hour to cover the distance and incurred no casualties as they did it.

They were not alone. Ahead of them were the 9th Essex and the 5th Royal Berks and immediately behind them were the 7th Suffolks. Ahead were other battalions of the 12th Division. An army was on the move underground. Although the British bombardment had already started and the German guns were responding by lobbing shells all over the Arras area, this time, unlike at the Somme, the men were marching towards the enemy lines in relative safety. While they were underground, the Norfolks had lost only two men wounded – one of them hit by a shell as he stood guard on the entrance to a cellar at the museum.

At the end of the system, the sappers had driven narrow finger-like tunnels into no-man's-land underneath the thick belts of German barbed wire. They had worked so that the tunnels rose to near the surface, until they were only feet below the ground. They had then packed them with explosive which, when detonated, would create a new trench into no-man's-land. One tunnel which reached the German front line was loaded with 670 kilos of explosive. At zero hour, the mines would be blown and the attack could sweep forward. It was to be very different to the Somme where hundreds of men were killed just getting to the front line.

The battle order for the attack again smiled favourably on Herbert. The 12th Division had been allocated the sector on either side of the Cambrai road.

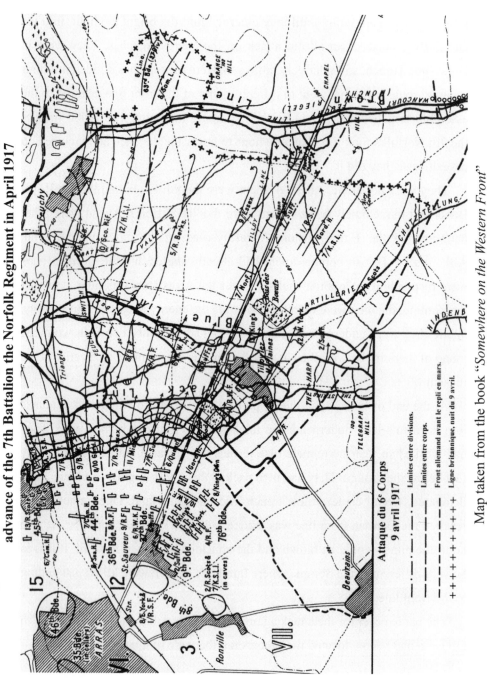

Map of the front line trenches at the opening of the Battle of Arras showing the line of advance of the 7th Battalion the Norfolk Regiment in April 1917

Map taken from the book *"Somewhere on the Western Front"* by Girardet, Jacques and Duclos published by Editions de George in 2003.

The first assault on the black line, indeed the attack all the way to the blue line, would be led by the 36th brigade on the left and the 37th brigade on the right, who, on reaching their objectives, would then allow the 35th Brigade to pass through them and continue the assault until the blue line was secure. The 7th Norfolks (part of the 35th Brigade) would therefore be part of the second assault and would continue until the final objective – the brown line – was taken.

At exactly 5.30 am all hell broke loose. The mines were exploded and the tunnels blown. Earth plumed into the air. The noise was deafening. All along the front thousands of men emerged and "went over the top" along a 21 mile front. The 36th and the 37th Brigades were among them. It was during this time that Herbert and the 7th were progressing through their underground positions and occupied the reserved trenches that the first wave of advance troops had just vacated. They arrived here by 7.30.

Ahead of them the sudden attack, in a storm of mortar bombs and swathes of machine-gun fire took the Germans by complete surprise. Few of the enemy reached their firing positions. Their infantry were trapped in their dugouts, hampered by the problems of narrow exit passages and widespread panic amongst the troops. The German artillery made a weak response; counter-battery fire had practically reduced the German guns to silence. The 36th and 37th brigades occupied the black line without serious difficulties and within the time allotted.

The 7th Norfolks, Herbert amongst them, could see the success of the attack from the reserve trenches and knew that their turn was about to come. At 10.05 am orders were received to be ready to advance. The Norfolks led the attack alongside the 9th Essex. The 5th Royal Berks and the 7th Suffolks followed behind. They advanced forward down a captured trench called Havant Lane. However they soon hit their first problem. At 11.00 they learnt that the blue line had not been completely overcome though according to the schedule, it should have been taken three hours earlier. They had to counter resistance from Germans dug in around Houlette Works. They were then held up by machine-gun fire from the ruins of Tilloy village on the right. These delays in capturing the first objective meant that the troops were always struggling to catch up to the timetable.

Nevertheless it was decided to press home the attack even though the 7th Norfolks were the only battalion to go forward on time. Their objective was the "Maison Rouge" on the Cambrai road. The official battalion history takes up the story:

> At 8 minutes after noon the attack was launched. The Norfolk men went forward with great dash and quickly silenced the machine guns and snipers from whose attention they had been suffering. The Germans began to surrender freely. In Tilloy quarry 90 of them stood up with hands up and were taken freely. In a "camouflage" trench 15 Germans and 3 machine guns were taken and ground was made secure enough for Battalion HQ to be established. The battalion commander then added rather poignantly "some delay had been caused by the taking of some prisoners".

The blue line was now secure but the real task of that long bloody day was to capture the brown line over 3,000 yards further along. The plan required that first of all the Feuchy Redoubt should be captured. It was a large fortified bunker along the Cambrai road (see Photo 37). Leaving the blue line, the 7th Norfolks were the only battalion to set off on time. They attacked and surrounded without difficulty their objective, the farmstead of "Maison Rouge". The German resistance proved much weaker than expected and many soldiers simply raised their hands and asked "where they ought to go". The Suffolks and Essex were less fortunate for they had started three hours later (the reason is unclear) and met fierce resistance. The Norfolks had moved so fast that they had caught up with their own creeping barrage. They started to take casualties from their own "shorts". British shells were killing British soldiers, not uncommon in the confusion of battle. Herbert was being shelled by his own side. Still they moved forward until the Essex and Suffolks could pass through them to continue the assault. But the work was still not done. Darkness fell. The day was over but the final objective, the brown line, had not yet been reached.

Herbert spent a long and uncomfortable night in a recently captured German trench. The Norfolks quickly "turned the trench around" and took up fully alert positions on a quickly improvised firing step. Shells and mortar bombs were being exchanged by both sides all through that long night. The German front line was less than 200 yards away. There was no sleep for anybody that night. It was bitterly cold.

Dawn the next morning saw a continuation of light snow and a cold wind but the final assault on the Feuchy Redoubt could not wait on the weather. Brigade had issued orders at 3.15 in the morning that the assault was to be renewed. By 8.15 pm the 7th Norfolks with two machine-gun crews attached had assembled and were ready to go. The 9th Essex and 7th Suffolks were on either side of them. There was a "let's get this over" attitude pervading the whole Battalion.

The Norfolks had been ordered to probe the German line but, if the wire was uncut, not to attack it but to wait for a flanking movement from other units that would turn the German line. There then followed one of those strange lulls that sometimes happened on the Western Front – a period of inactivity in the midst of frenetic action. The whole battalion was much troubled by a solitary German sniper who began to pick off Herbert's colleagues, almost at random. The crack of a rifle was immediately followed by a man going down. Some 30 men were hit.[36] The attack was postponed for four and a quarter hours. The whole Battalion was waiting, waiting, waiting for the order to be given.

It was not until 12.30 that the 7th Norfolks moved forward. They found the wire uncut and waited for the flanking movement. They then rapidly bombed their way up the trench known as Tilloy Lane. They moved so fast the Germans were completely surprised. Those that survived either surrendered or fled. The brown line was now taken. The Feuchy Redoubt was in British hands.

Herbert had survived another major engagement. He, in B Company, was in the thick of the action. He would remember the caves and tunnels, the snow and sleet, the attack on Houlette Works, the Germans with their hands held high

---

36 The sniper was captured a few hours later and made prisoner. His life was spared on the basis that he was merely doing his duty – another example of the humanity that was shown to the enemy in the midst of such carnage.

in Tilloy Quarry, and the assault on Maison Rouge. He would remember that sniper who wreaked havoc and he would remember the amazing bombing run up Tilloy Lane. Most of all he would remember dead and wounded Germans in the trench and the terrified looks on their faces. They were infantrymen, just like him. He had taken part in what was arguably the 7th Norfolks' finest hour. He had survived the day. Around him, the Norfolks had lost 21 men killed and around 130 injured. In so doing they had moved forward over three miles. Feuchy would stay in his memory alongside Delville Wood, Mash Valley and Thiepval. Swaffham was a million miles away, another world, another life, and another time. When would this war end?

He had only been back in France for 10 days.

The next day, the Norfolks went back to the support line around Maison Rouge, the same area they had captured only two days before. In spite of their victory, they were not happy. Tired and exhausted from the two days of frontal assault and with no sleep and little food, they found that all the best dugouts had already been taken up. It was still snowing. The weather was wet and very cold. Herbert found himself trying to get shelter in a wet, shallow foxhole full of slimy mud. It was his only protection against flying shells. Herbert did his best to sleep but it must have been almost impossible.

The dawn was a long time coming but when it did the sun shone again although it was bitterly cold. The leaving behind of the extra protective clothing did not seem like a good idea but who could have foreseen such a cold snap in early April. However, Herbert's lot started to improve. The order came to withdraw and by the next day the whole Battalion was back in billets. Their new temporary home was the old prison in Arras which, before the war, had housed the most violent of Artois criminals. Now it provided very welcome relief. On arrival everybody had a late breakfast, the first warm meal in seven days. A general clean up was ordered. The men were able to have a warm bath. They were provided with clean shirts and fresh underwear to go underneath their uniforms. Things were really getting better.

At 7.00 the next morning, April 14, the Battalion was ordered on parade. Just when they thought they might get some rest, they went on a route march nine miles westwards to a village that Herbert had never heard of and couldn't pronounce – Wanquetin. At one point, the divisional band played stirring regimental marches as the battalion passed by. The men were encouraged to sing in order to keep their spirits up. The next day, they covered another 13 miles to a place called Halloy. The weather continued to be atrocious. The whole march was carried out in a constant downpour of heavy rain. Herbert was soaked through to the skin – all the men were – but he took comfort in the fact that they were leaving the front line miles behind them.

What was going to happen next? Herbert was under no illusions. He could see some telltale signs. A number of new recruits were joining the battalion to make up for the casualties of the recent action. He noted that the brigadier "addressed the new men with a few words and said how well the brigade had just done, pointing out that they had a great reputation to live up to now that they had joined the four best regiments in the British Army". Herbert certainly realised that they were not in for a quiet time when on the next day they retraced their steps all the way back through the same villages they had just come through, back in the direction of the front line, back towards the sound of the guns, back to the mud and blood of Artois.

***

While the Norfolks had been regrouping and reorganising in the relative safety to the west of Arras, the attack on the stronghold village of Monchy further to the east had continued with great ferocity for over two weeks. The British Army continued to move eastwards and thousands of men of VII Corps strove to defeat the stubborn defence of the village. On occasions the attack became confused. In the many attacks on the village, infantrymen were supported by the new weapons of war (tanks) and by the vestiges of a past age, cavalry mounted on horses. Still to this day there is a debate as to which troops eventually entered the ruined village, but enter it they did and, by 24 April, the front line had moved to the east of Monchy and the whole of the village was in British hands. The front line trenches now faced out across no-man's-land from Monchy Wood, a small wooded area in the grounds of the rubble of what once was Monchy Château. Yet again, Herbert Barnes' war was to be associated with another wood.

There now occurred one of those small engagements that happened all over the Western Front during the long years of the First World War. They were engagements which seemed, with the benefit of hindsight, pointless. They were engagements where co-ordination completely broke down and men died in their hundreds for no purpose. The British High Command were concerned that the front to the north east of Monchy was not "straight". The Germans still held onto a salient and salients were bad news. They were an area of weakness that the enemy could exploit and attack and thus slow down or completely reverse the forward movement of the attack. Sir Douglas Haig wanted the line straightened where two trenches, Rifle trench and Bayonet trench, penetrated into the British lines. The task was entrusted to the 35th Brigade of the 12th Division, specifically to the men of the 7th Norfolks and the 5th Royal Berks.

Herbert and his colleagues moved forward into Arras on 24 April. This time they would travel to the front on double-decker buses. A cavalcade of "omnibuses" were lined up on the Doullens–Arras road. Over 20 of them chugged their way to the Faubourg d'Amiens, from where the men marched to billets in the Grand Place in Arras (see Photo 34).The Grand Place is the central square of Arras. The cobbled stone "place" covers an area roughly the size of eight football pitches and is surrounded on four sides by a continuous façade of buildings. Each building had an arch which the Tommies had partially blocked up to give them protection from both artillery fire and the biting wind. Herbert and the 7th did their best to get some sleep in the rubble that had once been a beautiful city. They drew full battle equipment from stores.

The next morning at 8 am they boarded a light railway that had been laid out in the last few days. It was another example of how quickly the engineers constructed communications systems once ground had been taken. In just a few minutes, they went over the ground that they had fought so hard for two days to capture a few days before. Now that the front line was four miles further east, the caves and cellars no longer offered protection. Getting to the front was a very dangerous business. The battalion was handed over to guides who took them through the labyrinth of captured trenches. They moved through the area where the battle had raged over the last two weeks, a land of burnt out tanks and blown up war equipment. As they approached Monchy village they saw the bloated remains of hundreds of horses and the shattered hulks of two tanks. Many bodies still lay where they had fallen. The Cambrai road itself was clogged with men and equipment moving backwards and forwards – units like the Norfolks moving to the front, wounded men and German prisoners coming the other way. It was a wasteland of death and destruction. Eventually they reached their positions in Monchy Wood.

Herbert had of course seen it all before and probably closed his mind to this moonscape that he was passing through. Every now and then a German shell would whistle overhead. The enemy knew exactly where the road was. They knew exactly where all the trenches were – after all, they had dug them all. When the 7th Norfolks reached Monchy, there was not much of a village left at all, just the usual pile of stones and bricks (see Photo 38). They reached Monchy Wood to the north-west of the village where battalion headquarters were established. The battalion itself moved and occupied the very front line trenches just beyond the wood that looked out over no-man's-land. The other side of the shell holes were Rifle trench and Bayonet trench.

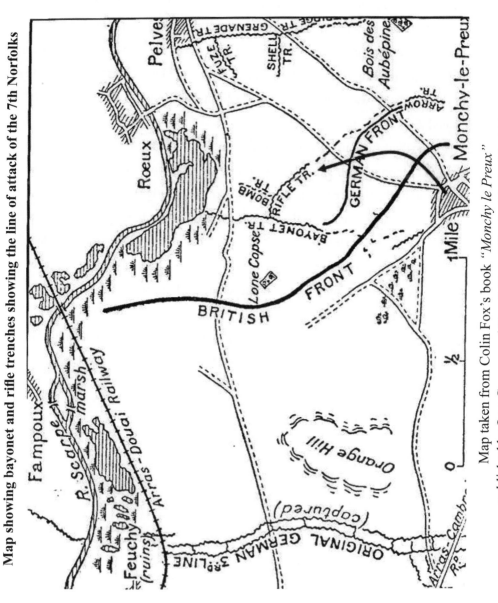

Map showing bayonet and rifle trenches showing the line of attack of the 7th Norfolks

Map taken from Colin Fox's book *"Monchy le Preux"* published by Leo Cooper and Pen & Sword Books Limited in 2000.

For two days Herbert and the 7th waited. For two days they manned the firing step on full alert and in full battle order. For two long days they were subjected to machine-gun fire, artillery attack and the attention of snipers. They were sitting and waiting. They sent out strong patrols that reported that Rifle trench was held in strength. During this time of waiting, they lost two men killed and 11 others wounded, two of whom were officers.

Today the Wood is a pleasant peaceful place. In spring the flowers blossom and the first shoots of the ground plants produce a canopy of colour. But if you look very carefully, you can still see the line of the trenches where the Norfolks sat out their 54 hours waiting to go over the top.

The omens were never good for Herbert right from the start. He was in B Company which took up a position to the left front with A Company to the right front. C Company took up the left support position with D Company in right support. Herbert was in the very front line trench closest to Rifle Trench. The battle orders, when they were received, said that A and B Companies would advance on the left towards Rifle trench. Zero hour was set for 4.25 am, Tuesday 28 April – just before dawn.

The Battalion Diary merely states that "the attack was not successful". In truth it was a fiasco. Nearly everything went wrong. At midnight, before the attack began, the Germans launched an attack of their own. The 7th Norfolks sent up SOS signals and asked for artillery support that was forthcoming and that, together with rifle and machine-gun fire, checked the attack. The Battalion Diary proudly stated that "No Germans reached our trenches but it meant that no sleep was had that night". Then the planned preliminary bombardment failed to materialise. Protective wire in front of the German trenches went uncut. The enemy had a clear uninterrupted view of the broad swathe of no-man's-land. The ground itself was wet, covered in mud and waterlogged shell holes. And Rifle Trench had scarcely been damaged at all by artillery.

When the whistle blew, and the Norfolks went up the ladders, they were immediately met by heavy machine-gun and rifle fire from Rifle trench. They were cut down in swathes. Many of them never made more than 50 yards of ground before crumpling. The left wing of the battalion was almost annihilated.

Others moved doggedly forward, trying to dodge the barrage of bullets. Amazingly some of the men made it just short of Rifle trench itself before being shot down.

Herbert went "over the top" on the left flank closest to Rifle trench. How far he got is not known but it could not have been far. Men around him went down like ninepins. He must have moved forward into a hail of machine-gun fire. Somewhere out in no-man's-land, two bullets from a machine-gun ripped into the top of his left leg, passed straight through and exited out the other side. He fell, fully conscious, bleeding profusely from the leg wound. He crawled into a shell hole. He somehow managed to get a medical dressing from his pack and fix it around the leg. In pain he lay in the gentle rain hoping fervently that an artillery shell would not find him, hoping that he was hidden from a sniper's view.

Herbert and many of his colleagues were now in that nightmare situation so dreaded by infantrymen throughout the war. The attack had failed. The trench ahead was still in German hands. No-man's-land was swept by machine-gun and rifle fire. Anything that was seen to move was immediately shot at. Herbert was wounded. He could not move forward, he could not crawl back. No help could reach him. Stretcher-bearers and men of the RAMC were themselves pinned down. He was stuck in a new kind of hell.

He was not alone. Nearly 1,000 men were scattered all over no-man's-land. Many were dead and hundreds like Herbert were wounded, many of them dying (the Battalion Diary stated that nearly 250 men fell in those few minutes). Bodies were strewn over the whole area and the cries of the wounded and dying could be heard all over the battlefield.

Herbert lay in his shell hole all day. He might have been alone. He might have had others with him. Sniper and machine-gun fire was rife, and every now and then an artillery shell exploded nearby. For over 12 hours he lay there working hard at stopping the loss of blood from his leg. Nothing moved. There was nowhere to go.

As night came and darkness fell, some furtive shadowy activity began to take place. The men who had not been hit crawled slowly back to the safety of the jumping-off trench. They moved as silently as they could from shell hole to shell hole, fearful lest they attract a sniper's bullet or an artillery shell. Some of the wounded made it back too, dragging their broken bodies across the sodden ground. Stretcher parties did their best to locate the fallen men and bring them back, but without very much success. The Germans throughout the night constantly used Verey lights which lit up the ground as if it was daylight. As the Battalion Diary coldly says, "many of the wounded cannot be brought in". Herbert lay out in his shell hole for the whole of the night. He had no idea how severe his wound was but he knew he was alive. It can only be imagined what must have passed through his mind as he watched the firework display going off all around him, the Verey lights and the constant tracer shells lighting up the sky. And all night the cries of men were asking for help which could not be given. Herbert lost a lot of colleagues during the night.[37]

The next morning, 29 April, a new attack was ordered. This time, it was the turn of the 9th Essex supported by attacks on the flanks with bombs, rifle grenades and mortars. This time, a heavy bombardment attempted to pulverise the German resistance. Men of the Essex swarmed past the shell holes where Herbert and many of his colleagues lay. More men fell but for a while, the attack was successful. Rifle trench was taken, if only for a short time.[38]

The work of the Essex men now enabled the stretcher-bearers to go to work. They emerged under fire from the front line trench and from the shell holes in which they had been pinned down. They quickly advanced over no-man's-land, doing their heroic but dangerous job. They located the dead and wounded. They decided who they could help and who they would have to leave. They found Herbert. They picked him up and placed him on a stretcher as the bullets and

---

37 Two soldiers in the 7th Norfolks born in Swaffham died that day. Private Alfred Couzens and Lance Corporal Horace Howard had been shot down as they moved forward towards Rifle Trench, Herbert knew them both well, both as youngsters and as soldiers.

38 The attack by the Essex which had given Herbert the opportunity to get back to safety was only partially successful. The central part of Rifle Trench was stormed, but its capture was only temporary. Aggressive counter-attacks by the Germans forced the Tommies to retreat back to their own lines once again. The checking of the general advance at Rifle and Bayonet Trenches was one of the many factors that convinced General Haig and the British High Command that the Battle of Arras was rapidly running out of steam.

shells fell around them. Bending low and running as fast as they could, they took him back to his own lines. They dropped him back into the trench in front of Monchy Wood that he had left the previous day.

He had lain out in no-man's-land for 31 hours. He was still alive.

It is not known which evacuation route Herbert took to get back to hospital. Once again, he had been "lucky". The leg wound was severe. Machine-gun bullets tended to smash bones and tear up ligaments but Herbert's wound was only a "flesh wound". However, it is almost certain that he could not walk and was once again in the hands of the stretcher-bearers. They carried him back along the same trenches that he had advanced through in the last few days. It is likely that he went to one of the advanced dressing stations that were a part of the underground labyrinth of caves and quarries in Arras. These were an integral part of the "subterranean world" and once he had arrived there he was in relative safety. By May 1917 these stations had achieved considerable sophistication. They were able to accept up to 700 men at any one time, they had waiting rooms, operating theatres for the most urgent cases, rest rooms for the stretcher-bearers, store rooms and of course they all had a morgue. Some were equipped with kitchens and electric lighting.[39]

He could not have stayed in the advanced dressing station for very long. He was carried by motorised ambulance back to a Casualty Clearing Station at Agnez-lès-Duisans and then by light railway to the number 6 Stationary Hospital at Frévent. He was rapidly transferred into an improvised and temporary ambulance train, TAT number 112.

Temporary ambulance trains were very different from the ambulance train Herbert had travelled in after his first wound after Thiepval. These were no more than ordinary French passenger carriages and were staffed by medical officers and orderlies only. They did not carry a complement of sisters and nurses and were drawn into action only when the number of wounded coming from the

---

39 One of the more sophisticated of these ADTs was called Thompson's cave, tunnelled out at the back of Rue St Quentin. It was manned by the field ambulances of the 3rd Division and ceased to operate on April 11 when it was hit by a large shell which burst the water main, causing the roof to collapse. Even the caverns were not completely safe.

trenches was too great to be brought down by proper ambulance trains. They were supposed to carry only those whose wounds were less severe although it frequently occurred that grave emergencies could occur on them. These temporary ambulance trains had no couchettes on them. Men were forced to sit in an upright position. They were therefore extremely uncomfortable and painful. However, the fact that Herbert was allocated to a TAT means that he was officially classified as "walking wounded". He could support himself with difficulty on crutches.

The TAT took Herbert to the Dannes-Camiers General Hospital on the coast five miles to the south of Boulogne. Herbert himself must have been surprised and very grateful at the speed that all this happened. His army documents showed that it took less than 18 hours from the time that he was brought out of no-man's-land to the time that he arrived at the General Hospital. This was a truly remarkable achievement by the Royal Army Medical Corps and compared very favourably to our post-war world.

The General Hospital, as its name suggests, was sited half way between the small settlements of Camiers and Dannes alongside the main coastal railway line. It stood back from the English Channel by about a mile with the rolling chalk hills of the Pas de Calais behind it. Herbert had, of course, been in two General Hospitals before at Rouen and Boulogne. This one was very similar – a sprawling "village" of marquees, tents and wooden huts. There were over 3,000 men being treated there, the demands for beds being swollen by the Arras offensive.

Herbert was treated there for six days. It was longer than is normal. The explanation is not clear. It is possible that he had picked up some contamination or inflammation on the wound. He had, after all, lain untreated in a dirty, muddy shell hole for a very long time and it would not have been surprising if infection had set in. It is more likely however, that the doctors were trying to avoid sending him back to England. The wound was not life threatening and if there were no complications, Herbert would be expected to recover. Every soldier was needed at the front. They would have made every effort to "get him back on his feet again".

However, it was not to be. The 6 May was his birthday and he received one of the best presents he was ever to have. He was told that he would be going back home to England, to an English hospital. His wound needed more attention. The doctors at Dannes-Camier would not be able to patch him up. And so, two days later on the 8 May he was stretchered onto a train to Boulogne and once again boarded a hospital ship for Newhaven. He had been in France for only 37 days.

CHAPTER 10

A STAY IN SHROPSHIRE

MAY–JUNE 1917

Rose did not know where Herbert was. Two weeks before his birthday, she had packaged up a parcel and sent it off to him. Amongst other things, it contained a letter from her and scribbled notes from Alf and Phyllis. It also contained a photograph of the family which included Emma, her sister, and her father, George. The parcel chased Herbert around France and by the time it found its way to the 7th Norfolks he was back on English shores. He never did receive it and it was lost somewhere in Artois.

The offensive around Arras had been fully reported in the *Norwich Mercury*. Again the reporters used rose coloured glasses. Rose would have read headlines such as "big new British advance" which screamed from the newspaper on April 10 with a sub-heading "first blow in spring campaign on a 12 mile front". "Nearly 1,000 prisoners taken up to 2pm yesterday" it continued and boasted of "the biggest cannonade of the war so far". It yelled out "portents of victory", "great sequel to the Somme victory". It is amazing that even in 1917 the Somme was being heralded as a huge success. It is also of interest that on the preceding page of the same newspaper was an article giving spring hints to gardeners on how to get the most out of the coming season.

The newspaper reports continued to be glowing and very positive as the month progressed although the casualty lists were getting more frequent and depressingly longer. Rose probably read them every so often, but she did not need a newspaper to be aware of the continuing impact of this dreadful war on her small town. It appears she learnt of Herbert's second wound on his birthday, 6th May, two days before he crossed the Channel. She knew enough to know that again it was a mixed blessing. It told her and the children that once again Herbert had survived. On the other hand she had no information as to how severe his wound was and what repercussions it would have on their future life. A few days later, Rose saw the extensive list of casualties among the Norfolk men. The list was divided into columns. The first column was bluntly headed up "Killed", the second "Died of wounds" and the third "Wounded". This time Herbert's name was included – Barnes 22345 H (Swaffham) (see Photo 39). The complete list came to nearly 200 men, nearly half of them from the Norfolk Regiment. Again they came from all over the county. Next to Herbert's name were A. Baldwin from Norwich and A. Bloomfield from the nearby village of Foulsham. There were two other men from Swaffham, one called Gazeley and one who was just described by his initials, E. J. In the British Army even the smashed bodies of the wounded were listed in stark alphabetic order, a name, a number and a place. There had never been a war before like this. It was progressively ripping the manhood from the cities, towns and villages all over the nation.

Yet life still went on. Amazingly, people at home were still concerned about everyday events and had to take care of the minutiae of their lives. Indeed the column in the *Norwich Mercury* right next to the sad and tragic list of killed and wounded was devoted to reporting the unusually dry weather for the season and bemoaned the fact that there had been a drought for several days.

The ambulance train pulled into the little village station. It had been another long, slow, painful journey for Herbert across the heartland of England. He was now officially classified as "walking wounded". He had been issued crutches. His left leg had been plastered and he held it out rigidly in front of him. He was not on a stretcher and had spent the night sitting in a "standard" railway carriage doing his level best to get his leg in a comfortable position without having other wounded soldiers and other passengers bang into it. It hurt a lot.

The station carried the name of Berrington. He had never heard of it. He had no idea where it was. He probably did not care much. What he did care about, and what disappointed him beyond words, is that he knew he was not going home to Norfolk. As his train clattered through the night, as he watched the stations go by, he quickly worked out that he was moving away from Swaffham, away from his wife and away from his children. Why was it not possible for him to recover in one of the many war hospitals in Norfolk, or at least in Suffolk, so that Rose could pay a visit and his beloved children could see their Daddy? It was all too much.

He was in Shropshire. The little station was built into a cutting (see photo 40), the banks rising high on either side, cradling the ticket office and waiting room which stood back from a neat, tidy platform. The whole scene nestled beneath a bridge that carried a winding country lane over the tracks. There was a square signal box and a few sidings alongside the track.[40]

Herbert had travelled down the Severn Valley Railway from Shrewsbury. Berrington was the first stop along the line. This line had been built in 1872, only 45 years before and had been extended in 1898. When Herbert arrived it was still quite new and, by 1917 standards, represented a modern development in transport.

However, there was nothing rural and sleepy about Berrington station when he arrived just after 11.00 am on Friday 8th May. It was a hive of activity with medical staff, railwaymen, ordinary train passengers and villagers all dashing about their business. The cause of such organised chaos was that Berrington, or more exactly the little hamlet of Cross Houses, had been chosen as the location for the Berrington War Hospital, an establishment which was equal in size to the London War Hospital in Epsom and was going to be Herbert's home for the next 10 days.

---

40 Berrington station was closed in 1963 as part of the Beeching closures. It is now a cattery, well tended and every bit as tidy as when Herbert arrived there in 1917. The tracks had been removed but the station platform still survives.

GRANDDAD'S WAR

The extensive, somewhat rambling buildings had started life in 1834 as a humble workhouse for the Atcham (later the Atcham & Shrewsbury) Poor Law Union. Built to the classic H-shape design of a workhouse, it had for 80 years housed the poor and dispossessed of the area. It had been considerably extended in 1871 to accommodate up to 500 inmates. In 1901 a new chapel had been built. By 1916, the huge demands on hospital beds by men flooding back from the Western Front persuaded the War Office to turn their eager eyes to this substantial building. Almost inevitably, in March of 1916, it was handed over to the military authorities and all the inmates were unceremoniously moved to other workhouses in the locality. Some of the staff transferred to the military while others moved with the inmates. The master and the matron stayed to look after the Tramp wards, the only part of the building still left performing its original function. More buildings were erected and a conversion to a fully fledged military hospital was achieved at breakneck speed. By the time Herbert arrived the hospital was in full swing (see photo 41).

New staff was drafted in. The official photograph taken a few days after Herbert was there (see photo 42) shows nearly 100 men of the RAMC and the sisters and nurses that must have cared for Herbert. In true Edwardian style, they pose formally for the photographer; their uniforms pristine, with polished buttons; their eyes looking straight ahead and their peaked caps perched precariously on their heads. All looked to be in their 40s. The men were too old to be sent back to the front but could now play a critical caring role, looking after the wounded. The hospital Chaplain, of course, sits in the front row.

The arrival of the "soldiers' train" at Berrington Station was a much practised and efficient routine. Some 10 minutes before the scheduled arrival, the large and resonant hospital bell would ring out to be heard throughout the rambling buildings and grounds. It heralded the staff to go and meet the train. Two motorised ambulances were started up. Stretchers on runners were pushed out of the main gate. Orderlies scooped up stretchers and nurses gathered bundles of crutches in their arms. A veritable armada progressed the 300 yards down the little country lane, some running, some walking. Everybody knew that they had to be on time. If they were late they would have to answer to Matron. Along the road they went. They turned left down the slope that led into the cutting and they swarmed onto the station platform. It was this hustle and bustle that Herbert met as he gingerly tried to descend from the train. He was met by a babble of voices – orders being shouted out, the soft cajoling of nurses doing their best to help the badly wounded mixed in with the hiss of steam from the train and the chatter of local onlookers. Herbert was in no doubt that he was back in England.

Stretcher cases were laid out on the platform so that they could later be placed in the motorised ambulances. Others were gently laid on the wheeled stretchers. Hand-held stretchers were picked up by burly RAMC orderlies. The more severe of the walking wounded were given new crutches and a friendly shoulder to lean on. The whole procession returned up the hill, back along the little road between the thick hedgerows and made its way back to the hospital. The whole operation took less than an hour.

However, staff was short and so the walking wounded were encouraged to proceed under their own steam. They took a short-cut – a footpath that left the other end of the station platform and made straight for the hospital, bypassing the hill and country lane. It is likely that this is the route Herbert took, limping painfully and slowly for about 300 yards, turning a corner and seeing for the first time the sprawling edifice which was the Berrington War Hospital.[41]

It is not known to which ward Herbert was assigned. We have no details as to the nature of his treatment. For the brief time that he was there he recovered well. His mobility slowly returned. Before too long, he was able to enjoy the Shropshire countryside. Over the fields he could enjoy the view of the Wrekin standing proud on the horizon. He was able to walk to the sweep of the River Severn as its heavy spring waters flowed under the beautiful medieval bridge at Atcham. It was a peaceful, rural scene that made him think of his native Norfolk. He paid at least one visit to Shrewsbury itself, sending off a postcard

41 Many of the buildings have since been demolished but the original workhouse and some of the early extensions still stand and have been converted into apartment buildings. The small but attractive chapel built in 1901 now makes an excellent village hall. The footpath that Herbert walked still survives as a shortcut from the cattery to the village. After the war, Berrington served as a General Hospital until it was finally closed in 1986.

to Rose and the family. Once again, it was all in stark contrast to the mud and blood of the trenches of Arras from which he had been so cruelly dispatched only a few days before.

However, the flow of wounded from France continued unabated. There was intense pressure on hospital beds all over the country. A wounded man who could walk and whose recovery was predictable could not be allowed to take up a precious bed for very long. After only 10 days, Herbert learnt that he was to be moved to a convalescent hospital 15 miles to the north.

On the 18th May, a motorised truck pulled up at the front gate of the hospital. A group of men, including Herbert, some on crutches, some still in wheelchairs, some with accentuated limps, were helped into the truck and the driver set off through the countryside of the Severn Valley. After a short drive the truck swept through pretentious and impressive gates. It passed a large lodge house and chugged up a long winding drive with trees on either side. Herbert's eyes were out on organ stops. He had entered a new world, one that he had heard about but of which he had never been a part. This was the world of aristocracy, the world of masters and servants, of country estates and rolling parkland. It was a million miles from the two-up-two-down of Ash Close, Swaffham. This was Shavington Hall.

The motorised ambulance climbed the drive that led to the front of the house. Herbert, all agog, took in the splendour of his new surroundings. The two-storey mansion, built of red brick, consisted of a grand central recessed front, the two extensive symmetrical wings stretching out on either side. Herbert looked in wonder at a façade of no less than 27 bay windows. They extended out before him. The whole of the first storey was covered with green rambling ivy (see Photo 43). The wings enclosed a large croquet lawn that stood overlooking extensive parkland. A huge formal parterre stood off to one side. Nearby was the stable block, equally impressive, and beyond that a huge walled garden. The rolling parklands covered over 1,500 acres and were dotted with statues. There was a large ornamental lake, appropriately called the Big Pool.

Shavington Hall has been described as the finest stately home in Shropshire. This is no mean praise for a county that boasts many palatial mansions. Built in 1685 by the 6th Viscount Kilmorey, it had been extensively enlarged in the early 1800s.[42] By the outbreak of the First World War, this magnificent edifice had passed to the Heywood-Lonsdale family, a military family that had served their country with great distinction.

The War Office had quickly turned its eager eyes on this huge building and the Heywood-Lonsdale family were only too pleased to help in the war effort. In 1915 they vacated all but a small corner and the whole establishment was rapidly turned into a convalescent hospital. There could have been few convalescent hospitals like it. The grand staircase that emanated from the entrance hallway might have been an impediment to limping and hobbling men, but the rooms were spacious and airy and the facilities more than adequate. The grounds might have become a little run down and tired – in war time Britain there were no resources for manicuring the extensive parkland – but they nevertheless offered outdoor recreational facilities the like of which the soldiers could only have dreamt.[43]

Herbert was bowled over. He could not escape the irony that it had taken a brutal war to bring the son of a working class man from his humble cottage to this glorious mansion. The irony was not lost on him and his contagious chuckle was working overtime. He was impatient to tell Rose his news, and the day after he arrived, he dashed off a postcard with a grand picture of the Hall on it. "This is a photo of the Hall," he told her (see Photo 44). "Fine one too," he proudly added. "I am going on fine, hope you are all well at home. Love to you and the little ones."

Indeed, he was going on fine. His leg was healing well and as the days passed he was comforted in the certain knowledge that no lasting damage had been done. He became an expert at walking on crutches but, after some time,

---

42 The Kilmoreys were descended from the Needham family who in the 15th century had strong connections with Needham Market in Norfolk. Herbert would, no doubt, have loved the quirk of fate which took this very different son of Norfolk to this house.

43 Shavington Hall was demolished in 1959. The Heywood-Lonsdale family took the view that the cost of upkeep was too much and was prohibitive. The only remains to be seen today are a rather dilapidated stable block, the walled garden and some of the lodge gates. Where the magnificent house once stood is now flat open ground.

he was able to throw them away and hobble around under his own steam. He explored the acres of parkland and the miles of walks through the huge estate. He made at least one visit to the nearby market town of Market Drayton. Spring was in the air. The leaves were fresh and the woodland flowers were blooming all around him. Birds were nesting in the trees and there was everywhere the beauty of life. In Arras or on the Somme there were no birds, there were no trees or flowers. Indeed there was very little grass. Here there was beauty and peace. Herbert loved Shavington Hall.

His stay at Shavington lasted for a little over four weeks. Rose did not travel to see him. Neither did the children. The letters between man and wife were frequent. His were short and to the point. Hers were longer and full of the news of the family and of what was happening in Swaffham. No mention was made of the heavy shadow that hung over his head. He was almost fit again and even though he was now 36 years and one month old, he was an experienced and war-tested soldier, and therefore needed by the army. There was no end in sight to this war. There could be little doubt in either of their minds that he might well be sent back to France. It was a horrible prospect, made worse by the peace and comfort of his surroundings. A return to the training battalion at Felixstowe beckoned and from there no doubt a transfer to the trenches of France. Rose stayed silent and stoic at this prospect.

———◆———

At the same time that Herbert was recovering in Shropshire, back in France, the Battle of Arras came to a stuttering halt. The dramatic and considerable gains in the early stages of the battle had raised hopes that a significant breakthrough could be achieved. There was talk of opening up a route to Cambrai and rolling up the German lines. Like all the other high expectations that had gone before, it never happened. As supply lines lengthened, the British Artillery was unable to keep concentration or accuracy. The Germans rapidly moved reserves to strengthen resistance. Under Baron von Richthofen, they took control of the skies. In addition, German defensive tactics were reshaped. The British advance faltered. Casualties grew and the total effort became paralysed. The offensive degenerated into a shambles. By the end of May 1917, the Battle of Arras, the forgotten battle, marked up average daily losses that exceeded all other battles of the Great War. By the time General Haig ordered a halt, the number of British dead exceeded 150,000 for the six miles of ground that had been won. Herbert's 36 days in Artois, like many thousands of others who marched through the tunnels of Arras was, in the end, to no avail. The failure at Arras meant that another major offensive would be needed in 1917 to break the German strength. Herbert would be going back across the Channel.

On 13 June 1917, the bitter news came through. Herbert was advised that he was required at Felixstowe. However, to his surprise and delight the order was sweetened by a very acceptable pill indeed. Before reporting to Felixstowe, he was to be granted 10 days' home leave. What a piece of news this was. He could hardly believe his good fortune. A full 19 months had passed since he left Swaffham on that cold November morning in 1915. Nearly 600 days had gone by since he last saw Rose. A lifetime of hope, fear, pain and deprivation had passed since he last held his children. Now he was going home. It might only be for 10 days but he would at last see Swaffham again. His eyes filled and his voice choked. He might be a hardened, battered soldier but nothing was ever more important to Herbert than his family.

On the 15th June, he packed his kit bag. Before he said goodbye to Shavington Hall, he went through a ritual that all the soldiers went through. In 1886, over 30 years before, Earl Kilmorey had created a visitors' book. All guests who stayed the night at the Hall were expected to sign it. It was thick and had a maroon cover with the words Shavington Hall proudly embossed in gold (see Photo 45). Before the war, it had been signed by Lords and Ladies, Dukes and Duchesses and the very best of England's high society. When the Hall was converted to a hospital, Lord Kilmorey insisted that it was signed by all the soldiers who convalesced there, whatever their rank and whatever their station. There were to be no exceptions. It reflected the pride that this military man felt in all the fighting men of the British Army. So in the book, after Earls and Viscounts were written the names of Privates and Sergeants. And Herbert Barnes.

Herbert signed in his clear precise handwriting. He wrote "22345 Private H.E. Barnes, 7th Norfolk Regiment". Some soldiers indicated where and when they were wounded. Herbert, in his characteristic way, refrained from any elaboration. Number, name and regiment were all he put. Ahead of him on the line on the same day were Private Howard of the Middlesex Regiment and Sergeant Horsley of the Lancashire Fusiliers. Following behind him, as he went to the desk on which the book stood, was Bill Robertson of the 7th Scottish Rifles. Herbert was once again living and serving with men from all over the country.

He signed the book, left the Hall and climbed onto a truck to go to the nearby station. He was going home.

———◆———

Photo 33 – The Rubble of Arras – April 1917: *The ruins of Arras in April 1917.*

Photo 34 – Billetts in the Grand Place – Arras: *The Grand Place in Arras in April 1917. Herbert was temporarily bivouacked under one of its many arches.*

Photo 35 – Men in caverns Arras – April 1917: *Some of the 22,000 men living underground before the battle of Arras. Herbert spent 3 days in conditions such as these.*

Photo 36 – Underground Service before the Battle of Arras: *An artist's impression of the underground service held on Easter Sunday 1917, the day before the battle of Arras began.*

Photo 37 – La Chapelle de Feuchy: *A modern photograph of La Chapelle de Feuchy, the German strongpoint that was a major objective of the 7th Norfolks in April 1917.*

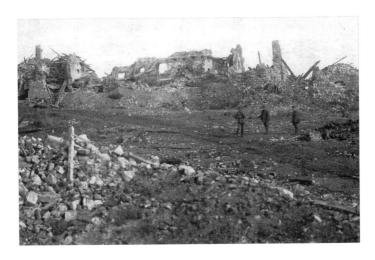

Photo 38 – Monchy-le-Preux: *The shattered ruins of the village of Monchy-le-Preux where Herbert passed to get to the front line in April 1917.*

Photo 39 – Norwich Mercury – Report of Herbert's wound: *The report of Herbert's 2nd wound in the casualty lists in the Norwich Mercury in May 1917.*

Photo 40 – Berrington Railway Station: *Berrington Station on the Severn Valley Line. Herbert hobbled off the train on crutches while others were laid on stretchers on the platform to the left. The station is now a cattery.*

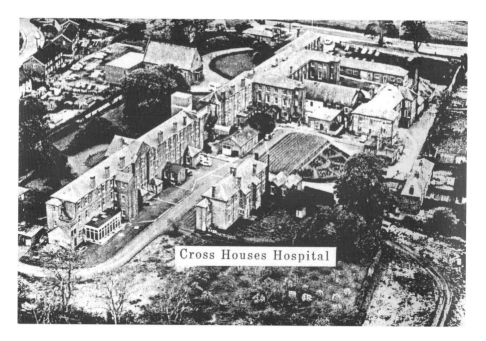

Photo 41 – Berrington Hospital: *The huge complex of the Berrington War Hospital now partially demolished. The chapel in the top left hand corner is now the village hall.*

Photo 42 – The Staff at Berrington Hospital: *The staff and nurses of the Berrington War Hospital photographed in June 1917 a few days after Herbert was a patient there.*

Photo 43 – Shavington Hall: *The Magnificent Shavington Hall where Herbert convalesced in May 1917.*

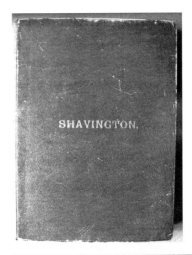

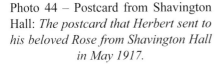

Photo 44 – Postcard from Shavington Hall: *The postcard that Herbert sent to his beloved Rose from Shavington Hall in May 1917.*

Photo 45 – Visitors' book from Shavington Hall: *Lord Kilmorey's visitors' book and Herbert's entry in May 1917.*

Photo 46 – Poperinghe Town: *The central square at Poperinghe as it looks today.*

Photo 47 – Poperinghe Railway Station: *A modern view of the railway station at "Pop". The railhead for troops going to the front at Ypres and where Herbert disembarked in September 1917.*

Photo 48 – Talbot House: *The peaceful back garden at Talbot House where Herbert spent some relaxing hours before going to the front during 3rd Ypres.*

Photo 49 – Switch Road, Poperinghe: *The modern sign for Switch Road that the 8th Norfolks used on their way to the front to bypass potential artillery fire in Poperinghe town centre.*

Photo 50 – Crossing the Yser: *A makeshift pontoon bridge built on sunken barges on the Yzer canal similar to the one Herbert and the 8th Norfolks crossed on their way to the front line trenches.*

Photo 51 – Duckboards – The Advance to Poelcapelle: *A duckboard across the terrible quagmire that was 3rd Ypres with an inset of a poor Tommy who had fallen into the mud and died.*

Photo 52 – Pill Box: *A captured German pill box similar to the one in which Herbert was blown up by a direct hit by an incendiary gas shell.*

Rose went to the station to meet him off the King`s Lynn train. It was late on a Friday afternoon and the children were already home from school. Emma, Rose's sister, was given the job of looking after them, although Alf, now 10 years old, was quite capable. Rose was, in truth, very excited and a little nervous. Her nervousness was made the more intense because she was not completely sure which train Herbert would be on. The letter received only the day before, had been a little garbled. Nevertheless, she prettied herself as best she could – she had not seen her husband in such a long time – and rushed off to the station. Her excitement and apprehension reached fever pitch as the train pulled in. The doors opened and closed, the smoke and steam hissed from the engine, people came and went but, as the train disappeared, there was no sign of Herbert. He was not on the train.

It was as if all the pent up emotions of the last 19 months came rushing to the surface. All the pain, worry and stress of living alone, and bringing up the children, of making ends meet, of holding the family together, at that moment just got too much for her. This very strong woman finally snapped. She burst into tears and sobbed. She cried all the way back to Ash Close, much to the dismay and distress of the children, especially young Bert who recalled the incident years later. Emma tried to console her but she was inconsolable. It was all too much.

It was just at that moment that they heard the sound of army boots as they made contact with the hard ground of Ash Close. Looking out of the back door, Rose could see Herbert turning into Spinks Yard. She could see her husband resplendent in his army uniform which she, of course, had never seen before. He walked along, upright, proud and every bit the soldier.[44]

It was an emotionally charged moment for everybody. There were kisses and hugs aplenty. By his own later admission Herbert was "all watered up". When the excitement of the first meeting had passed, the first thing that struck Rose was Herbert's appearance. She was shocked at how he had changed. In the 19 months since she had seen him he seemed to have aged 19 years. His hair, normally thick and wiry was thin and wispy and his brow line had receded a good one and a half inches. He was beginning to go bald. His moustache, which he took pride in

---

44   It transpired that Herbert had travelled from Kings Lynn to Swaffham in an army transport with other soldiers and had never indeed intended to be on the train at all.

keeping neatly trimmed, was thin and unkempt. He had lost nearly two stone in weight. Although fit and well, he seemed to her to have passed from youth to late middle age in just a few months. Rose had to remind herself that since she last saw him he had been shot in the neck within an inch of his life. He had been shot in the leg. He had suffered a severe bout of influenza. He had lived on army rations in appalling conditions. Perhaps it was not surprising that the experiences of the last few months had taken their toll. However, she was still taken aback.

Herbert's home leave in Swaffham lasted 10 days but he never really settled. It was indeed a holiday from the war, and Herbert had never been on holiday in his life before. He also knew that when the 10 days were over, he would have to go back. He visited his old haunts in Swaffham. He went to the pub but none of his mates were there. They were all away in the army. Some were dead. He went down to the football ground but he knew nobody there either, apart from a few elderly men who remembered him from before the war. He noticed that there were hardly any men in Swaffham between the ages of 18 and 40. They were all away doing their bit. He noticed that it was a town of old men, children and women. He noticed that all the jobs once done by men were now done by the ladies. He noticed that all the spare land, the parks and the allotments had all been ploughed up and planted to produce food for the war effort. He did not feel that this was the Swaffham he knew and loved. The war had changed everything. Even Mr Fayers, the tailor where he used to work, was no longer tailoring suits for the menfolk of the town. There was no call for that either.

He spent his time with his family. He kept popping next door to chat to Rose's father. Always upbeat and laughing, George Drake always looked on the bright side. He was always cheerful. Herbert travelled up to Wells, to the Buttlands, to visit his own father who was busy raising a second family. They commiserated on the death of young George and they talked about Alf. His father was still working even though he was in his late 60s. He had postponed his retirement in order to put food on the table (he and his second wife Ethel would have six children, all half brothers and half sisters to Herbert) and because the country needed old engine drivers to keep the railways running. Nearly all the young railwaymen were over in France.

The greater part of his 10 days was spent with Rose and his children. Little Teddy was getting to know his father for the very first time. To him, this man was almost a stranger. Alf, Phyllis and Bert loved having him around again. They played cards and dominoes. They walked in the woods to the north of the town. Herbert delighted in childhood pranks which included placing sweets in a tree and pretending they had grown there. The children loved it. For Rose, it was an all too brief resumption of the loving relationship that they had known before he left home. After the children had their usual bedtime story from their mother and were tucked up in bed and asleep, the couple could enjoy their private moments together. (As this story unfolds, it will be seen that Rose became pregnant during Herbert's home leave, and exactly nine months later a little girl, who was christened Ivy, was born.)

The war was never mentioned to either Rose or the children. Herbert did not talk about his experiences at all. Nothing was said. Not even in passing. There was no mention of Mash Valley or Delville Wood, of Thiepval or Arras. There was no talk of the hospitals or the ambulances. There was nothing about the shelling or machine-guns. No mention of bullets or mud or shell-holes or trenches. There were no references to dead or dying men or putrefied bodies. Herbert was already starting the process of locking away in another part of his mind his experiences of war. They would never be allowed to impinge on the peace and happiness of this respite.

Ten days is, however, a very short time. As the clock ticked and the hours passed, Monday 25 June got closer and closer. Rose knew and was resigned. In their own way, so were Alf and Phyllis. They knew that their father was going to leave again. They knew that he was probably going to go back to that dreadful war across the water. They knew that he might not come back, that they might never see him again. The 10 days of having him there just made the parting that much harder, that much more gut-wrenching. How would they all be able to bear it?

It is worth dwelling a little on Rose's situation at this time. This soft-centred, artistic mother of four looked around at her family with bewilderment. Her husband was about to leave home to go off to the war for a second time. Her eldest brother, Arthur, had died in the first year of the war (in King`s Lynn hospital, from dropsy).

His son (Rose's nephew) called Cecil, had been captured in France in 1914 and was languishing a prisoner somewhere in Germany. Her third brother, Ted, had been shot and critically wounded in France in 1916. Her fourth brother, Alexander, was part of a Lewis machine-gun crew and was somewhere in the trenches (he was subsequently killed in 1918). And, of course, her mother had passed away in early 1916. However, for Rose, it did not end there. Her brother-in-law George had been killed in 1916. Her second brother-in-law, Alf, had been shot and critically wounded at Thiepval. Her third brother-in-law, John, had been hit by shrapnel at Delville Wood. For Rose the impact of the war went even further. Her second sister, Maud, had married a man called William Brundle who was in France fighting for King and Country. If this was not enough, five more of her Negus cousins were fighting at the front and one had been killed in 1916.

For Rose, the war stretched its tentacles into every aspect of her life. She had, of course, the not inconsiderable support of her sisters and her father. However, she was the one who brought up the boisterous and growing family. She was the one who made ends meet, managed the family budget, educated the children, cooked the meals and mended the clothes, sometimes until late into the night. She was the one who hammered nails into the soles of their shoes. She grew stronger because she had to. She became more self-reliant and more resilient as the days and months went by. She would feel the incredible pain of Herbert going off to war again, but she would dig deep in order to help the children get through it all. She was every bit as strong as her husband.

Monday 25 June came all too soon. The family rose early, as they always did, and Rose helped the children get ready for school. The goodbyes were long and tearful, especially for Phyllis, but eventually all the children ran off to school. Herbert picked up his kit bag. He popped next door to say his farewells to Emma and his father-in-law. He and Rose walked together to the station, arm in arm. Ten minutes later he was gone.

She did not know whether she would see him again. She walked back home, tearful and grieving but she was determined to keep the home fires burning, determined to do right by the children, determined to soldier on.

CHAPTER 11

THE BATTLE OF 3RD YPRES (WIPERS) – THE ULTIMATE HORROR

JUNE–OCTOBER 1917

Herbert was shipped back to France on Tuesday 29th July. Ever since he had boarded the train at Swaffham, he had been resigned to his fate. There was an inevitability about his return to the trenches. Although he was now over 36 years old, he felt comparatively fit and well. His body had recovered from its wounds. He was not so sure about his mind. Whatever lingering hopes he might have had that he would be retained at Felixstowe in the Training Battalion were soon squashed. He was in billets in Walton for only four weeks, the amount of time that it took to get him fighting fit again. His time in hospital and convalescence meant that it was nearly eight weeks since he had been on active duty. His life again might depend on him getting fighting fit quickly so for a third time he went through the mind-numbing routine of sit-ups, forced marches and intense physical training sessions. He was soon in top condition again. He was able once again to enjoy the "social" evenings in the YMCA marquee but he knew it would not last long. He enjoyed once again the home comforts of sleeping in a real bed in a real house (his billets) but he knew that that would not last long either.

There was, perhaps, only one compensation. His brother Jack was also at Felixstowe and Herbert was able to spend some time with him. Jack had been pretty badly bashed about at Delville Wood but had escaped with his life. He had been shipped back to England and had spent months in hospitals and later in convalescence. At one stage there was doubt that he would ever walk again but he had made a slow, painful recovery. He was officially classified as an "invalid" and walked with a pronounced limp. After being discharged from hospital he had spent time back in Swaffham with his wife Alice and his family. He had, of course, seen Rose and the children although he talked very little of his experiences on the Somme. They were to remain a secret for some time.

Jack, however, was not discharged from the army. He opted, or perhaps was ordered, to stay in uniform and he joined the 3rd Norfolks at Felixstowe to help the war effort in whatever way he could. He was to stay in the training battalion for another two years.

So Herbert's and Jack's paths were to cross again. Herbert had not seen his brother for nearly a year since the march under fire to the front line trenches at Delville Wood in July 1916. Then Jack had been fit and well, as had Herbert, just as they had when they both played together in the Swaffham Whippets football team. Now both of them knew that their footballing days were over. Both had been injured, both were in their middle thirties. But Jack was staying in England, while Herbert was going to France for a third time.

After the stalemate at Arras, the British Army was planning yet another major offensive. Manpower in France was again being rebuilt to support another push which would, it was hoped, achieve that elusive major breakthrough. Like Somme and Arras before it, the attack to the east of a small Belgian town called Ypres would punch a hole through the German lines. Herbert had heard it all before.

Herbert had also been on the cross-Channel boat twice before but this time his route to the battlefields was different. The moment his train chugged into Dover, he knew that he was not going back to Boulogne. This time he was heading for Dunkirk, the most northerly of the embarkation points for the Western Front. As he waited on the dockside to board, lightning cracked and thunder rumbled from an early morning thunderstorm. Was it prophetic? By the time the boat headed into the waves, the storm had abated, the weather was calm, the sun shone and he wistfully watched the famous white cliffs of Dover fade into the distance. He said goodbye to England yet again.

Herbert felt differently this time. The elation and curiosity of his first Channel crossing and the apprehension of the second were now distant memories. This third crossing was much more painful. He had no hope in his heart and he carried no aspirations as to his future. He was resigned and stoic. He did not complain, neither did he ever put into words what he felt. His mood was solemn, his demeanour downbeat. The soldiers on the boat all felt the same. There was nothing to celebrate and nowhere to hide. A fellow soldier was brave enough to write in a letter home what thousands of other men were feeling and thinking at this time:

> *The last flickers of our early credulous idealism had died in the Arras Battles. Although we were docile, willing and biddable, we were tired beyond hope. Indeed, we knew now too well to hope, although despair had not yet overwhelmed us. We lived from hand to mouth, expecting nothing and so disappointed nowhere. We were no longer decoyed by the vociferous patriotism of the newspapers. We no longer believed in the purity of the politicians. We were as fed up with England as they were with France and Belgium. The best we could count on was a blighty good for a year; the next a little breathing space to stretch our legs and fill our lungs in some back area, a village with good estaminets. The worst – we knew so much now that we dare not envisage worse, yet we felt worse did exist and we might even now be ripening for it. Our speech has grown coarser, our humour threadbare.*
>
> *Guy Chapman, 13th Royal Fusiliers.*[45]

Dunkirk was a hive of activity, but Herbert's wide-eyed wonder when he first saw the frenetic activity in Boulogne 16 months before had long since faded. He was quickly disembarked, and with other soldiers, made his way to Base Depot 17, a few miles inland. Base Depots were huge facilities that had been established initially by each Division as they arrived in France, and all men arriving in France passed through them on their way to their Battalions.

---

45   Letter from Guy Chapman – 13th Royal Fusiliers.

Much of the matériel needed to support the Division's war effort also found its way to the base camps. They were therefore a forest of men and equipment covering hundreds of acres.

All the soldiers, whether they were new recruits or men returning from hospital, had already been passed in England as fully trained. Nevertheless, the General Headquarters had stipulated that at least 10 days of additional training be given at the Base Depots. Quite why that requirement existed is not clear and in many cases it was not enforced. The pressure to get men to the front as quickly as possible was intense. There seemed little point in spending valuable time retraining soldiers that were already declared trained back in England. It was also a requirement that a further strict medical check be carried out.

All this was of course news to Herbert. No such process had been followed on his arrival at Arras where he had found himself marching to the front line within three days of disembarkation. No such "additional training" had occurred either in 1916 when he was in a front line trench within days of landing at Boulogne. This time, however, he was held at Base Depot No. 17 for no less than 17 days. Initially, it is not clear why. However, what went on in those 17 days of early August turned out to be very critical to Herbert's survival of the 3rd Battle of Ypres.

Why did Herbert not go straight to his Battalion? Why was he delayed for those critical 17 days? It is possible that the army were following to the letter the process laid out in the army manual. This meant putting Herbert through further training but this is highly unlikely. He was now a veteran of both the Somme and Arras. He had experienced the realities of fighting in the front line trenches at least six times. He had three times passed through the training rigours of Felixstowe. Is it possible that the medical check turned up something? A bullet in the neck and a machine-gun shot through the leg might have left the 36 year old man with some disability. That would not have been surprising. However, again it is unlikely. There is no reference to such a problem in his army records. It is not a credible explanation.

The most likely reason, in the light of future events, is that Herbert was indeed being retrained but this time for a different role. He was being instructed in the role of Battalion stretcher-bearer. When a battalion went "over the top" the wounded were initially found and cared for by stretcher-bearers who risked their lives to get to their colleagues as quickly as circumstances would allow. These heroic men came principally from two sources. The Royal Army Medical Corps provided men who were allocated to the attacking battalions. They were fully trained soldiers in their own right but also they were trained medics. All through the war they did outstanding work locating wounded men and bringing them back to the relative safety of their own trenches.

However, they were not the only stretcher-bearers. There were others who were members of the attacking battalions themselves. Men from the ranks were chosen in advance of an attack and given rudimentary training on how to locate and approach fallen comrades, how to apply field dressing and bandages and then how to get the wounded back to a home trench. It was highly dangerous work. Often it had to take place in no-man's-land swept with machine-gun and artillery fire. On many occasions, these brave men went out at night to collect up their cargo of shattered bodies. Thousands of men, Herbert included, have had to thank stretcher-bearers for saving their lives.

An experienced Tommy like Herbert, who had already passed his 36th birthday and whose mobility might have been partially impaired by the bullet wound in his leg, would have made good material for a stretcher-bearer. He was a staunch soldier, not easily flustered. He had a caring nature, developed in childhood. He might have volunteered for such a role. He might have thought that it was the best thing for him. He might have also been influenced by the fact that Rose would appreciate the few extra shillings that would go into his pay packet. It is more likely however that Herbert had nothing to do with it at all. The army, in its inimitable way, probably just told him what was expected of him. Whatever the reason, Herbert left Base Depot No. 17 on 18 August to rejoin the 8th Battalion the Norfolk Regiment as a stretcher-bearer should he be needed.

GRANDDAD'S WAR

Back in Swaffham, Rose, after saying goodbye to her husband for a second time, quickly returned to her daily routine. Although permanently tired and sometimes on the point of exhaustion, she never wavered in her resolve. Her children would not want for food on the table or love in the home or a story to hear. She would always do her bit. After Herbert had been gone for a few weeks, she knew that she was pregnant. Contraception was not yet widely known and Herbert's short home leave had resulted in the inevitable. It must have been the last thing that Rose wanted. She loved children. There was rarely a more loving, caring mother. She gained satisfaction and fulfilment from being with them. But nine months of pregnancy and another mouth to feed must have filled her with apprehension. She had no idea for how long Herbert would be away and in 1917 there was no prospect of an early end to the war. Indeed she knew that there was a very good chance that Herbert would not come back at all. Another baby! Another mouth to feed!

If she was frightened, she did not show it. She "soldiered" on. Emma and her father were there, her sister Maud was there. Her father-in-law was a few miles away. Her many friends at the Baptist Chapel were there too to give a helping hand when it was needed. Rose would get through somehow. She would not be defeated. She would have this baby and Alf, Phyllis, Bert and Ted would have a little sister or brother. The children would hold the future.

All the children were fun-loving, boisterous and, sometimes, quite frankly, a handful. They were up to all sorts of mischief and Rose was sometimes at her wits' end keeping order. Bert especially loved playing games and, war or no war; he had a good time with the other lads in Ash Close. Many years later he recalled the games they used to play:

Children's games came around in the same old order every year in Ash Close. Marbles were perhaps the most popular. Great skill was needed to hold your own and a good player was held in high esteem. You could buy a dozen for a hapenny from any decent shop and some boys made them from clay, sticking them in their mother's ovens. The boy's school playground on the Campinglands was riddles with holes where "Drollems" and terms like *"bux" and "spits" could be heard. We would play `Pinkums` all the way to school along the gutterings and through the churchyard to the Campinglands. If a marble disappeared down a drain that was a good excuse to heave off the grating and search among the mud and leaves for whatever treasures happen to be there, like coins, if we were lucky. Hoops were popular with the boys, iron ones were preferred to those made of wood, with an iron "croom", as they were called, to guide them. Running along with a hoop you could be a pilot of a plane or even the driver of a steam engine over at Sturridges.[46]   Then the spinning tops would have their turn, and conkers, of course, and hopscotch, cricket with a dustbin lid as a wicket. Tippit consisted of two bits of wood, one about 6 inches long and the other rather longer. The shorter one was tapped on the end, causing the other to fly up in the air. On its way down it was struck and sent as far away as possible. All kind of games with skipping ropes and bouncing balls, to the singing of old ditties. One went "one, two, three O'Leary". A fascinating pastime was the making of peepshows. These consisted of a piece of glass, surrounded by flower petals, skilfully arranged, with perhaps a picture of something or other in the centre. To peep at it you had to use a pin. These could be obtained by paying a visit to Well Yard where Mrs Goodrum, the dressmaker, would inadvertently shake them out of her tablecloth. Or Mother would get them as change from Aldiss, the draper. If an article was three shillings, the change for 2/11d would be pins or pieces of ribbon. Cigarette cards collecting and swapping was a real business conducted with expertise – we knew the swapping value of every card. Arrangements were made to visit one each others houses for swapping sessions and mother would grant privacy for these to take place.*

Bert was into everything, as no doubt were Alf and Phyllis too. They ran everywhere and very rarely walked. On occasions they played Rose up as most children do with their mother from time to time and the stern voice of their

---

46   Sturridges was the timber yard over the wall at the back of Spink's Yard.

father was not there to keep them in check. Rose had her hands full and, on occasions, it clearly was too much for her. Bert recalls:

> *Sometimes, when we had been quarrelling and making things difficult for her she would walk out and leave us. We never knew where she went but it was probably next door into Grandfather Drake's house. How relieved we were when she walked in again. Sometimes we thought she had gone for good.*

As normal family life continued as best it could, the war was casting a huge shadow over everyday life in the towns and villages of England. As summer passed to autumn in 1917, things were piling up on the Nation. The German U-boat offensive in the Atlantic was wreaking havoc with the lifeblood of supplies coming from America and the Empire. Food was getting short and prices were going up and even staples were in short supply. Rose, on occasions, found herself joining queues at the grocery store, at the butcher's and at the market stalls. She was more fortunate than most. Her Father, all his life a self-employed agricultural labourer, knew where to go and who to approach. He knew his way around the local community and Rose and the children would not want for much if he had anything to do with it. Others were not so lucky and the townsfolk of Swaffham were mumbling. There was discontent in the air.

The discontent was fanned by the never ending list of casualties coming from the front. Rose noticed that the reports in the *Eastern Daily Press* and the *Norwich Mercury* were not now so positive. The gloss had gone off the headlines. There was more talk of mud and poor conditions at the front. There was more talk of casualties and deaths. There was more talk of a long war of attrition. Nearly every street and every family knew men who were no more. They all knew many more who had, like Herbert, been shot or gassed or blown up. Politicians were held in low regard and there were mumblings about the Generals. The women and the old men were prepared to keep the home fires burning but they were beginning to ask for how long and for what purpose.

Rose was not in the least bit interested in politics. She knew where the future lay. Her children were the future and more specifically her eldest boy,

Alf. He was continuing to do well at school. The teachers were pleased. Rose was concentrating on her ambition that Alf should go to Hammonds Grammar School in Swaffham, even though there was a huge social gap to bridge and even though there was no extra money. Rose was relentless and she worked hard with the teachers at the London Road School. Mrs Mary Hornsby, the Headmistress, and Mrs Minnie Josh, the senior teacher, also had ambitions for Alf and had recognised his potential. They went out of their way to encourage him and they worked behind the scenes to give him extra tuition. Rose might be pregnant, she might have three other children to care for, but she still found time to read and write with Alf in the evening and at the weekends. She had talked it all over with Herbert during his home leave, but he could do little over in France. If it were to happen, it would, as always, be down to Rose. If she had anything to do with it, Alf would sit his scholarship in 1918 and he was going to pass. Now that was a future on which to focus.

The major offensive that history refers to as the 3rd Battle of Ypres was in full swing by the time that Herbert set foot in Dunkirk. It was to be a momentous struggle.

Sir Douglas Haig's battle plan was simple in the extreme.

Map showing the progressive advances of the British Army during the 3rd Battle of Ypres in the late Summer early Autumn of 1917

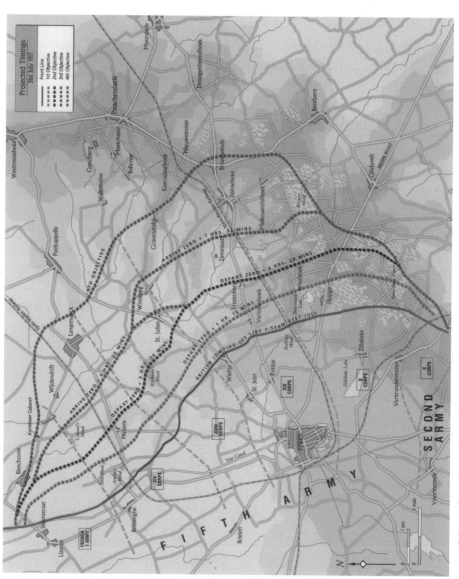

Map taken from Peter Barton's book *"The Somme"* published by Constable in 2006.

He tried to learn as many lessons as possible from the Arras offensive of four months before. He would focus all his forces at Ypres. The famous Salient was some two miles deep and four miles from north to south with the town sitting in the middle. The Yser Canal, running north to south through Ypres was considered to be the eastern edge of the salient.

General Haig planned three stages to the battle. Firstly, he would attack and take the southern end of the salient around the villages of Wytschaete and Messines. This was high land and had been troublesome for some time because it gave the Germans an unencumbered view and artillery control over the salient itself. Secondly, he would then punch a hole through the German lines in the centre of the salient, aiming eventually for the ridges on either side of the village of Passchendaele. Thirdly, he would drive on, capture the rail and road links and drive northwards all the way to the North Sea coast and, with the help of a large amphibious landing, would take the Belgian ports of Nieuport and Antwerp. He would outflank the German Army and roll them up.

It was a grand design which, in a depressingly familiar way, was modified, changed, played with and rewritten. The essence of the plan stayed the same but the timetable slipped back. Indeed it slipped back substantially. In all, the start date for the offensive moved back by as much as six weeks and these were six weeks that would have dire repercussions to the whole of the British Army:

> *These decisions were baffling for Haig was fully aware of the treacherous nature of the Flanders geology and the criticality of using the prime dry campaigning months. Early June may have been earmarked for Messines, but that still left the second half of that month and more than half of July before restart. The British had at their disposal 80 years worth of Belgian meteorological records. Choosing to delay the Ypres assault was a serious gamble.*
>
> *Peter Barton, Passchendaele.*[47]

---

47 *Passchendaele* by Peter Barton published by Constable in 2007.

As the world knows, by the time the second part of the offensive began in August, September and October, the warm summer weather had passed and the rain came. And it rained, day after day after day. The low-lying Flanders battlefield turned into a quagmire of mud. Men went to the front on duckboards laid across swamps rather than in trenches. They took shelter from artillery in water filled shell holes rather than dugouts. The wounded drowned before they could get support. They fought in the most abominable conditions in the history of warfare and they fought and died in unprecedented numbers.

In the history of warfare, men had never fought in conditions like these before:

> It is quite impossible to describe in words what the situation and the state of the country was like up there. It rained steadily the whole time and the darkness at night was intense. This added to the usual confusion and uncertainty that reigns on a battlefield, rendered reorganising and relocating of troops a super - human job. Even in daylight it was almost impossible to find out where anyone was. Battalions were scattered over many square miles without a landmark anywhere. The country was one mass of shell holes and it was very easy to end up head over heels in a shell hole full of water and arrive soaked to the skin in one mass of mud from head to foot. Battalions were shoved into the middle of a mud waste with just a few shelters.
>
> *R. T. Fellows, 1st Rifle Brigade.*[48]

The mud, the squalor, the rain, the death and destruction went on for nearly three long months. There had never been any thing like it before and there would never be again. "Wipers was the ultimate horror." This was what lay ahead for Herbert as he set out to rejoin the 8th Battalion, the Norfolk Regiment on the 18 August 1917.

———————•◆•———————

48 Letter from Lt Col R T Fellows – 1st Rifle Brigade – *Passchendaele* by Peter Barton published by Constable in 2007.

Herbert had not seen any of his pals in the 8th Battalion since the glorious but costly offensive on the Schwaben Redoubt nearly a year before. (At Arras he had been in the 7th.) After he had fallen in that attack, the 18th Division had kept up the assault and eventually the impregnable Redoubt was taken. The 7th had then been caught up in a number of other Somme actions in and around the village of Miraumont. They had been moved up to the Arras area but had not been called upon to take a major part in that battle. Nevertheless they incurred casualties in an abortive attack on an empty German trench (according to the Battalion history, 64 men were killed or wounded). The Battalion had then moved north again to the Ypres Salient in preparation for the upcoming offensive.

Herbert's 17 days at Base Depot 17 turned out to be very fortuitous indeed. When he joined the 8th (at the Rubrouk training area) he found that they had been through a very rough time indeed. While he was being retrained, his new colleagues had been involved in a bloody action that had left them seriously depleted. As part of General Haig's plan to punch a hole through the middle of the German defences, on 10 August the Battalion, with other Battalions of the 53rd Brigade, were ordered to take over the front line in the area around Glencorse Wood. The War Diary indicated that there had been considerable confusion in this operation. This was an understatement. The men had been on the move for almost 22 hours before they got to the front line. Having at last gained their positions, the Germans launched their own attack on a strongpoint that the Norfolk men were holding. The strongpoint was lost. The Germans managed to break through a part of the line. A counter-attack was ordered and the strongpoint was recaptured and held for the next two days in spite of repeated, strong, German attempts to recapture it. Casualties were heavy on both sides. On 13 and 14 August the Norfolks had withdrawn to dugouts but were severely mauled by an enemy bombardment. A gas shell penetrated the dug out occupied by the officers of C Company. Seven of them were seriously wounded and four others were injured, most of them because of gas. If that was not enough, on the night of the 14th the Battalion took refuge in a shelter called Crab Crawl, "which was one of the most terrible shelters imaginable, a place in which anyone with the slightest inclination to claustrophobia must have gone mad". It was a long, oval tunnel in Observatory Ridge, from which, in places, there led out T heads and recesses for troops. There were eight or nine entrances by passages six feet high and one foot broad so that a man had to move sideways in them (hence the name Crab Crawl). The T heads were ventilated by blow holes leading to the hillside, but many of these had been blocked up by the shells which were constantly falling on the neighbourhood. There were ventilating pumps, but they had broken down. In some of the recesses the air was so foul that a candle could not be kept alight. These traumatic experiences from 10 to 16 August resulted, according to the Battalion War Diary, in 194 casualties, 52 of which had been killed. Many men had been gassed. By the time the Battalion was relieved and returned by train to the Rubrouk training area, they desperately needed time to recuperate and rebuild.

Herbert missed all this action. He missed Glencorse Wood and he missed Crab Crawl even though he was only a few miles away at Base Depot 17. That 17-day delay was truly a blessing in disguise and was another example of survival sometimes depending on good fortune. Certainly infantry men were required before the Glencorse Wood action and there was ample time for him to rejoin the Battalion before it was sent to the front line. He was incredibly lucky, if that is the right word, that because of his age and because of his previous wounds he was being trained to be a stretcher-bearer behind the lines, out of harm's way. Whatever the explanation, his 17 days at Base Depot 17 meant that he did not get involved in these bloody encounters and did not become a casualty like many of his colleagues.

When Herbert rejoined the 8th he found that he was not alone in joining the Battalion. The Ypres offensive was now in full swing and the casualties of Glencorse Wood had to be replaced quickly. As an important part of Maxse's 18th (Eastern) Division, the Norfolks would be needed again in the front line – and soon. On the same day as Herbert, 118 other men left the Base Depot and joined the Battalion; on the 22nd there were seven more, followed by four more the next day and three days after that an additional 71. Indeed between the 18th and 31st August, no fewer than eight Officers and 200 other ranks joined the Battalion, to make good the casualties. Whatever illusions Herbert might have had that his third tour of duty in France was in some way going to be less demanding, they were being dispelled by the day. "Something was up!"

For the next five weeks, the Battalion stayed at the Rubrouck training area. Rubrouk is a small Flanders village some 10 kilometres south of Dunkirk and 20 kilometres to the east of Ypres and it is well out of range of the heaviest of the German guns. Herbert got to know his colleagues again, some of them the same men he knew from Delville Wood and Thiepval. However some of the men were new to him. The whole Battalion was recuperating and rebuilding. New officers were getting to know their men and all four companies were reorganising. Herbert was to see again someone else at Rubrouck.

Only a few days after saying goodbye to his younger brother in Felixstowe, he met again his elder brother Alf in Rubrouk. Fate was determining that the paths of the brothers were crossing and recrossing as the war progressed. After being seriously wounded at Thiepval Alf had, like Jack, spent many months in hospital in England. He also had recovered and in due course had rejoined the 8th Suffolks which was a sister Battalion to the 8th Norfolks in the 53rd Brigade, part of the renowned 18th (Eastern) Division. They too were at Rubrouck rebuilding for the next offensive. The two brothers had not met since the days at Autuille Wood prior to the attack on Thiepval village. They knew of each other's experiences. The family grapevine and the letters from home made sure of that. They now met again as veterans of the Western Front but at heart they were both still men from Norfolk. They were both Swaffham men. Again there is no record of what was said, and for how long they met. It can be imagined that the two of them would hide their emotion behind a veneer of calm. They would catch up on family news, talk about their ageing father and poor dead George. They would talk about Jack and his smashed legs. They would pass on news of Swaffham. There would be the jokes and the contagious chuckle. They would have smoked a pipe together. They may even have swapped stories about their injuries. They would wish one another well and shake hands. That would be it. Inside they would be burning with concern for one another. They would not see one another again until well after the war was over.

While the 8th Norfolks were regrouping at Rubrouck, there occurred an incident which had an extremely sobering affect on Herbert and all the men of the 8th. One of their number was arrested for desertion, tried, convicted and shot by firing squad. He was John Abigail who had been born of poor, uncaring parents in a slum area of Norwich. He had been ill-treated as a child and had grown up with poverty and hunger as constant companions. He had never been much of a soldier, indeed he had never been much of anything. He had deserted, left his post and gone AWOL. He had been quickly captured. It had all got just too much for this undisciplined, poorly educated 20 year old. He couldn't cope any longer with this terrible war. But army regulations were unbending and an example had to be made and the death sentence was duly carried out on the 12 September. Whether Herbert knew John Abigail is not known but he certainly knew about of the execution – everybody in the 8th Battalion was made fully aware of it. The whole point of Abigail's death was to make an example of him "pour encourager les autres". (Note – John Abigail received a pardon from the British government in 2006 along with 303 other British Tommies that were executed for various offences during the First World War. Ironically, John Abigail's name still appears on the roll of honour on the Norwich War Memorial and is recorded on the war memorial in St Augustine's Church in the city.)

———◆———

It was not until 22 September that the Battalion was ordered to move again, by which time Herbert had been in France for a full eight weeks. His days had been taken up with the general activities of a soldier behind the lines. However the move on the 22nd seemed to him to be significant and he must have known that it was the beginning of the painstaking process that would result in the Battalion being in the front line yet again. He had after all been through it all before.

The Battalion, indeed the whole of the 53rd Brigade, left Rubrouck in the morning, marched to a railway station in the small village of Esquelberg, where they entrained and journeyed to Poperinghe, a journey of 10 kilometres which somehow, in the congested mayhem of wartime travel, took over three hours.

Poperinghe is only 10 kilometres to the west of Ypres but it will always hold a special place in the hearts and minds of thousands of British Tommies. They could never wrap their tongue around its name. They had better things to do than fathom the mysteries of the Walloon language. So they simply called it "Pop". This small market town (see Photo 46) was the last relatively safe railhead for men and matériel before they moved eastwards to the horrors of the waterlogged battlefield. It was here that they snatched precious moments of rest and relaxation before their date with destiny.

Herbert and the Norfolks detrained at Pop railway station, but it was not a place to dwell (see Photo 47). As a centre for military comings and goings, it was a target for spasmodic long range enemy artillery fire and could, on occasions, get very uncomfortable. The Battalion quickly headed for Road Camp in the nearby Hamlet of St-Jan-ter-Biezen. As they marched through Pop, Herbert saw once again the sights and sounds of a town at war:

> *The town was always swarming with Officers and men. There were mess presidents and mess cooks buying provisions. There were people going on leave or coming back with no objections to wasting a few days. There were large garrisons and nearly always at least a division billeted. Besides this there was always a vast mass of people simply there for "a day out". The traffic passing through Poperinghe would have made Oxford Street in June look sleepy, and every lorry, limber, car or tender from whatever direction it was coming shed a few people more into the mass. You could have your hair cut in a shop which warned its customers laconically "we do not work when the Germans are shelling". You could buy all the things you had been needing for months – puttees and razors, shirts and studs and toothpaste. You could buy omelettes and vin blanc or fish and chips. In a word, the resources of civilisation left no dizzy joy to be desired.*
>
> *F. R. Barry*

They arrived at Road Camp just before midnight, having been on the move for 18 hours. They stayed there for a whole 14 days. With the attention to detail that was the trademark of General Maxse and the Eastern Division, Herbert and the Battalion went through more preparatory training – as if more was required. It was not all work however. Herbert visited "Pop" a number of times. Many years later he mentioned it in passing to one of his grandsons. Perhaps he went for a hair cut or had his moustache smartened up a little. He almost certainly went into one of the many cafes. He certainly visited Talbot House (see Photo 48) which, then and now, had gained a justified reputation as a place for relaxation for the stressed British soldier.

Talbot House was, in 1917, in its prime. This extraordinary club, open to all ranks, was named after Gilbert Talbot, son of the Bishop of Winchester, who was killed in the Ypres Salient in 1916. Run by Phillip "Tubby" Clayton, the House had the atmosphere of a home where all men, whoever they were, weary and frightened from fighting the war, could come and be refreshed physically and spiritually. A cup of tea cost one penny. There was a tea bar and a small grocery store. There was a dry canteen which sold hundreds of different things from cigarettes to toothpaste. A welcoming notice above the door proclaimed, rather indelicately, "If you spit on the carpet at home, you may spit on the carpet here". The army signallers, using their special skills, shortened the name of the place to Toc H and it thus became the byword for a celebrated worldwide movement that continued to operate long after the war was over.

Herbert and his mates visited it at least once. They probably had a cup of tea, played some cards, most likely crib, and put their feet up for a while. As it was a home for all ranks, it was for Herbert as for many others a surreal period of fun and good company. Just a few miles down the road, the most vicious battle of the First World War was being played out.[49]

---

49 Talbot House is now open to the public. It is little changed to what it must have been like in 1917. In particular, visitors can sit in the peaceful small garden where once soldiers whiled away a quiet hour or two. They can also go into the small theatre where entertainment was once put on for the troops. Anyone can now sit where once Herbert and his mates once sat.

Whatever the pleasures that Pop offered, Herbert could not escape his feeling of foreboding. He knew that he would soon be back at the front. Morale needed a lift and after a few days, the Battalion was called on parade and medals were given out for conspicuous bravery during the battles for Glencorse Wood that Herbert had so narrowly missed. There were five Military Crosses, two Distinguished Conduct Medals, and nine Military Medals. The men of the 8th Norfolks were being recognised for the fighting that they had done. During the month, further reinforcements arrived from the Base Depots, no fewer than 14 more officers and 92 other ranks swelled the Battalion to a fighting strength of 1,043 men. "Something was clearly up."

On 8 October the orders finally came. The Battalion under a new commanding officer was to move forward to the front line area in three stages. Herbert had done this at least five times before and he recognised the signs. The memories of the quarries of Loos, of Mash Valley, of Delville Wood, of Thiepval, of Feuchy and of Monchy were still vivid. He knew the process and he knew what it all meant. He would indeed be in a front line trench before too long.

A Battalion on the move is a formidable sight and it is an equally formidable logistical operation. The orders were quite precise. One billeting officer per company was ordered to move on bicycles ahead of the men to ensure that billets were available when they arrived at their destination that night. The men would have their kits ready by 2.30 pm or else, and they would stand clear of the billets by 1.15 pm. They would parade at 2.15 pm. Tents and huts would be thoroughly cleaned out, rubbish burnt, latrine buckets emptied and the camp left in a sanitary condition. The location of the division bomb store, the brigade bomb dumps and the proposed dumps of weapons in the forward positions was identified. The weapons in each of these dumps were specified – 2500 SAA, 190 Mills Rifle Grenades, 125 Other Grenades, and 40 Verey Pistols. The way in which weapons would be carried forward to reach the dump was detailed – a carrying party of four privates from A Company, five from B Company, six and one NCO from C company and five and one NCO from D Company would carry weapons forward when ordered. 800 petrol tins filled with water would be drawn from the brigade headquarters and four water carts would be kept in case of emergency. Orders went out that "all ranks must realise that petrol tins are very valuable and the supply is very limited and must on no account be thrown away".[50] Salvage dumps were established and orders issued that "every man, animal and vehicle returning from the line must bring back some article of salvage". Men must also notice the position of captured guns and whether these guns are capable of being moved by horse teams by night or by day. Directions were given as to where prisoners of war should be taken. The Quartermaster was instructed to hand out sufficient shovels (44) and that the men had a sufficient supply of tommy cookers but the cookers should not be used until the Battalion was in the front line. The Quartermaster was also instructed to issue every man with a pair of dry socks. Whale oil was to be issued daily and every man was ordered to rub it into his feet well to prevent trench foot on pain of court martial.

A Battalion on the move numbered over 1,000 men. They carried all the equipment for fighting and living and dying. They carried everything by hand into and across a battle area where the normal rules of transport did not and could not apply. The Tommy was both a fighting machine and also a beast of burden. It was he, with the occasional help of horses, that must get the wherewithal of war to the front line.

Herbert had a very special interest in the "medical arrangements". They were very clear. When the Battalion got to the front line area, the initial collecting points for the wounded would be located just behind the front line at places called Malta House, Bulow Farm and Mon-de-Rosta. Advance dressing stations had been set up at Minty Farm, and at 3 House and St Julien.

It was ordered that four stretcher-bearers from the RAMC would be attached to each regimental aid post. However, conditions out on the battlefield were very bad and the distance to safety much longer than normal:

In view of the heavy work that will be thrown on stretcher - bearers during this operation, each company will arrange for a minimum number of 8 stretcher - bearers per company (Herbert was of course one of the 8 stretcher - bearers

---

50   Brigade orders.

from B company), to assist those from the Royal Army Medical Corps. This is
rendered necessary owing to the length of the carry. These men will report to
the medical officer this afternoon at 3.00pm at the medical instruction room
for instruction on bandaging. All ranks are to be informed that the divisional
sign adopted for marking the position of wounded men is a piece of bandage or
paper stuck on the end of a stick or bayonet. Wounded men showing this sign
will be found quicker than those who do not show it.

The last order was perhaps the most brutal. "Each unit will be responsible for the dead in its own area. All ranks must be instructed that the upper (green) identity disk must be left on the body and the red disk together with private effects forwarded to headquarters."

On 9 October, the Battalion set out from Road Camp. Herbert's day began early and by 11.00 am his battle kit was prepared and ready. By 1.45 pm his billets had been cleared and cleaned and ready for inspection. At 2.15 pm he stood on parade with the 8th Norfolks. Alongside him were the 8th Suffolks, his brother Alf standing somewhere in their ranks. At 3.00 pm he reported to the medical inspection room and was given instructions on the medical arrangements that he would need to know to do his job as a stretcher-bearer in the front line area. He was given rudimentary instructions on locating the wounded, applying field dressings and bandaging. He rejoined his company and the Battalion set out at 3.30 pm. Their route took them around the north of Pop (to avoid both congestion and bombardment) on what was called the Switch road (see Photo 49), along the lanes to the crossroads to Brielen. They marched in company order with the 8th Suffolks following up behind. They marched for three and a half hours, fortunately unmolested by enemy artillery and arrived to bivouac at Murat Camp as the sun was setting.

The next day they were on the move again, this time a short distance to one of the thousands of dugouts sunk into the west bank of the Yser canal. The Yser canal was a boundary in the mind of the army. To the west was relative safety; to the east were the killing fields of the Ypres Salient. The men found their way across the canal on a number of improvised bridges which were constantly targeted by artillery bombardments. Consequently many of the bridges were held up by sunken barges that were more resistant to shelling (see Photo 50). In other places tunnels had been cut below the canal but these were largely ineffective in the wet weather. All along the western bank of the canal were dugouts, one after another, sheltering thousands of men. Many were reinforced with concrete. The raised levee of the canal bank offered real protection from shells and shrapnel. Also sunk into the bank were medical facilities for treating wounded men coming back from the front. (Many, like Essex Farm, have been preserved and are now open to the public.) In October 1917, the west bank of the Yser canal was a bustling hive of activity with whole divisions of soldiers sheltering beneath it.

Herbert and the Norfolks stayed cooped up in the dugouts for four nights and three days. The front line was nearly six miles away across the quagmire to the east. The noise of gunfire was incessant and the dugouts themselves were subject to spasmodic bombardment. They were small, inhospitable, damp and unpleasant. Herbert did not care. They were safe. The Norfolks incurred no casualties during those four days.

The 14 October dawned cloudy and the rain continued to fall. The ground was waterlogged, the men damp and unhappy. But there was a job to do. The Battalion had been ordered to relieve units of the 11th Division in the front line near the village of Poelcappelle to the north east of Passchendaele. It was a six mile march from the dugouts. This time the 8th Suffolks, brother Alf included, had gone to the front two days before. At 1.30 in the afternoon the Norfolks started out and they quickly discovered the conditions here were very different to those at the Somme and Arras. There were few communication trenches and no tunnels to protect the men here. The approach was along duckboard tracks that wound their way through and over the water-filled shell holes. Some were wide enough to take two lines of men. Others were just big enough for single file. Many were fitted with anti-slip wire that the men could grab at. It stopped them dropping into the mud and water on either side. Being sucked into the quagmire was a constant fear. From time to time, Herbert passed the decomposing bodies of men who had been wounded and just could not escape the clinging mud (see Photo 51). The duckboard was slippery and wet, some of them tilted sideways, some on a slope and some stretches were missing altogether or shattered by bombardment. Herbert had never seen anything quite like this before. To make matters worse, the men were visible for miles around and enemy gunners were on constant lookout for units of men moving forward. They quickly became a target for artillery. There were few places to hide and almost nowhere to seek cover. Even General Haig was becoming aware of the shocking battlefield conditions for reports were hourly coming in of horses, mules and men drowned, wagons and even railways sinking into the mud. Up ahead, a man of the 8th Suffolks Private S. T. Fuller recorded in his diary what he found.

Two signallers heard cries for help, and after a search, found two men stuck in the mud. They were not wounded in any way, but were unable to get out of their own accord. The signallers "tapped in" on the line and phoned us for stretcher-bearers – as the men could not walk even after they had been extricated. Had our phone wire not run past the spot, those two men might have remained there, fast in the mud, until they died of starvation or exhaustion.[51]

Progress for the Norfolks was painfully slow. The Battalion Diary merely states that the "ground was very wet and muddy which made the going rather difficult". A Company led the way; B Company followed leaving a gap of about 200 yards. Soon a long thin string of men were winding their way along the duckboard track. After two hours a halt was called in a trench called "Cane Trench". This was an old German trench that had been captured a few weeks before. It had been "turned around" and was in good enough condition to give some protection. "Teas" were issued to the men. Crowded in the trench, they ate bread and sipped on hot drinks. They then moved forward again by platoon with bigger gaps between the men. They crossed another two miles of a moonscape of desolation and destruction until they reached the front line that was little

---

51   Quote from Pt S T Fuller – 8th Suffolks – *Passchendaele* by Peter Barton published by Constable in 2007.

more than a line of mud-filled shell holes. Herbert and B Company fanned out to the left and D Company went off to the right. A Company and C Company were held in support. It was another of those quirks of fate that the Battalion they were relieving were the 8th Suffolks. In the fading light, the two brothers passed each other, one going forward, the other going to the rear. These two men who were so close in every sense were now no more than shadows that passed in a twilight world. They might even have seen one another in the gloom. When they were kicking a football about in the park in King's Lynn all those years ago, they could never have dreamed that their lives would bring them together in this god-forsaken place.

As if by miracle, the relief operation had been carried out without attracting any hostile shelling and amazingly no casualties were incurred. The men settled into their positions as best they could. Herbert, sometime that evening, withdrew from the front line with B Company and went back a few yards to a solid stone and concrete pillbox that had been captured with heavy casualties a few days before. The Regimental First Aid Post had been established in the pillbox. Herbert's duties as a stretcher-bearer had begun.

The relief operation did not go unnoticed for long. In the early hours of the morning "all hell broke loose". The dark sky was lit up by the arching fire of shells and tracers. The Germans opened up a heavy bombardment with 77 mm and 5 cm gas shells. They kept it up all through the day. Casualties started to climb. The Norfolks were losing men. The stretcher-bearers were kept busy. They were locating the wounded and carrying them back to the Advance Dressing Station at Bulow Farm. Herbert was busy running his wounded colleagues from the front to the pillbox.

Sometime during that day, during the bombardment, he was in the Regimental First Aid Post in the pillbox (see Photo 52). With him was the medical officer, Captain W. A. Todd of the RAMC, and his orderly. Also in the pillbox was a stretcher-bearer, Lance Corporal Everitt, a man who in civilian life worked as a pharmacist at the Norfolk coastal village of Mundesley. They were probably in the process of bringing wounded men to the post and were for a short time in the relative safety of one of the few concrete structures in the area.

Safety, however, in a battlefield is a relative term. Herbert's good fortune ran out. The pillbox received a direct hit. A large gas shell penetrated the walls of the structure and exploded inside. A sickening crash and a blinding flash were followed by mustard gas that filled what was left of the pillbox. All four men were blown off their feet. All four were peppered with shrapnel.

When help came running, the scene that confronted them was one of devastation. The Regimental Aid Post was no more. The pillbox was a mess as was everything inside it. Equipment lay strewn over the ground. On the floor were four bodies. None of them moved. None of them made a sound. Surely this time, Herbert Barnes's war had come to an end – a sudden, bloody end. It was surely over now.

The orderly and stretcher-bearer Everitt were killed instantly, blown to pieces by the explosion. Captain Todd was knocked unconscious. Private Herbert Barnes was lifted into the air and also lay on the ground unconscious. He was hit by shrapnel and bathed in mustard gas. They were both surely dead. It was not reasonable to expect flesh and blood to survive such an explosion.

CHAPTER 12

HOME AND AWAY IN SCOTLAND
OCTOBER–DECEMBER 1917

Good fortune is a gift. Lady Luck spreads her favours in frivolous ways. In the front line, it was never a question of bravery, or cowardice, or courage, or any of those virtues that are associated with the fighting soldier. It was not heroics that kept some men alive and killed others. It was a merely a matter of random chance.

When Herbert's colleagues got inside the pillbox they found that the stretcher-bearer Everitt had been killed instantly. He had been blown to pieces by the explosion. The medical orderly was also dead, killed by the shrapnel that had ricocheted around the enclosed area. Captain Todd had been knocked unconscious and also hit by shrapnel. Herbert Barnes had been lifted in the air and also lay on the ground unconscious. He too had been hit by shrapnel and bathed in mustard gas. However, in spite of everything, both Captain Todd and Herbert Barnes were still alive. They were both in bad shape but, amazingly, clung on to a fragile strand of life.

The evacuation procedure for the injured, so meticulously laid down by the battalion commanders before the men moved up to the front, now kicked in. Stretcher-bearers, men who had attended the self-same briefing as Herbert had attended back at Road Camp, carried the two wounded men back to Bulow Farm. This was the closest collecting point for the wounded from the left flank of the front line allocated to the 53rd Brigade. It was a carry of not more than 1,000 yards. From there they were taken back on a longer carry across the exposed duckboards to the relative safety of Minty Farm, nearly two miles away, the nearest advanced dressing station.

How long the evacuation took is not known, but it was probably no more than a few hours. Neither is it known when or if Herbert regained consciousness. If he ever did come to on that long hazardous journey, exposed to enemy artillery, he would have been in excruciating pain. Three pieces of shrapnel, all about the size of a rifle bullet, had got embedded in the top of his good leg, the right one, and come to rest close to the bone. His uniform was blood-soaked from the waist down. Mustard gas had sprayed his face and was attacking all the soft skin around his eyes and nose. Blistering was occurring. The gas attacked his conjunctiva and his eyelids, causing them to close. Herbert could not walk, neither could he see and the burning sensation was spreading all over his face. When he came to, he wanted to vomit and probably did. Before he was carried back to Minty Farm, the medics had covered his eyes with a water-soaked bandage to ease some of the pain. Mustard gas was a terrible weapon.

There was no farm, of course, at Minty Farm. It had been blown to smithereens during the advance into the salient and the pile of building rubble was little more than ground high. However, the farm cellars had been reinforced and provided subterranean cover from the constant shelling (see Photo 53). Outside, on the ground surrounding the cellars, were scattered the stretchers and crutches that were used to get men further back behind the lines. There was a temporary cemetery for those Tommies who would be going no further. Their makeshift wooden crosses represented what once had been a person. It was to be hoped that Herbert would not be one of them.[52] Even as he was carried into the cellar, shellfire was exploding all around the farm but the underground cave provided enough protection for the surgeons and medics to get to work on him and Captain Todd. Here he got his first serious medical treatment. The surgeons, using scalpels and tweezers, dug out the metal from Herbert's leg. For reasons best known to him, the surgeon thought that Herbert might want to keep some of the metal chunks as a souvenir.[53] He carefully placed it in Hebert's "baccy

---

52 Minty Farm is now rebuilt and is a prosperous working farm. Nestled up behind it is the peaceful, well tended War Graves Commission Cemetery with its rows of white headstones.

53 It had become common practice to keep pieces of shrapnel or rifle bullets as rather macabre mementos of an action survived.

tin" and tucked it back into his uniform pocket. It was an act of kindness in a brutal world. He then sewed Herbert's leg back up again.[54]

The gas damage was less easily treated. It was quickly diagnosed that Herbert had not ingested sufficient gas that would result in the bronchial tubes being attacked. If he had, he would certainly have died a painful lingering death a week or two later. Fortunately the internal damage was limited. The external damage, the blistering to the face and eyes, was going to need more treatment as would the restoration of his eyesight.

Herbert would have to go back down the line, the same way as he had come only a few hours before. The stretcher-bearers took him back along the duckboards, all the way to the west bank of the Yzer canal. It was the "long carry" that Herbert himself had been briefed on a few days earlier and one of the major reasons he was in the Regimental First Aid Post in the first place. Where exactly he was taken is not known (it could perhaps have been the famous Essex Farm). Wherever it was, a decision was made that Herbert needed extensive treatment that could only be found in one of the general hospitals on the coast. He was, for the fourth time, on his way out of the war zone.

The hospital that he went to seemed somewhat of a strange choice. The 10th General Hospital at Rouen was over 200 kilometres from Ypres to the north-west of Paris on the River Seine. It was another long, uncomfortable and painful journey in an ambulance train. To Herbert it seemed to go on for ever. Still unable to walk, and still unable to see, it must have been a long haul indeed. It took a little more than 24 hours as the train stopped and started along the congested railway lines of Eastern France. However, it is still to the credit of the RAMC, and the well-used, well-practised evacuation procedure, that Herbert was admitted to the hospital less than 30 hours after the gas shell blew up his pillbox.

The 10th General Hospital in Rouen was located on the racecourse on what was then the outskirts of the city. Here Herbert could expect the best of care

---

54 The small piece of round metal eventually found its way back to Rose who kept it nearly all her life. She eventually passed it on to her eldest daughter Phyllis, who in turn passed it to her daughter, Barbara, who still has it to this day (see Photo 54).

and attention. One of Rouen's specialities was the treatment of mustard gas victims. It looked much like many of the other General Hospitals that Herbert had been to in the past. Temporary huts festooned a huge grass area, most of them accommodating the medical staff and nurses. The wounded men were accommodated in a forest of large white marquees, each with between 50 and 60 beds, all of them full with wounded soldiers. A Sister held sway over each tent and with the help of the trained orderlies and Voluntary Aid Detachment nurses ("VADs") she tended to the men's needs. On arrival, Herbert was once again cut out of his lice-infested bloody uniform. He was washed, bathed and dressed in the blue outfits that he knew so well. He became, once again, what the nurses called, a Blue Boy. His personal belongings (including the piece of shrapnel) were put in a clutch bag that was hung on the wooden frame of his bed. He was given a hot drink which he found painful to get down his throat. He was then put on the "S list" which indicated that he was a serious case. For this Herbert was no doubt grateful. There was also a D list which was reserved for dangerous cases, men who were going to do very well if they pulled through.[55]

Herbert was very ill. He continued to be in intense discomfort, principally from the pain to both his face and eyes. The shrapnel gash in his leg, normally a severe wound, seemed almost incidental as the staff went to work on the gas burns. His blistered face was treated and his eyes constantly bathed and the dressing changed. The other symptoms of mustard gas poisoning, severe headaches, a rapidly increased pulse and a high fever, were brought under control. Herbert gradually began to recover from this, his greatest ordeal.

He stayed in the marquee on the racecourse at Rouen for a full week, from October 17 to 24. The length of his hospitalisation was influenced by a number of factors. Initially, he might well have been in too much discomfort to be moved. There might also have been some hope amongst the medical staff that he could be patched up and returned to the front although that does seem

---

55 Frances Cluett – *The Diaries of Mary Wilson*. Frances Cluett was a Canadian VAD who was present at the 10th General Hospital in 1917 and in her letters home describes life in the marquees in some detail. 'The patients were grateful to be in hospital and tucked up with the hope of a "Blighty".'

rather a long shot. It might be there were no ships available to take him back to England. Whatever the reason, it was not until after six days of being at Rouen that he was told that he did indeed have a "Blighty" and that he was going back to England. For a third time in less than 12 months he would cross the English Channel in a hospital ship.

His transport this time was the SS *St Patrick*. By coincidence, it was the sister ship of the SS *St David* on which he had crossed after his gunshot wound at Arras. Before the war this twin-funnelled steam ship had spent peacetime as a cross-Channel ferry plying between Fishguard and Rosslare across the Irish Sea. On the outbreak of war, she had been greedily snatched up by the war department and converted into a hospital ship. She was supposed to carry only 180 patients at a time and she had been going backward and forwards between Rouen, Le Havre and Southampton ever since the war started.

The journey across the Channel was not without its difficulties. He and the other stretcher cases were loaded aboard on the evening of 24 October, followed up the gangplank by the walking wounded. There were far, far more than 180 wounded men and the boat was uncomfortably crowded. It was intended that it would sail across at night-time to avoid the attention of German U-boats that were by this time openly torpedoing hospital ships. However the sailing was cancelled at the last minute. The ship's log book indicates that the walking wounded were ordered to disembark. However, the stretcher cases, Herbert among them, stayed on board all that night and the rest of the next day. Again, at dusk the walking wounded embarked yet again and the *St Patrick* set out for Southampton. The crossing was rough and unpleasant but by the morning of October 26 1917, Herbert was once again on English soil.

It is not clear at what stage Herbert's sight began to improve, or when in this long journey he began to see again. A heavy exposure to mustard gas invariably results in blindness and skin being scarred for life. Herbert was lucky. He had been gassed but not as badly as some of his less fortunate colleagues. Herbert's face blistering was improving day by day, as indeed were his eyes. His leg wound was mending and he had not contracted any infection. However, he was showing some strange symptoms. He had been very badly knocked about and was feeling rough. The impact of the explosion had "shaken him up" very severely with the result that his heartbeat was irregular and he was showing mild signs of nervous disorder. In spite of all that, he could only have felt deep down some elation. He had survived the front line trenches yet again. He was back in England and he was alive. Everything else he knew he could cope with. The landing dock at Southampton, in no way picturesque, must have seemed beautiful to him, if indeed he was able to see it at all.

As the new day dawned, Herbert's stretcher was transferred from boat to hospital train. He did not know where he was going. His hopes must have been high that this time he could perhaps go back to Norfolk, perhaps to the war hospital at Norwich. All through the day the train moved on. It stopped and started and for many hours Herbert could hear the clickety-clack of the wheels against the points. The journey seemed to go on forever. He would have known from the nurses on the train that he was heading north. He would have quickly worked out that he was going nowhere near Norfolk. Somewhere along the way, perhaps at Peterborough or York or Newcastle he was told or deduced that he was going all the way to Scotland.

He had never been that far north before. To him, Scotland was a far-away place. In 1917 it was almost the equivalent of "going abroad". Late at night, some 18 hours after he left Southampton, the train pulled into the sidings that served the Edinburgh War Hospital at Bangour in West Lothian, 15 miles to the east of Scotland's capital city. For the next few weeks this was going to be his new home.

Rose already knew that Herbert had been wounded yet again. She had received a telegram from the War Office while Herbert was at the General Hospital at Rouen. She also knew that he had been gassed but she did not know the details. She did not know how badly he had been affected but she had been told enough to know that he would survive. Gas conjured up all sorts of injuries in the minds of the civilian population back in Britain. They knew about blindness, scarring, damage to internal organs and a whole host of the terrible afflictions that could result in a slow, lingering death. Rose had seen gas victims in Swaffham and the surrounding villages. She would have to wait and see whether the Herbert who came back to England was the same Herbert who had kissed her goodbye on Swaffham Station a few weeks before. Such was the fear of gas, so much did it preoccupy her mind, that it was some time before she knew about the pieces of metal that had come close to taking away Herbert's leg. Alf and Phyllis were old enough and aware enough to breathe a big sigh of relief that their Daddy might well be coming home again. Young Bert had another great story to tell his mates at school.

The *Norfolk Mercury* included Herbert in their long casualty list the very next week. It was a list that filled a full column. There he was – Barnes 22345 (Swaffham). He was sandwiched between a Sergeant A. T. Barton of Norwich and Private A. C. Bayes also of Norwich. Lance Corporal T. A. J. Everitt of Mundesley was also in the list but he was under the killed column. He had been standing only a few feet from Herbert when the shell hit. But for a piece of good fortune, Herbert might well have been in that column too. One man lived while another next to him died.

While Herbert was being cared for at Rouen, the 8th Battalion the Norfolk Regiment were in the thick of the fighting to take the villages of Poelcappelle and Passchendaele. They were involved in one of the most bizarre attacks in the whole of the Battle of 3rd Ypres

The "Chinaman attack" carried out by the 8th Norfolks in October 1917 showing the approximate position of the pillbox which received a direct hit and in which Herbert was severely wounded

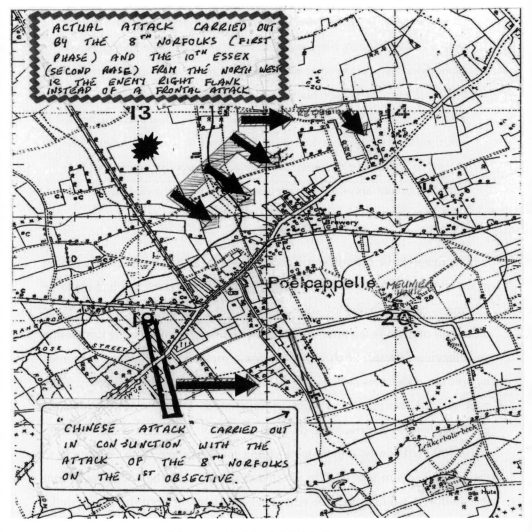

Map provided by Mr Dick Rayner.

Following Herbert's injury, the Battalion had withdrawn to Cane Trench for a few days but had then been moved forward again to the front line at Poelcapelle. The Battalion Diary takes up the story:

> *Of the village, there was practically nothing left, hardly a brick remained upon a brick, and only here and there where the Church or Larger House (Brewery) stood, was the sight marked by a larger heap of rubbish, amongst which pillboxes had been planted by the enemy. Everywhere the whole area was pitted with shell holes and even the metalled road was practically unrecognisable. The attacks hitherto had been from the south; this time it was decided to attack from the north, at the same time deceiving the enemy by a "Chinese" attack towards the south which consisted in drawing the German fire by the use of dummy figures.*[56]

The imaginative commander General Ivor Maxse had been up to his tricks again and had devised what was nothing more than a stunt. He had made up dummies, cut-out shapes of soldiers made out of millboards. He had made thousands of them in ten different attitudes of attack, from kneeling to shooting and charging forward. Each was a full size representation, elaborately painted by women in factories back in England to look like a determined enemy. They were pegged into place and wires, springs, ropes and pulleys were attached enabling them to be raised and dropped at will by a two man team sheltering some 200 yards away. Others were spring loaded to appear to be leaping to their feet. The aim was to give the impression of a full blooded attack from the southwest while in fact the real attack was coming from the 8th Norfolks and the 10th Essex of the 53rd Brigade from the northwest. These diversionary tactics helped the village of Poelcappelle to be captured but not before the 8th Norfolks had suffered some 224 casualties, of which 34 were dead. However, the triumphant Norfolk and Essex men tramped back to Cane Trench to hear the whole division and General Maxse singing their praises. It is perhaps fitting

---

56 *The History of the Norfolk Regiment* by F Loraine Petre OBE, published by the Empire Press.

that the "Chinamen" attack was destined to be the 8th Norfolks' last great action. It was about to be disbanded. Its survivors proceeded to join the 7th and 9th (Service) Battalions of the Norfolk Regiment. In the duration of the war it had lost some 770 men killed according to the Battalion Diary records. The Battalion Commander on its dissolution recorded that "the comradeship and harmony can never be forgotten".

Whether Herbert echoed these sentiments can never be known. As his train pulled into the single platform at Bangour he had other, more pressing things, on his mind. He wanted to be able to see and he wanted to be able to walk.

The Edinburgh War Hospital had many similarities to the London War Hospital at Epsom. It had been purpose built in 1904 although it was not officially opened until 1906. It too had been a mental asylum for the "distressed of Edinburgh". It is a matter of irony that it had been modelled on a German asylum in Leipzig and was lauded as a pioneering "colony" plan psychiatric hospital. While the nursing staff was housed in huts, the patients were accommodated in individual villas, 32 in all, scattered around the hilly but beautifully landscaped estate of the Earl Hamilton of Bangour (see Photo 55). Each villa was an imposing structure of stone-grey granite, three storeys high, built to take advantage of the views across the Scottish moor side. They were each self-contained and accommodated around 30 patients. They had been built in the 17th Century Scottish Renaissance style and would have done any stately home proud. This was a modern, forward-thinking hospital, wonderfully well equipped and offering to its inmates facilities beyond its time. It had a working farm, extensive workshops, a cricket field with its own pavilion, a school, a shop, a well stocked library and a massive laundry. It also had a large concert hall built in an Edwardian Baroque Style with an elevated stage and a huge velvet red curtain. Standing over the site was a large purpose-built church.[57]

---

57 This beautiful place is now at the time of writing a sadly neglected site of dereliction – a blot on the landscape. The M8 cuts through its southern boundary. Each villa is boarded up, the concert hall is falling into disrepair and the church is locked and bolted. The author was fortunate

Needless to say in 1915 the whole institution was requisitioned by the War Office. Its patients were scattered around other institutions of Scotland and before long the grounds were festooned with temporary marquees and prefabricated huts dotted between the stone villas. By the time Herbert arrived on October 26 1917, the staff was caring for over 3,000 men, all war casualties. The vast majority were victims were from the Western Front. The hospital had its own, single platform railway station at the end of a short terminus line from Edinburgh together with a turntable to turn the trains around to get another load of wounded men.[58] In 1917 trains carrying wounded men were routed directly from the Channel ports to this little railway station. The wounded men had no need to be carried from train to train. They could travel undisturbed for nearly the whole length of the country. It was a very long journey indeed and Herbert was very ready to disembark the train and get to know his new rest home.

He quickly learnt that the hospital had a pedigree in the treatment of gas victims especially eye wounds. It also had experience in the treatment of shell-shock, a condition that was becoming recognised as a serious result of artillery fire.[59] Herbert was beginning to show some signs of shell-shock, his blood pressure was permanently high and he had a stuttering heartbeat. The trauma from his experience was not severe but it was evident. The doctors diagnosed it. He knew that he was in the best place to ensure that he returned to good health. He was a relatively happy man.

He was treated at Bangour for nearly four weeks. In that time he started to walk again and his eyesight progressively improved. With the help of a crutch he was able to move around the villas and mingle with the other soldiers, many of them much worse off than he. Shell-shock can produce terrible symptoms and gas poisoning left an indelible mark. Herbert could see at first hand the shattered minds and battered bodies of some of those around him. He knew he had cause to be thankful. He was able to attend concerts in the recreation

---

to be given a guided tour by a friendly security man – the only person on the whole property.

58   The railway line was closed in 1921.

59   The Army had come to the realisation by this time that shellshock was a treatable medical condition and not a sign of cowardice.

hall. He knew his footballing days were over but he was able to watch football matches that were played on a pitch squeezed in amongst the marquees. He watched the men at work in the hospital workshop. He even took occasional slow walks in the grounds around the hospital.

On 20 November Herbert was well enough to leave the intensive care of the Edinburgh War Hospital. The wound in his leg was well on the way to healing and it was becoming evident that he would be left with little worse than a slight limp. One of the pieces of shrapnel which caused the wound was in fact no bigger than a large marble and he had it safely tucked away in his baccy tin, not so much as a trophy but more as a souvenir of the Ypres mud. He would present it to Rose when next he saw her. The effect of the gas shell explosion was not so easily shaken off. Even after four weeks in the fastidious care of the doctors and nurses at Bangour, his heartbeat was still wildly irregular. Notwithstanding all of that, he was on the mend.

His luck was to continue to hold. Indeed in the short term it was to get substantially better. He was advised that the remainder of his recovery and convalescence was to take place at Wemyss Castle in the old Scottish Kingdom of Fife. He had never heard of such a place before and in his postcards home he took a while to master its strange Gaelic spelling. He travelled the 20 miles from Bangour by train, chugging his way through the industrial heartlands of Scotland, passing through Falkirk, and disembarking at the Scottish mining town of Kirkcaldy.

Herbert found himself in a magnificent location. Wemyss Castle itself was not so much a castle, more a baronial mansion. It stood high up on a cliff top overlooking the Firth of Forth on its northern shore (see Photo 56). The building, somewhat dilapidated before it was taken over in 1915 by the War Office, is rich in history and had been in the hands of the Wemyss family for hundreds of years. Herbert, even with his aches and pains and the periodic playing up of his recent wounds could not but appreciate and enjoy the splendour of where he was. He was "tickled pink" that a working class tailor from Swaffham was eating and sleeping in the self same building where Mary Queen of Scots had first set eyes on her future husband, Lord Darnley, and where 15 generations of the Wemyss had held sway over the local populace and spread their influence over all of Scotland.

The castle itself matched its rich history in every respect. The old palace – the eastern part of the present day building – dated from the 16th century and was built in the same architectural style as the old parts of Holyrood Palace in Edinburgh. The western two thirds of the mansion were built in the 18th century by Lord Wemyss in a style completely sympathetic to the original. The total effect is an archaic country home at one with its beautiful surroundings.

This was where Herbert found himself in November of 1917. The immense rooms with their yards of wood flooring had been stripped of their former splendour. The dormitory rooms at the front were filled with beds lined up in regimental style. In the common rooms, the men could sit in comfortable chairs, talk, play cards and dominoes or just read, sleep and convalesce. Herbert enjoyed those long, lazy days and was in his element, especially at the crib table.

When he woke up on his first morning and looked south across the Firth, he could see the massive bulk of the castle at Edinburgh in the distance silhouetted against the background of The Pentlands Hills. He could see the Bass Rock standing proud in the waters of the Firth and on a clear sunny day he could almost touch its white rock face. In the distance, across the water, he could see the Lammermuir Hills and to the left the wide expanse of the water that was the North Sea. Even though the Firth itself was full of merchant vessels and warships going about their wartime business, this was for Herbert a long, long way from the mud and mayhem of Flanders.

His convalescence at Wemyss Castle was to last for four weeks and he came to love the place. As his mobility returned and his eyesight improved, he explored the grounds of the parkland around the castle with its soaring trees, some of which are still there today. It was late autumn, and the oak, ash and beech leaves had turned a burnished gold and on sunny days magically caught the sunlight. He sat on the cliff top, staring across the water with the waves crashing on the rocks 75 feet below. He explored the old windmill stump that stood (and still stands) at the eastern edge of the parkland. He ventured into Jean

Green's cave, a cavernous hole in the cliff face just below the castle grounds. He looked down on the improvised salt water swimming pool as miners from the local coal pits would come for recreation and a wash up.

As he got fitter he travelled even further afield to the "Man in the Rock" at Dysart and then in early December all the way to Edinburgh itself. His trip to Edinburgh was not an accident. He had arranged the trip to see again a close member of his family for the first time in a long time. His elder sister Mary – the one who had helped to bring him up, who had held him on her knee and played with him at Kirby Street and later at Swaffham – was now temporarily living in Edinburgh. This was the same Mary who had received the last few letters from young George before he was killed. Before the war she had married and had gone to live with her husband, adopted daughter and son in Lowestoft on the Suffolk coast. Her husband had subsequently been sent up to Edinburgh on war work and the family were now living in Kier Street in Edinburgh's south side. The adopted daughter little Constance Hall, or Connie as she was called, was nine years old. Evacuation to her was a big adventure and Edinburgh a magnificent city with which she quickly fell in love.[60]

It was no doubt a joyous meeting. Brother and sister were both a long way from home and both were caught up in a life disrupted by war. Mary had grown up to become somewhat the matriarch of the family, very upstanding and prone to seriousness. After the war was over she would enter politics and become a pioneer amongst North West Norfolk women entering politics. She would become a founder member of the North West Norfolk Labour Party and even in 1917 was often seen in those large brimmed lady's hats that so epitomised the times. Although a woman to be taken seriously, she was still a Barnes, with that sense of humour and twinkle in her eye that seemed to be carried in the

---

60   Connie's story is a remarkable saga in its own right. She was not aware that she had been adopted until she was over 16 years old and the shock of it had a lasting affect on her. She grew up thinking that Herbert's children were her cousins only to find out that they were nothing of the sort. Indeed they were not blood relations at all. She began to look at them in a new light and some years later she fell in love and married Herbert's eldest son Alf. They had four children, the youngest of whom is the author of this book. For Herbert, of course, this little girl, who he looked upon as his niece, would one day be his daughter-in-law. Truth is often stranger than fiction!

family genes. She was pleased to see Herbert doing so well and immediately wrote to Rose to tell her of their meeting. There was lots of laughter and also some tears but neither Mary nor Herbert was given much to shows of emotion. This was a deep but quiet affection that came from a shared family upbringing. Connie was very pleased to see her uncle. Herbert was a natural with children, able to play with them and entertain them, even though his body hurt and his mind was tired.

The visit brought home to Herbert how much he was missing Rose and the children. Even though his surroundings were so enjoyable the fact that he was back in Britain and close to them made the ache even more acute. The postcards home reflected how much he loved them but he was at pains to assure them that he was all right. He did not want them worrying over him. On November 23, three days after his arrival at the castle, he sent postcards to Phyllis, Bert and Alfred. "Dear Phyllis," he wrote "This is the place where I am now – don't you think it is a fine place. The sea comes right up to it. Don't you wish you were here? I do hope you are well. Love and kisses." And he signed himself "Daddy". The card to young Bert, now six years old depicted The Man in the Rock at Dysart. Bert was far and away the bubbliest of the children, and Herbert's choice of words reflects the closeness between father and son, despite the enforced absences. "Dear Bertie," he wrote, "this is a nice post card and it is quite near where I am now. It is lovely here. Oh, I do wish I could take you to the seaside. I hope you are quite well. Love and kisses."

The one to Alfred depicted an impressive view of Wemyss Castle from the sea. Alfred was now 10 years old and studying to do the unthinkable and win a place at Swaffham Grammar School. Herbert was immensely proud of his eldest son's potential and encouraged him to keep up with his lessons (see Photo 56).

"Dear Alfie, I hope you are going on well with your lessons. I am anxious to hear. This is a fine view of the castle …" And then in case little Ted, who was only four years old, should feel left out at not being sent a postcard of his own, Herbert added, "Kiss little Teddy for me. Love to mother and yourself."

Herbert's health continued to improve. His eyesight particularly was returning to normal and he was increasingly able to enjoy the pleasures of his surroundings. He was not unhappy when the medical staff took the decision to keep Herbert at Wemyss Castle for a few more weeks because of the irregular nature of his heartbeat which even by the middle of December had not returned to normal. His medical records from this time also show that he still had a mild form of conjunctivitis but it was not severe enough to keep him out of the trenches. His leg wound was by now completely recovered. Only the shock impact of the shell on his heart was keeping him in hospital. Even in the magnificent surroundings of Wemyss Castle an imminent return to the battlefields of France for a fourth time was raising its head.

On December 17 1917, Herbert was finally told that he was to be posted back to the 3rd (Training) Battalion of the Norfolk Regiment at Felixstowe. The long dreary process which he had endured three times before was about to start all over again. Once in 1916 and twice in 1917 he had gone through this routine that each time landed him eventually in a front line trench and with a serious wound. It was about to happen all over again.

But there was some good news too – some very good news. The Regiment had granted Herbert 10 days' home leave – he was not to report to Felixstowe until 28 December. He was going to spend Christmas in Swaffham. He was going home to Ash Close to be with Rose and the children over the festive period. He was jubilant. He was overcome with joy. Rose and the children were excited as well. This was simply the best Christmas present that any of them could possibly have.

The next day he packed together his few belongings and was taken to the station. The journey home could not go quickly enough. He hardly had time to marvel at the engineering splendour that is the Forth Rail Bridge as he glided across it. He didn't notice the hustle and bustle of Waverley Station as he made his connections. Changing again at Peterborough, he arrived at Swaffham in the late evening. It was dark and cold but Rose was there at the station. She was now six months pregnant and in a woman less than five feet tall her condition was very obvious. But it had not prevented her walking to meet Herbert. She was glowing with happiness, with love and excitement.

They walked back to Ash Close. The children waited with anticipation at their Grandfather's house and were in the yard when their Mother and Father turned into it. The emotion of the moment was intense.

Many years later, when she was in her 80s, Phyllis (eight years old at the time) recalled on tape the magic of it all:

I don't know where we got them from, probably from Mr Fayers and they would be sawn up but there was nobody to saw them up so the logs were out there and they were nearly as high as the fence. I know I sat on these logs waiting for Mother to come back from the station with Dad. I assume that Bert was there as well, it might have been Alf. We were all sitting on these logs waiting for Mother to bring Dad back home. And I can remember them walking down the yard.

At this point in her memories, Phyllis's voice cracks with the emotion even though 80 years had passed. "Mother was crying. I remember we were all kneeling on the floor. I was bending down undoing his puttees and rolling them up. We were taking his puttees off."

Herbert was to spend Christmas at home.

CHAPTER 13

A CLOSE RUN THING

DECEMBER 1917–JULY 1918

Christmas Day 1917 was a most memorable day in the life of the Barnes family. Having Herbert at home with his wife and children during the Christmas celebrations was a joy beyond their wildest expectations. It was as unforeseen as it was wonderful. Such was the impact that it would establish a pattern that would be followed in the Barnes family for the next 40 years. Every year from now on in, with a very few exceptions, Herbert and Rose's children would congregate at his house on Christmas Day. Wherever they were, they would do everything in their power to be with their parents. As they grew up and scattered to the four corners of the country, they would nevertheless make their way back home on this special day. It was, after all, the day they got their father back from the trenches. Later still, it would not just be his children – it would be his grandchildren too. Christmas with Granddad and Grandma would become an event that would shape the lives of all his offspring and their offspring too. It was an annual event that bound them together, that made them a family, that gave them a shared experience. It all started on Christmas Day 1917.

The children's natural excitement at the Christmas festivities was enhanced many times over by having their father home with them. However, with the best will in the world, they could not have failed to notice the significant change in his appearance since last they saw him. They noticed that his face was pale and he looked tired and drawn. They noticed that he had some ugly blemishes on his skin. They could not ignore the fact that his hair was considerably thinner than it had been six months before and that his hairline was receding rapidly. (Hair loss was a side-effect of gas poisoning.) They might have commented on the fact that his thick, bushy moustache was a little less thick and a little less bushy than they remembered it to be. They noticed also that he walked with a limp – not a very pronounced limp, but a limp nevertheless. He had lost a lot of weight and he seemed a little less confident in himself. He had a tendency to be a bit more nervous about things going on around him. This strong sturdy father was not quite as robust as he used to be.

The children didn't let their natural concern bother them too much because they also noticed that Herbert had not lost his infectious sense of fun. He had not lost his sheer delight at being with children again, and his own children at that. His wonderful ability to play with them, entertain them, amuse them and laugh with them had survived the horrors of trench warfare and bloody carnage. All that he had learnt helping to bring up his younger brothers and sisters back in Kirby Street in Kings Lynn all those years ago had not been lost in the mud and filth of France. Inside, he was still able to cope, able to live and love, and able to give and take.

Even during the rigours of wartime, Christmas was going to be celebrated. The Victorians had already established many of the Christmas traditions which we now hold dear and which we celebrate today. During the First World War, although money was scarce and material goods were hard to find, people were going to have a good time anyway. Father Christmas would come, war or no war. At the age of 10, young Alf had long since worked out the truth about that. He had blown the gaffe to his young sister Phyllis, as elder brothers always do, much to her annoyance. But young Bert was quite convinced that Father Christmas would bring him something exciting. Young Ted would experience his first real Christmas with his Dad.

Rose was six months pregnant. She was a delicate, small woman and the baby she carried weighed heavily on her. However, it would still be down to her to make all the arrangements. There would be Christmas stockings, not filled with material things but filled with excitement nevertheless. Herbert would have bought some cigarette cards home for Alf and Bert. Granddad Drake would find some walnuts he had dashed from trees earlier in the year. Rose would have got some crayons and pencils and maybe a colouring book and they would all have been stuffed into one of Granddad Drake's stockings. A book would have been bought or found for Phyllis who avidly read anything she could lay her hands on. Rose would always make it wonderful for her children and Herbert would bring it all alive for them, war or no war.

Rose would have made some form of Christmas pudding, maybe with the help of her sister Emma from next door. She served it up at the end of the Christmas meal. She would have taken a farthing or two from her savings and hidden the coins in the Christmas pudding as she spooned out each portion so that the children could find them, as if by magic, as they tucked into their bowls. Alf was old enough to be puzzled as to why all the children found their farthing but the grown-ups did not. There might even have been a tree if Granddad Drake had been able to locate one and he knew his way around the local woods. There was a small box of decorations – brightly coloured streamers that they would stretch from the corner of the ceiling to the central light and Herbert would have put them up on Christmas Eve after the children had gone to bed so that they could see them, wide eyed and wonderful, on Christmas morning. Together, Herbert and Rose could make Christmas enchanting for everybody. For 24 hours this terrible war was forgotten.

The family was, of course, quite large. Within a few doors lived Rose's sister, Emma and her father, George. A little further down Ash Close lived her sister Maud and her sister-in-law Alice. On Christmas Day they would have visited one another's houses and they might have had Christmas lunch all together. In all the celebrations, it was difficult to escape the fact that around the table were many more women than men. With the exception of Rose's father George, Herbert was the only man at home during Christmas 1917. Brother Alf was in the trenches in France with the 7th Suffolks. Brother Jack was in Felixstowe with the 3rd Norfolks. Brother George was dead. Brother-in-law Ted was in hospital, recovering from his wounds. Brother-in-law Alick was somewhere in the Middle East fighting the Turks. Brother-in-law William was also in France. Nephew Cecil was in a prisoner of war camp somewhere in Germany. The Christmas lunch was indeed a celebration but there were many familiar faces that were not there.

GRANDDAD'S WAR

There were of course lots of jobs to be done around the house. There had not been a man there for so long. Logs needed sawing, and coal shovelling. Rose's father was never a shirker and did what he could but things piled up nevertheless. But Herbert was never one for the homely chores and I expect that Rose just got on and did whatever was needed and what she could not do was left undone. When he was not with his children, Herbert spent his Christmas leave in and around Swaffham. The Greyhound pub had not changed one little bit, except, of course, all of his friends were dead or in France. The football club had suspended its fixtures for lack of players. He paid a visit to Wells to see his Dad and Stepmother. They now had a rapidly expanding second family. Although they were his half-brothers and sisters they were about the same age as his own children and there was very little common ground with this 36 year old war veteran. He found Swaffham a relatively lonely place where all the men of his age were away at war and the only ones left were the very young, the very old and those that had already been invalided out of the army. He felt strangely separated from the places and people who, only two years before, had been his life. Fayers Bespoke Tailors had closed its doors. Herbert was beginning to be aware that Swaffham was changing. This war would change everything.

He was at home for 10 days – a blissful 10 days for him, for Rose and for the family. As 28 December drew near, he was forced to look ahead yet again. His future was unsure. He had recovered from the explosion in the pillbox at Poelcapelle, but he was not completely himself. He had no idea whether he would be sent back to France and for 10 wonderful days he did not even think about it. But the time passed and eventually that dreadful day arrived yet again. The pain was very real, for him, for Rose and for the children. The tears flowed in buckets. Phyllis could not talk about it, even later, in her old age, it was all too much. They all went through the same sad ritual that they had already experienced two times before. Firstly, he said a choked goodbye to the children and then walked the short, sad steps with the pregnant Rose to Swaffham station, followed by a tearful and quick farewell. He was gone yet again. He was on his way back to Felixstowe. For all he knew, he was on his way back to France.

The next few weeks of Herbert's life as a soldier were covered in confusion and uncertainty. On arrival at the 3rd (Training) Battalion at Felixstowe he was, of course, on familiar ground, made more familiar by yet another reunion with brother Jack, by this time a nearly permanent member of the training battalion. He went through the same routine that he had experienced no less than three times before. He was billeted in a private house in the back streets of Walton, the northern suburb of Felixstowe that was the temporary home of so many Tommies. It is unlikely that the billets were the same as he had enjoyed before but, as far as is known, he was very comfortable sleeping in clean sheets in a hospitable home. He was of course now a real veteran and he knew the ropes about as well as anybody and certainly better than the hundreds of raw recruits that were being trained up for service in France. He knew he had to get fit quickly and at 36 years old it was all getting just a little bit harder. He went through the routine of physical jerks and route marches that he knew so well. He became for the fourth time a soldier fit for active duty. He had no doubt where his future lay. He was destined to return once again to the killing fields of France.

In spite of, or perhaps because of, all the activity, he was desperately tired in both body and mind. Getting fighting fit again at the age of 36 was very demanding and it took its toll. Try as he might, he found it difficult to drum up enthusiasm for the daily routine that stretched his battered body to the full. More significantly, his mind had become numb at the huge wear and tear of the last three years. He had no illusions as to the future. There was no excitement left. There were no dreams remaining to keep his motivation intact. He had one hope and one hope alone – that somehow he would survive and that one day he would come home to Rose and the family and start living a normal life again.

The demand for men on the Western Front was as acute as it had ever been. The war of attrition was bleeding the manpower of Britain, France and Germany day by day. Casualties were sapping the strength of all the combatants. Conscription, introduced in 1916, drew into the army all able-bodied men once they reached the age of 18. Many younger conscripts lied about their age.

Herbert was surrounded by men 18 years his junior – he was nearly old enough to be their father.

The offensive at Ypres had, like many other offences before it, petered out into a stalemate. The villages of Passchendaele and Poelcappelle had both been taken but at huge cost in men and matériel. Both place names would become synonymous with mass slaughter on an unprecedented scale. The knock out punch through to the town of Roulers and beyond had proved beyond the capability of the British Army. The loop around to the Belgian ports never happened and the amphibious landings were cancelled. By November 1917, it became evident that, in spite of the carnage of the 3rd Ypres, the offensive had achieved little more than to deepen the salient and to leave the British troops in a yet more exposed and perilous position. General Haig now knew that the new front line, so expensively won, was in itself a new nightmare. The Germans, now free of the burden of the Russian front, began to plan a counter-attack. Britain needed every available soldier at the front.

Herbert had every expectation that he would return to France. However, as January turned into February and March heralded in the spring, it became evident that his situation might be changing. There could have been a number of factors in what happened next. We have seen that in February 1918 the 8th Battalion of the Norfolk Regiment had been disbanded and its men sent to the 7th and 9th (Service) Battalions. In March 1918, the United States had joined the Allied war effort and Americans started to arrive on the Western Front, first of all a few thousand at a time and then in greater numbers. Then they came in their hundreds of thousands.[61] The Germans were running out of time and, in desperation, they launched a massive counter-attack on the Somme and around Ypres in the spring of 1918 designed to deliver a knock-out blow before too many Americans arrived. Ground that had taken years and thousands of casualties to win was given back to the enemy in a matter of weeks. Every man was needed at the front during this critical time.

---

61 Such is the quirk of history that one of the American privates was an 18 year old New Yorker called Ignacio Montaperto whose grand-daughter would one day marry one of the grandsons of Herbert Barnes – the author of this book.

Herbert expected to cross the Channel for a fourth time. Exactly when he learnt that he was to stay in England is not known. It is not recorded in his documents. What is clear is that sometime between January and March 1918 while at Felixstowe, he had yet another medical. This medical declared that he was unfit for service overseas. Subsequent documentation confirmed that he was diagnosed with DAH (see Photo 57); this was an army abbreviation for "disorderly action of the heart" which was also called "irritable heart". In modern day parlance, it would be referred to as Post-Traumatic Stress Syndrome. In the Tommy's language, it was called shellshock. The most significant symptom of DAH was an abnormally high pulse rate that showed considerable variation over small periods of time. This pulse rate rocketed upwards during periods of high anxiety, even though there were no outward signs of physical injury. In 1918, a pulse rate of over 100 was considered sufficient grounds for a soldier to be rejected for service and this rule was applied quite rigorously during the initial enlistment process. With veterans however, the medical officer had some discretion and, on detecting a rapid heartbeat would carry out a more thorough examination before arriving at a conclusion. The horrific explosion in the confined space of the pillbox at Poelcappelle had taken its toll on Herbert. It had resulted in a less than optimum performance by his vital organ, his heart. This was hardly surprising. In the last two and a half years, he had contracted influenza, he had been shot by a sniper, he had been mown down by a machine-gun, he had been blown up by a shell, he had been riddled with shrapnel and he had been bathed in mustard gas. His body had absorbed all this and now his heart was saying "enough is enough". He was 37 years old.

Herbert was declared unfit for overseas service early in 1918, some 26 months after he enlisted and 20 months after he first went to France. It was a momentous moment for him – one of the most momentous moments of his whole life. Having a "dodgy heart" could not be considered good news, but it paled into insignificance when compared with what the diagnosis meant to him and his family. It meant that he would not be going back to France. It meant that in all probability he would survive the war. It meant for the first time in years he dared think about his future. He dared plan ahead in his mind rather than live only for today. He could allow himself the privilege of thinking about middle and old age. He could think about living. For the first time in a long time, he now had a future.

He wrote home to Rose. Her relief knew no bounds. She told the children – all of them apart from Teddy knew the significance of the news. A very heavy burden lifted from Ash Close, a burden that had jaundiced all their lives for the last three years and which was now gone, they hoped, forever.

Life is not so simple though. Herbert had not been declared disabled and unfit for all service. His condition meant that he would not be going back to the trenches, but the army needed every soldier that it could muster. When Herbert had enlisted all those many months ago, he had signed an "attestation" that he was willing to service His Majesty "for the duration of the war" and that even after the termination of hostilities he would be asked to stay on "until your services could be spared". Herbert might have been relieved of the horrors of trench warfare but his days as a Tommy were a long way from being over.

However, in the first three months of 1918, the good news for Herbert just kept on coming. On the 10th March, a telegram arrived to say that Rose was safely delivered of a healthy baby girl. The little baby had been born at Ash Close where Rose had been assisted by her sister Emma and a local midwife. All were well. Herbert was granted a 36 hour home pass and hurriedly caught the train back to Swaffham. He had time on his way back home to contemplate this new development. Herbert always favoured the boys. He loved his daughters dearly but he was a man's man and his sons always came first. It was his way. He was very much a man of his time. However, privately, he was happy that Phyllis now had a little sister and that the "family had better balance". Rose was of course delighted. Nothing was taken for granted. The loss of baby Ruby still weighed heavily on both their minds, so the new arrival was cosseted from the very start. She was named Ivy Emma Barnes – Ivy because Rose liked the name and Emma after the aunt who had done so much to support the family over the last few years. To the day he died, Herbert always saw Ivy as the gift that accompanied his release from the trenches.

Another welcome development came at the same time. Rose might have been pregnant and she had her hands full looking after the four children, but she had never given up her dream for young Alf. She had been working away with the teachers at the National School. She had learnt that the Governors of Hammonds Grammar School in Swaffham offered 12 precious scholarships a year to working class boys from elementary schools in the town and surrounding districts. Examinations were scheduled for July of each year. Twelve places was not a lot and competition would be fierce, but Rose knew that Alf had a chance and the teachers agreed. It was decided that Alf would be one of the boys who would sit the examination. Yes, 1918 had begun very well indeed.

Herbert stayed with the 3rd (Training) Battalion of the Norfolks until the 19 July 1918, a little over six months. Exactly what he did during that time is not clear. Thousands of raw recruits were passing through on their way to France. All were being urgently trained for trench warfare as well as carrying out the routine duties of a garrison battalion. Herbert was an experienced front line soldier who had extensive knowledge of what it was like to be on active duty in France. It is inconceivable that the officers did not make productive use of him. It is highly likely that they appreciated his friendly way with the young soldiers and harnessed those abilities to help in the training process. Herbert, who had gone through so much training, became in part a trainer himself. He would have been good at it too – a comforting word here, some advice there, and a few chosen remarks of support to calm the fears and build a little confidence. He would have been in his element.

There is also some anecdotal evidence that he spent some time at the Royal Arsenal at Woolwich. In the height of the war, the Arsenal employed over 80,000 people to develop and manufacture the never-ending supply of munitions that were needed to support the war effort. There is no documentary evidence that he was ever there but members of the family have recalled that he reminisced about it in one of his rare private moments. It is certainly true that for the rest of his life on a Saturday afternoon, the football result that he would want to know before all others, after his beloved Norwich City of course, was that of the Arsenal.

Herbert must have settled into a comfortable routine at Felixstowe. He was there long enough to build up camaraderie with his colleagues. The euphoria of having a permanent "blighty" could only enhance his stay there. He might well have gone back to Swaffham a few times to see Ivy, but if he did it is not on his record. He was granted no home leave during this period, neither is there any evidence to suggest that Rose ever went to Felixstowe.

However, his peace of mind did not last for long. On 9 July Herbert was suddenly transferred to the 18th Battalion, the Welsh Regiment, which at that time was based at Aldershot in Hampshire. The move seems to have come completely out of the blue and the reasons for it are unclear even to this day. What is not unclear, however, is that Herbert, from the relative comfort of Felixstowe, appeared to be on his way back to France.

The 18th (Service) Battalion of the Welsh Regiment had first landed in France in June 1916 in readiness for the opening of the Battle of the Somme. It had fought with distinction through to late April 1918 when it had been very badly mauled indeed, suffering horrific casualties. It had been reduced to cadre status only, repatriated back to the UK and based temporarily in North Walsham in Norfolk. However, after a few days it was decided to fully reconstitute the Battalion, absorb troops from a number of other battalions, move it to Aldershot and, much to Herbert's alarm, prepare it to move back to France. Plans were well advanced. The embarkation date had been set for 29 July 1918. Herbert, to his amazement, was a part of this build-up.

He packed his kit bag on the 9th July, said goodbye to his colleagues at Felixstowe and marched off once again to the railway station. He made his way across London, something that he had done many times before, and reported to his new Regiment. It is not known what he had been told. What he found on arrival was a Battalion very much going through the frenzied activity and preparation for an imminent transfer to France. It was due to set sail in only 20 days' time.

Perhaps he had had another medical. Perhaps his heart condition had improved. Perhaps the more relaxed atmosphere of Felixstowe had brought about a recovery. Whatever the background, the transfer came as a bombshell. He thought he was through with trench warfare. He thought he had finished with shells and machine-guns. He thought he had put all of that behind him. However, the Welsh Regiment needed men and he was one of the hundreds who had been drafted into it.

It is not known what or how he told Rose and the children. Or if indeed he told them anything at all. Rose knew he was moving to Aldershot and knew he was changing regiments but it appears that's about all she knew.

On his arrival at Aldershot he found that preparations were indeed in full swing. Nearly 1,000 men had been very quickly assembled from all over the country and were being rapidly trained and equipped to be a fully operational combat battalion. Herbert knew none of his new colleagues. They were all new faces to him. He needed to integrate rapidly and effectively and it is likely that his role was one of a stretcher-bearer, taking advantage of his brief but valuable experience at Ypres. In less than three weeks the Battalion would cross the Channel and join the fighting troops in the Cambrai sector of the front where yet another major push was being prepared.

He had been in Aldershot for only 10 days when his world turned upside down yet again. Having prepared himself for a return to France and having started the difficult challenge of attuning himself psychologically to the rigours of trench warfare for a fourth time, an order came through that his transfer to the Welsh Regiment had been a mistake. An error had been made. There had been a bureaucratic mix-up. His documents clearly show the transfer order with a black line drawn through it and the words "cancelled – error" in black ink written against it (Photo 58).

Errors of this nature were not unknown in the First World War. Five million men passed through the army from 1914 to 1919. There were many hundreds of army units. There were hundreds of thousands of casualties and hundreds of thousands of transfers. Against this background, it is not surprising that some administrative errors were made. It is in fact remarkable, and a credit to the army, that administration and documentary detail was as good as it was. This was, of course, an age without computers or electronic communications. Indeed, it was an age before the typewriter was in wide everyday use. Nearly everything was written by pen in longhand by an army of clerks. All of Herbert's documents that survive, on which this narrative is partly based, were meticulously completed in the neat legible handwriting of an army clerk.

The mistake came to light on or around the 18th July. Herbert's relief must have been immense. In spite of having psyched himself up for a return to France and in spite of still wanting to do his best for King and Country, there can be little doubt that he had no desire to cross the Channel. Even as he watched his new colleagues busily prepare for their date with destiny, he had no interest in being with them. He had done with all that.

The 18th Battalion the Welsh Regiment was later heavily involved in the Battle of Cambrai and was to suffer heavy casualties. It had been a very close run thing indeed.

For the first time since he enlisted, Herbert was now a soldier without a regiment and in the army that meant a soldier without a home. The army had temporarily "lost him". For the first time, he was to have some influence on what was to happen next. Ever since 1915 he had always been told what to do and where to go. This time where he would go was a result of a personal request on his part that was acceded to by the army.

Herbert knew he could not be sent to France and he had no interest in returning to Felixstowe. In the last three years, he had had extensive exposure to the Royal Army Medical Corps. Four times the RAMC had taken him from the front line as a casualty. Four times he had been through their Casualty Clearing Stations. Four times he had stayed in their hospitals in France. He had travelled on their hospital ships and been looked after in England in their hospitals and convalescent homes. More recently, as a stretcher-bearer he had worked with them in a Regimental First Aid Post and in Advanced Dressing Stations. Indeed he had spent a significant proportion of his war with the RAMC. The demands of the Corps were an easy fit with his character. He had a caring nature and enjoyed watching over his younger colleagues. Sometimes he found himself playing the role of a father figure. In 1918 millions of men were in hospitals and convalescent homes in England recovering from their wounds and needing care.

Herbert therefore requested to join the RAMC and made arguments as to his suitability. Desperate for manpower, the army agreed and on 19 July 1918 he was transferred yet again. He was no longer Private H. E. Barnes, number 22345, of the Norfolk Regiment. Indeed he was no longer Private H. E. Barnes, number 78443, of the Welsh Regiment. He was now Private H. E. Barnes, number 144676, of the 7th Training Battalion of the RAMC. He was on the move again.

He had missed going back to France by a mere 10 days.

CHAPTER 14

LOOKING AFTER OTHERS

JULY–NOVEMBER 1918

Herbert was becoming a much-travelled man. He had spent his childhood and his early life in Norfolk and had not journeyed far. This long war had changed all that. Now he had seen a large part of Northern France. He had spent some time in Suffolk. He had convalesced in Surrey. He had visited Shropshire. He had journeyed up to Scotland. Indeed he had criss-crossed England many times. A man who previously had only mixed with people from his home county had now lived and fought with men from all over Great Britain, indeed from all over the world. His horizons had been changed. Where would they send him next?

The 7th Training Battalion of the Royal Army Medical Corps was based at Blackpool on the Lancashire coast. Herbert's good fortune was still looking after him. If he was going to be away from home, if he was going to be estranged from his children, if he was going to be separated from his beloved Rose, there were much worse places to be than Blackpool. Herbert had been posted to the Kings Lancashire Military Convalescent Hospital which was at Squires Gate just to the south of the town. The hospital had been set up in 1915 to look after the many wounded men whose homes were in Lancashire or who belonged to the Lancashire regiments, most notably the Royal Lancashire Fusiliers. The establishment consisted of a few permanent buildings which had been supplemented by the usual forest of marquees and Nissen huts (see Photo 59). It had all been constructed on the Clifton Park Racecourse just to the south of the town and bordered on to the sand dunes. It looked out over the sand flats and the Irish Sea. By the time Herbert arrived there on 19 July 1918, the area called Squires Gate provided beds for some 4,600 men.[62]

Herbert, on arrival, joined D Company and was housed in Number 3 Camp in a long wooden hut. The hut, basic in every respect, accommodated some 30 men, all RAMC privates and all veterans of the trenches. The hospital was, of course, huge and very different to those he had experienced at Epsom and at Bangour in Scotland as there were very few permanent structures.

Now, however, the shoe was on the other foot – he was the one doing the caring; he was the one looking after the injured. The old grandstand of the racecourse had been converted into hospital use and the old seating area had been roofed over to house the patients. The facility was nevertheless impressive. It had a cricket pitch and a bowling green. Indeed, it is during this period of his life that Herbert learnt to play bowls, a pastime that would give him much pleasure during the rest of his life. The hospital was also a training centre for new RAMC recruits, which is the principal reason that Herbert had been posted there. He was to get even more training but this time in the practice of caring for others.

Even in 1918, with the war now four years old, Blackpool had all the characteristics and facilities of a holiday resort. People still enjoyed a day by the seaside and the Zeppelin attacks on the eastern coastal towns had persuaded revellers that the west coast was a much safer place to be. Most of the attractions that we associate with Blackpool today had been built in the 30 years before Herbert arrived. They were all relatively new and hugely impressive, indeed a minor wonder of the Victorian age. Remarkably, they continued operations throughout the war years.

The famous tower stood tall over the town and the North Pier was in everyday use. The Tower Roof Gardens were a marvel to all who saw them and tram rides could be taken along Princess Parade. Pontin's holiday camp was open and operating. War or no war, the huge carousel was still turning. Herbert could not but look in wonderment at the playground on his doorstep. He must have

---

62   There are no visible remains of the First World War facilities. The site is now taken up by Blackpool's airport and is covered with terminals, runways and taxi-ways.

wondered what on earth all this had to do with the hell and filth of the trenches where he had spent much of his last three years.

However, there were reminders that a war was going on. There were soldiers everywhere. As well as the constant flow of battered bodies arriving at the hospital, there were 14,000 troops billeted in the town. Out to sea was the constant movement of merchant ships and Royal Navy men-of-war returning and leaving to run the gauntlet across the North Atlantic, dodging the U-boats as they went.

It is not known exactly what Herbert's duties were at Squires Gate or of what his day to day routine consisted. He was now spending his working day looking after other Tommies and he was able to identify closely with their discomfort, their hopes and their fears. After all, he had so very recently been in their position.

His many postcards home reflect almost jubilation in his demeanour – he had escaped the trenches and he was clearly enjoying his new posting. He had the added bonus of discovering the delights of Blackpool. He appeared to be thankful to a point where he could not believe his luck.

It is equally obvious that he missed his children and he sent them postcards at regular intervals. Even though he had been away from the family home for the last three years, he knew the individual character of each of his offspring. He picked a postcard that he considered suitable for each child. He would write a few words and then package them all together and post them off. For example, to little Teddy he picked out a picture of the Tower Café and wrote "this is where you get your cakes and ice cream that make your mouth water. I will get you some when I come home". He picked out another one of the paddling pool at St Anne's-on-Sea. "Dear Little Teddy," he wrote, "this is where all the little teddies go to paddle. It's just made for little boys and girls to go in with no boots or stockings on. They have some nice games in them" (see Photo 60).

Bert was always his favourite child. He loved his zest for life, his constant energy and his curiosity about everything. He always wished that Bertie was by his side. For him, he picked out a card of the new gardens at St Anne's-on-Sea. "I am sending you a nice picture of the gardens. It is only one end of them. There is a little river in them. Also a nice little bridge made with stones from off the beach, a nice little path and a dug-out." In another card to Bert picturing the South Promenade at St Anne's he wrote, "Tell Phyllis I am sending her some more nice silk pictures. I will send you some stamps as soon as I go to town. If you are a good boy I will try and come and see you." Phyllis, of course, was a girl and, try as he might, he was never as close to her but he picked out a card of the Palace Picture Pavilion, a sumptuous movie theatre built with all the elaborate decoration of a West End Theatre. Here the new marvel of moving pictures was shown. He wrote, "This is a nice picture house. Wouldn't you like to go in? I would take you if you were here." Cards to Alfie were far more perfunctory and matter of fact. The words were always much shorter. A picture card of the North Pier simply said, "I went on there on Sunday and listened to the band." And another of the Tower Menagerie, "This is only half the menagerie at the Tower. It is a splendid place with lots of animals in it." His letters and cards seemed to exactly sum up the characters of his children and this, too, he owes to Rose. Each package of cards was wrapped together with the one to Rose on the top. "I must just send you one as well," he wrote. "As you can see, it is the Pavilion and the corner of the tennis ground. Inside the concerts go on afternoon and night." He then added a phrase which was as emotional as Herbert could ever get in writing, "It sets the heart longing, I know. With love from Herbert."

The flood of postcards and their scribbled contents demonstrated that Herbert's heart was torn. He loved the new-found freedom that Blackpool offered – swimming in the sea, walking in the gardens, visiting the bandstands and enjoying the funfair. His natural zest for life was gradually being reawakened. His delight at being in this new and exciting playground was beginning to heal the scars of his terrible experience. Not even the steady flow of crushed bodies that continued to arrive at the hospital could dampen his rising spirits.

On the other hand, he continued to yearn for his home and family. Everything that he did he would rather have done with Rose, or with Bert or with little Teddy. Wherever he went, he wished desperately that they could be alongside him.

In the middle of August, he received a telegram from Rose. Its contents made this war toughened veteran fill with tears. Alf had passed that very important exam and would be one of the 13 children from the "working classes" who would be accepted into Hammonds Grammar School on a scholarship. Rose, Alf and the teachers had pulled if off together. They had, together, made the most unlikely happen. Herbert could hardly contain himself. This modest, unassuming man was filled with pride and his hope for the future, almost non-existent 12 months before, blossomed once again. He knew there would be financial repercussions. He knew that sacrifices would have to be made; there would be uniforms to buy, books to get, shoes to purchase. However, now was not the time to worry about that. Now was the time to enjoy the moment for what it was.

Alf wrote to his father to confirm the good news. His handwriting was neat but had all the imperfections of an 11 year old boy. Herbert sent back a card the next day. "Dear Alfie," he wrote, "I got your nice letter and was pleased you got on so well. Keep it up and always write and let me know how you go on and how you like it. I shall follow all with the greatest of interest and I hope I shall always be as proud of you as I am now. Well done!" He put in a badge with the letter. He had often sent Alf badges before and the boy now had quite a collection. Alf by return of post sent back another card. The picture on the card was amazingly the inside of the science laboratory at Hammonds School (see Photo 61). "Dear Daddy," Alfie wrote with a black quill pen in a flowing longhand that had a tendency to smudge "This is a room I expect I will spend much more time in. Thank you very much for the badge." And just to illustrate that children have not changed too much over the years, he added, "I would like one of the Black Watch next time."

Photo 53 – Minty Farm advanced dressing station: *A picture of the advanced dressing station at Minty Farm taken in 1917. Herbert was taken here after being wounded at Poelcapelleas.*

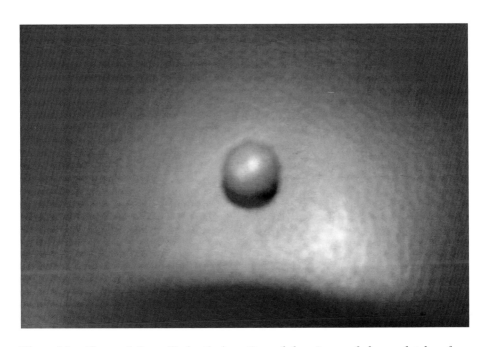

Photo 54 – Shrapnel from Herbert's leg: *One of the pieces of shrapnel taken from Herbert's leg after his wound at Poelcapelle which was preserved in his "baccy" tin.*

Photo 55 – Bangour War Hospital: *One of the many massive "villas" at the Bangour War Hospital where Herbert spent 4 weeks recovering from his wounds in October 1917.*

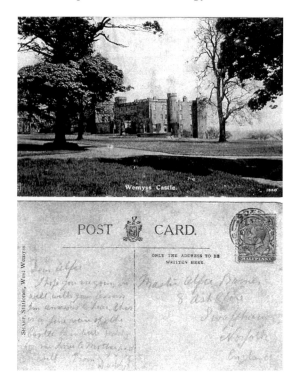

Photo 56 – Wemyss Castle: *A postcard of Wemyss Castle sent by Herbert to his son Alf in November 1917.*

This pension was ... increased by a bonus

Rank (for pension) Pte. Regimental No. 144676.
Name (Surname first) Barnes Herbert Edward
Regiment or Corps RA of B 19 Coy
Date of Trans 12.8.19 Age on Discharge 38 Marital Status M
Address on Discharge 8 Ash Close Swaffam Norfolk
Disabilities 1. D.A.H. 2. Chr: Conjunctitis 3.
State whether attributable, aggravated, or non-attributable. 1. Attrib 2. Aggrav. 3.
Degree of Disablement (in percentages) 20%
Weekly Pension or Allowance 5/6 fr 13.8.19 to 2.9.19 then 8/- fr 3.9.19 to be reviewed in 55 weeks. Nature of Award 6.
Allowances for 5 children 4/10 fr 13.8.19 to 2.9.19 then 8/2 fr
A. 19/2 for wife & 5 children

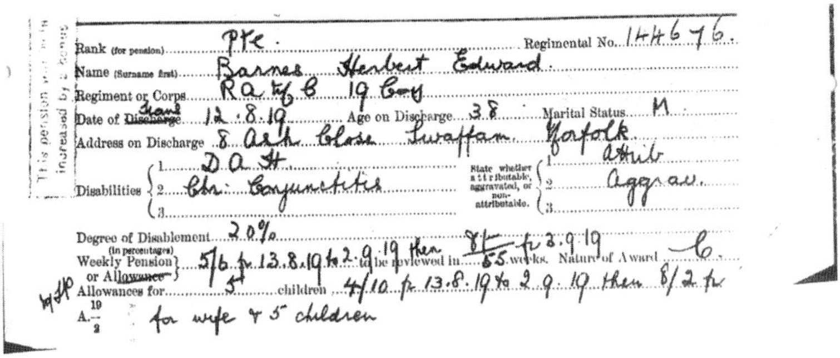

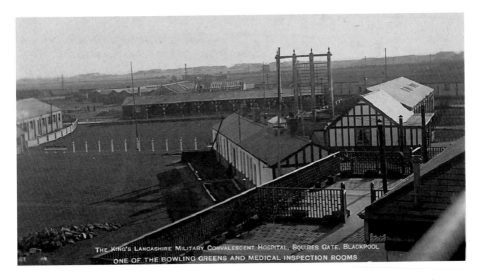

Photo 57 – Herbert's Pension document: *A document by the War Office in 1919 setting out Herbert's War Pension and outlining his injuries in a perfunctory fashion – note D.A.H.*

W 5313—2606 500,000 7/15 T. & W. Ld. NEXT OF KIN. Army Form W. 3080.

Relation	Name	Address
Wife	Rosa Barnes	9 Ash Close, Swaffham

AFW 3016 2/1 Pk 8' Furlough from 18.12.16 28.12.17 Duty
~~Transferred ...~~ cancelled - error
Trans'd to RAMC 19.7.18 & posted to 7th T.B.

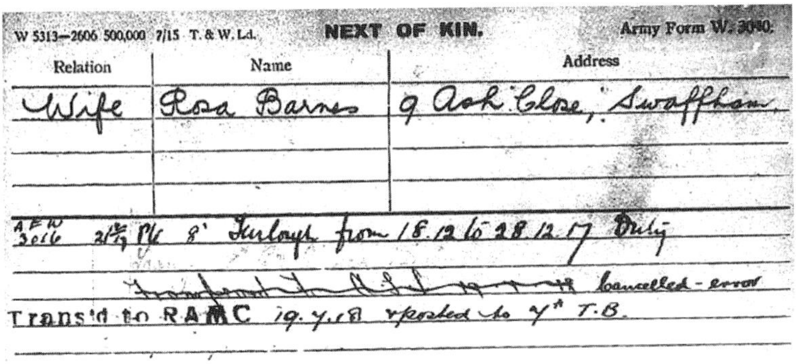

Photo 58 – The error in Herbert's orders: *Herbert's document of transfer from the Norfolks to the Welsh Regiment and then to the RAMC. Note the words "cancelled in error".*

Photo 59 – Squires Gate Hospital: *The Kings Lancashire Military Convalescent Hospital at Squires Gate, Blackpool where Herbert arrived in 1918. This is now the site of Blackpool airport.*

Photo 60 – Postcard to Teddy from Blackpool: *One of the very many postcards Herbert sent to all members of his family in Swaffham from Blackpool.*

Photo 61 – Hammonds School – Science Laboratory: *A picture of the science room at the Hammond Grammar School at Swaffham, sent by young Alf to his father in 1918.*

Photo 62 – Herbert's family 1923: *Herbert's family outside Burntstalks at Docking soon after moving in in 1923. The children, Bert, Phyllis, Ted and Ivy with their mother and father and Rose's father Alfred Drake standing behind.*

Photo 63 – Herbert as a postman: *Herbert in his postman's uniform outside of the backdoor at Burntstalks.*

Photo 64 – The Chum: *A picture and postcard of Herbert's unnamed best chum in the RAMC.*

HERBERT BARNES

Photo 65 – Herbert's platoon at Blackpool: *Herbert with members of the 7th training Battalion of the RAMC outside a billet hut at Squires Gate, Blackpool.*

Photo 66 – Herbert & Rose – 50th Wedding Anniversary: *Herbert and Rose's Golden Wedding Anniversary 1957.*

ur Party's

Scene of tragedy

'DRUNKEN DRIVER KILLED 2'

Then he tried to fight, court told

A DRUNKEN American Serviceman careered up and down a village street in his car at fifty to seventy m.p.h., mounted the pavement and killed an elderly couple, it was alleged at Hunstanton, Norfolk, court yesterday.

The American, Airman Second Class Ronald Joel Beseda, aged 23 stationed at Sculthorpe, Norfolk, was sent for trial and granted £25 bail.

He was accused of killing seventy-eight-year-old Herbert Barnes and his wife Rosa, 76, by dangerous driving and of driving under the influence of drink.

They Died

Near Home

Mr. and Mrs. Barnes died within a few yards of their home in the Norfolk village of Docking, said Mr. D. Williams, prosecuting.

Mr. Williams said: "For some fifteen minutes before the accident the driving of the car

Airman Beseda

American for trial

had excited the attention of passers by.

"It careered up and down the village street at speeds between fifty and seventy miles an hour crossing from side to side and with horn sounding," he said.

After mounting the pavement and killing the couple, the car ended up by colliding with an electricity pole and then crashing head on into a stone wall, said Mr. Williams.

Beseda, he said, was so helplessly drunk that he fought police when they reached the crash. Later he had to be held down while being examined by a doctor.

Dr. Patrick Laffman of Burnham Market, Norfolk, said: "I found Beseda very drunk, very aggressive and very truculent."

A Home Office scientist said that tests revealed that Beseda had consumed the equivalent of five and a half pints

of beer or one-third of a large bottle of spirits.

Police Constable Richard Green said he found the accused sitting on the roadway leaning against the side of his car with the bodies of Mr. and Mrs. Barnes in the road a few feet away.

"He was helplessly drunk," he said.

He Made

No Reply

Police Constable Francis Beales added that Beseda "sat waving his arms and shouting and wanting to fight."

The magistrates were told that eight hours after the accident when Beseda was told that two people had been killed in his car by him being his head and made no reply.

When formally charged in court yesterday Beseda replied "I do not wish to say anything at this stage."

Photo 67 – The accident at Docking: *The report of the tragic accident at Docking in 1960 in the Lynn News and Advertiser.*

Photo 68 – Newspaper article on the trial: *Newspaper coverage of the trial of Joel Beseda.*

Alf's life would now be changed forever. He would receive the education that all of the children deserved and of which all were capable. However, only one, the eldest, would be able to take advantage of the opportunity. Herbert and Rose would never be able to afford the same privilege for Phyllis, Bert, Ted or Ivy, even though they were just as able and their potential just as great. Without the scholarship, they would not even have been able to support Alf. At this time, opportunities for a family of five from the working class were very limited.

———— ◆ ◆ ————

In France, the terrible war of attrition continued day after day and week after week. On 21 March 1918 the German armies launched a series of massive attacks, aimed at winning a victory before the American intervention became decisive. There were 4.6 million German troops now amassed along the Western Front. The battlefield on the Somme, where Herbert had fought and thousands had died, was recaptured in a matter of days and the Germans stood once again in front of Amiens. The Ypres Salient was now totally untenable and all the ground gained in 1917 at the cost of hundreds of thousands of casualties had to be given up and was lost within a week. The Germans were back within one mile of what was left of Ypres town walls. The French collapsed to the south and for the first time the outskirts of Paris itself came under bombardment from heavy artillery. Throughout the long summer of 1918, while Herbert was in Blackpool, the Allies were staring at the potential nightmare of total defeat. Casualty rates rocketed upwards. The number of dead was higher than even during the 3rd Battle of Ypres. The flow of injured became a deluge. At the hospital at Squires Gate the number of beds was increased and new marquees were erected. Herbert worked and watched as hundreds of wounded arrived everyday. The British Army was close to defeat and France and the British Empire looked as if they would be swamped.

However, now it was the Germans' turn to feel the pain of high casualties, longer supply lines and ever-decreasing resources. They were now stretched to snapping point. General Pétain, now the Commander of the French forces, predicted, "If we can hold out until the end of July, our situation will be excellent.

We can resume the offensive. After that victory will be ours." This time he was right. The German army was close to exhaustion. All further attempts by them to move forward were absorbed and rebutted. Although it was not obvious at the time, the Allied armies would soon be able to deliver a "coup-de-grâce".

The counter-attack started in August and made significant inroads. In front of Amiens, the allied armies, employing 456 tanks and 13 divisions, took back 12 kilometres of territory in one day. This was equal to the total area captured in the three months of the Battle of the Somme in 1916. Advances were made all along the front. The final act was played out but not with speed and not without casualties. It was mid-September before Flanders was liberated. Troops swept across the battlefields of Ypres in less than two days. The German High Command now accepted the impossibility of victory and knew that they were at the end of their reserves. The war must be ended. Even so, until the Armistice could be negotiated, the fighting would go on and men would go on dying.

———————◆———————

On October 2 1918, Rose got out of bed early as she always did. The children were having their breakfast and getting ready for school. Alf was dressed in his smart new school uniform and looked every part the young man. The purchase had stretched Rose's family budget nearly to breaking point. Herbert's father in Wells had helped to cover the cost. After the chores were done and the children had left the house, Rose popped next door for her daily chat with her sister Emma. The scene that confronted her was heartbreaking. Emma was in tears and her Father's face was ashen white behind his long flowing beard.

A telegram had been received – the telegram that everyone dreaded and nobody wanted to receive. Rose's younger brother Alexander, who everybody called young Alick, had been killed in action two days before. He was a gunner in the Royal Field Artillery. He had joined the forces in May 1914, spent two and a half years in Egypt and had also seen service in Palestine. He had only been in France for three months. He and his gun crew had been moving forward as part of the general advance west of Ypres. They had been spotted by German artillery and the whole battery came under heavy shellfire. Alick Drake was one of the 10 men who were killed outright.[63]

Young Alick had been an outstanding gunner. His commanding officer wrote a commendation that was delivered a few days later to his father at Ash Close. "He was quite the best gunner in his detachment." None of this was of any consolation to the family. Rose, Emma, Maud and their father were grief-stricken. The futility of it all was difficult to bear. Everyone knew the war was coming to an end. Everyone knew that victory was very close. Why could the politicians not bring it all to a swift conclusion? Why did soldiers still have to die? Why did her brother have to die?

The end of the bloodiest conflict in the history of the world came quite quickly. The German army was finished. Now they vociferously advocated an armistice so as to avoid humiliation and to be able to claim that they had been "undefeated in the field". The plea to cease hostilities was delivered on 3 October; only four days after Alick Drake had been killed. It took another five weeks for the Germans to accept the Allies' crippling peace terms; five weeks during which both sides continued to take thousands of casualties. At the eleventh hour of the eleventh day of the eleventh month in 1918, the guns finally fell silent. The war was over. It was done.

In Swaffham, the celebrations were instantaneous. The bells rang out all over town and the people spilled onto the streets and into the market square. Young Bert's memories of the day were vivid, even 50 years later:

I remember the whistles over at Surridges factory blowing like mad and blaring out across the town. Everything that could make a noise was brought into service. Klaxons blew, horns blared and all the factory whistles went off as if in unison. I remember a big procession and I found myself waving a little Union Jack and I noticed that everybody looked happier. One of the carts had

---

63 Gunner Alexander Drake's remains are buried at Unicorn Cemetery at the village of Vendhuile and his sacrifice is commemorated on the Swaffham War Memorial.

an effigy of the Kaiser bound in a chair with two British Tommies pointing their bayonets at him. My most vivid memory is that we all had a holiday from school.

Bert also remembers that Rose was crying. He recalls that she cried off and on nearly all day. She might have been crying with relief that it was all over. She might have been crying with gratitude that Herbert had survived. She might have been crying because her husband was not by her side. Most likely, she might have been crying because of what she had lost. Since this dreadful war started over four years before, her family had been "mashed and mangled". Her mother was dead, as were her eldest brother Arthur and youngest brother Alick. Brother Cyril was somewhere in Germany, a prisoner of war and nobody knew where he was. Brother Ted was partially disabled and somewhere in France. Her brother-in-law George was dead and her other two brothers-in-law Alf and Jack were both recovering from their wounds. Rose had lots of reasons for crying that day.

Further north, Blackpool went crazy as only a seaside resort could. The celebrations filled the golden mile as thousands of people thronged the waterfront. The blackout was lifted and all the lights came on. However, on this momentous day that ended a war that had ripped Herbert's life apart, he was on duty all day at Squires Gate looking after the wounded of the Lancashire Fusiliers. We do not know if he joined in the celebrations. There is no record of what he did or what he thought on that day, 11 of November 1918.

CHAPTER 15

A LIFE FOR A HERO

NOVEMBER 1918–MARCH 1960

It was August 1947 and a long cold winter had passed. The warm summer days were much more to Herbert's liking. He had celebrated his 66th birthday and was having to think very seriously about retirement, something he did not even want to contemplate. For the last 25 years he had lived in the delightful village of Docking which stands on high land in north-west Norfolk. He was the village postman. He had grown to love this place and to love his life in it. He really did not want anything much to change, even though he knew that he could do nothing to stop the passing of the years.

His routine was well set. He lived about a mile outside the village and must rise early to cycle to the post office to collect the mail. Rose got up early and made him breakfast as she had always done. He said a cheery good morning to Mr Overton who managed the post office, although it was his wife who was the postmistress and prepared all the letters and parcels that Herbert was to deliver. They were both kind, considerate people and had become close friends over the years. Herbert was very fond of them. He climbed onto his bicycle, a sturdy, black upright machine with a basket strung on the front handlebars. He set off on his round (see photo 63). Docking is an extensive village and Herbert covered the outlying areas to the west, south and north. He had to cover over eight miles every day. It is also very hilly; Herbert always said that those people who think that Norfolk is flat should come to Docking. From the post office he cycled down to the station where, years ago, his Father used to drive the train. He pedalled all the way to Summerfield Farm. He returned back to the village and then down the hill to the small and very pretty hamlet of Fring. On his way to Fring he usually did a detour and went back past his house. He always called in to share a cup of tea with Rose.

Today, he had extra company in the form of his eldest granddaughter. Mary was Alf's eldest child and was a little over 12 years old. She was on holiday from school and liked nothing better than to spend time with her grandparents. Herbert loved having her with him. He had in all seven grandchildren (and would in due course have another two). They all adored him because he made them laugh, played with them, told stories and gave them his time. After his cup of tea with Rose, he and Mary cycled down the long green lane to Fring, free-wheeling between the high hedgerows that separated the lane from the fields. They delivered a few letters to the houses in the hamlet and then stopped at Fring Hall where the staff sometimes passed the day with Herbert and, if he was lucky, served him another cup of tea. He unlocked the red letter box that was sunk into the wall (it is still there), took out the letters and he and Mary cycled all the way back up the hill to Docking, chatting away to one another and sometimes stopping to admire the view.

Herbert was very happy with his life. He revelled in the fresh open air. He knew everybody in the village and everybody knew him. He had a growing family with grandchildren with whom he loved to spend time. It was as if he was making up for the war years he lost with his own children. He had Rose who was fit and well and looked after him as she had always done. At the end of the First World War, the political cry from a battered people was that Great Britain must become a country fit for heroes. Herbert never considered himself a hero but, with the help of good luck and a following wind, he had come through the dangers of the trenches. He now had a life "fit for a hero". He was quite content.

———◦◆◦———

After the guns fell silent in 1918, Herbert's life as a Tommy was far from over. He was to spend another long eight months at Blackpool with the RAMC. As long as there were wounded soldiers to care for, the Army needed men to do the caring. Just because hostilities were over, it did not mean that the wounded somehow experienced a miraculous recovery. Thousands, indeed hundreds of thousands of enlisted men were retained in the Armed Forces for months after the war was over. On the one hand, there was work to be done and on the other there were very few jobs at home. Herbert was no exception to this general rule. He stayed on at Squires Gate.

For the first time, he was able to develop real friendships with his colleagues. In France, there had been no evidence that he had forged any close or lasting friendships with anyone. He had been constantly on the move and he knew that life could be snuffed out at any time. At Blackpool however, in the more relaxed atmosphere of the camp, he mentions for the first time in his cards and letters, pals who served with him. On one of the cards he sent to Alfie was a picture of a heavily moustached, war-torn soldier of about 40 years old. "Here is one of my chums who is going to be a hospital orderly at Reading. He is a nice chum and has a little boy about your age" (see photo 64). He sent home another picture of his whole platoon, photographed sitting in front of their Nissen hut (see Photo 65). The photograph captures the impact that the war years had on Herbert. He looks old and drawn, as do all 16 of the men in the picture. His hair has become thin and wispy and he is turning grey. His hairline has receded dramatically. His moustache is a little straggly. His skin is a little blotchy and tending to wrinkle. Nevertheless he looks relaxed and content.

At first things went well for Herbert. The soldier's pay that Rose collected every week was more than welcome and much needed, especially given the demands of the children's schooling. Soon, however the separation from his growing family was difficult to stomach. A few short home leaves did little to ease the pain. The anguish felt by Herbert was being felt by soldiers all over the country. Men wanted to get back home but the army was retaining them. It became a serious problem. Indeed, there had been no open mutinies in the British Army all through the trench battles. The men had remained resolute in the blood and filth of the front line in France, but in 1919 there grew acute discontent among thousands of men in England who wanted and needed to be with their families. As the months passed and winter turned into summer, discontent turned into open defiance. The mind-numbing routine of Army life seemed to many to be without purpose and without reason. The authorities finally had to listen. Action was taken and men started to be demobbed.

In the middle of July 1919, over nine months after the war ended, Herbert Barnes was told he would have 28 days of home leave. He was going back to Ash Close. He packed his kit bag for the last time and said a protracted goodbye to his friends and the few remaining patients that were still in the hospital. The army gave him a £2 advance over and above his normal soldier's allowance to cover any immediate expenses. On 16 July he caught the train at Blackpool station to make the long journey to Swaffham. After the 28 days were over, he would be officially "transferred to the class Z reserve". This was the jargon used to indicate that he was being demobbed. He was also given permission to wear civilian clothing for the first time in three and a half years. He was however still a soldier and would not be discharged for another six months. However, in nearly every respect Herbert ceased to be in the British Army on 12 August 1919. He would be given an honourable discharge with a commendation on his character. He was awarded the Kings Medal and the Victory Medal.He was 38 years and three months old. He had been in the Army for 1,329 days.[64]

His coming home to Ash Close was a jubilant occasion. The children were very excited and a celebratory party was held at Ash Close with all the family there. Indeed, the whole family had a grand reunion. Brother Alf had already been demobbed on 21 March and had been home for three months. Brother Jack had been demobbed a month earlier on 26 February. It seems that Herbert's job in the RAMC of looking after the wounded had meant that he was retained in uniform for a little longer. The three soldier brothers were joined by the others. Charlie, who, being a railwayman, had been in a reserved profession and never

---

64 There is an unusual story associated with the two medals. For many years they disappeared and were considered lost. In 2012, while the finishing touches were being made to this narrative, the author's cousin, Anne, eldest daughter of young Bert, was spring cleaning through her house when she found an old shoebox given to her by her father many years before. Thinking that it was about time to empty and sort out the box, she found to her amazement the two medals, one with the original ribbon. Both were in good condition with Herbert's name, rank, serial number and regiment engraved around the milled edge. The medals had come to light some 95 years after they had been presented. Anne and her sister Nancy have very kindly donated them to the Author and they are now proudly displayed in a presentation box on his office wall.

enlisted, and the two girls, Mary and Jane came to visit too. They were together again, just as they had been at Kirby Street all those years ago. Only young George was absent. He would not be coming home ever again. His death cast a shadow.

Rose was deliriously happy and also very much relieved. Her family, many of whom lived in Ash Close came to visit on Herbert's return. Emma and Maud were there nearly every day anyway. Brother Ted had been discharged and was still nursing his wounds. Her nephew Cyril had returned from the German prison camp. Only young Alick would not be coming back. It was ironic that the ones who had died were the youngest in both families.

However, as happy as everyone was, there was not the same drama and pathos as was associated with those snatched home leaves in 1916 and 1917. The war was over and Herbert's life was no longer in jeopardy. Indeed conditions in Swaffham were beginning to return to what could be described as normal. In fact there is considerable evidence that Herbert's return after a long absence posed some challenges for the whole of the family.

Herbert had no job to return to. Mr Fayers' bespoke tailoring business had long since ceased to operate and his shop in Ash Close had been turned into a private residence. The mass production of army uniforms had made bespoke tailoring a thing of the past. Herbert never did much like the job as a tailor anyway. However, he knew that opportunities were limited as thousands of men were coming home and joining the workforce. Alf and Jack were in fact in the same position. They had no jobs to go to either.

Financially, it does not appear to have been an issue. Herbert's soldier's pension was paid to him on the day that he arrived back at Swaffham. He had completed all the necessary documentation. He had declared that he had five dependent children and his declaration was signed by the headmaster or headmistress of all the schools that they attended. He had declared that he had a dependent wife. His papers said that he had been discharged with two disabilities (see Photo 57). Firstly, a disorderly action of the heart which was, it was claimed, directly attributable to his war service. Secondly, it identified chronic conjunctivitis which had, it was also claimed, been "aggravated" while he was in France. It was a typical army turn of phrase to describe the business of being blown up by a gas shell as an "aggravation". The document went on to say that he was 20 percent disabled, whatever that might mean. There was of course no visible sign of this, other than a very light limp but it did affect the size of his pension. The army would pay him eight shillings a week for 55 weeks when the amount would be reviewed. In addition he would receive an allowance of eight shillings and two pence a week for his wife and five children. His soldier's pension was, therefore, in total 16 shillings and two pence a week. It was not a lot but it was sufficient to buy Herbert some time to find a job.

Herbert's coming home was a joy for everybody but it was not without its strains. All the children would recall in later life that a certain degree of adaptation was required. Their father had been away for nearly four years and, in that time, Rose had been in charge of all aspects of family life. She had, as a result, grown into her role and become a stronger more forceful mother. She had become accustomed to managing the finances of the family. She had become accustomed to disciplining the children. She had made all the decisions, both big and small. She had demonstrated a high degree of competence. She now had to get used to having her husband home again; a husband who saw no reason why he should not take over the management of the household. It is clear that this adaptation was not all plain sailing.

What is more, the children had to quickly get to know their father all over again. Little Teddy had to get to know his father for the very first time. Herbert's natural playfulness with young children made this a straightforward transformation but the bond between the children and their mother was strong and would remain so forever. They still looked to her to meet any needs they might have. Going to their father did not come naturally. However, they both got through it in a relatively short period of time. It was no more and no less than the transformation that thousands of families up and down the country experienced as the men from the army came home and picked up the threads of their lives.

It took Herbert just under six months to find a job, by which time he was completely integrated back into Swaffham life. He had joined the bowls club.

He spent an occasional evening in The Greyhound. He worked on his father-in-law's allotment and went to the Baptist Chapel with Rose. However, a life of idleness was not for him and his soldier's pension would not last for ever. In March 1920, he successfully applied for and became an auxiliary postman in the town. He was very pleased with this turn of events. He had found full-time employment in a relatively short time and it was a job he quickly came to like. Neatly turned out in his new uniform with his postman's cap firmly perched on his head (see Photo 6) he thrived on the daily contact with the townsfolk of Swaffham. They warmed to him too. The job was not particularly well paid but it supplemented his soldier's pension. He and Rose and the children could make ends meet. They were even able to find the extra expense associated with Alf's attendance at the Grammar School. Herbert knew the job was only temporary but he was happy in his work and at peace with himself.

His search for a better paid job went on through the rest of 1920 and into 1921. Opportunities were scarce and he had eventually to give up on getting a better job with the post office in Swaffham. He extended his search further, to the villages that surrounded the town. Thus it was that he applied for and was offered the job of village postman in the north-west Norfolk village of Docking.

This was not an easy decision for Herbert to make and it took much thought. He wanted and needed the job but he knew that the move would cause upheaval within his family. Rose was a Swaffham girl, born and bred. All her family lived in the town and she had known no other home. Furthermore, Alf was doing well at the Grammar School and after all the effort to get him there, taking him away was out of the question. Phyllis and Bert were settled in their respective schools too. After much discussion, and some argument, the decision was made – Herbert would take the job at Docking and would stay in digs there until he had found a home to live in. Then the rest of the family would follow; all except Alf, who would stay and live with his Grandfather and Aunt Emma and finish his schooling. The family would leave Swaffham where they had lived for 31 years. They would say goodbye to Ash Close with all its memories and all its associations. They would leave and make a new life in an unknown village.

On January 24 1922, on a cold, snowy day, Herbert began his new job as the village postman at Docking.[65] He took a room above the post office in the centre of the village, a room let to him by Mr and Mrs Overton. After a few months, he became aware that council houses were to become available in a converted disused workhouse a mile to the east of the village. The workhouse had the unusual name of Burntstalks.

Burntstalks was a very large building standing high on a hill with open fields all around it.[66] It was brick built and its robust form was silhouetted against the skyline from whichever direction you approached. It was a classic workhouse design, very reminiscent to Herbert of the Berrington War Hospital in which he had recovered from his wound after Arras. The conversion of the workhouse into 20 houses had been undertaken by the Docking Rural District Council. The houses were far from palatial but would more than suffice. There were three rooms downstairs: a drawing room, a kitchen big enough to hold a dining table, and a walk-in pantry. There were three bedrooms upstairs, one of which was quite large. Outside the back door there was a washhouse, a coal house and a bucket toilet. More importantly to Herbert, there was a large yard and garden at the back and an equally large garden at the front. The accommodation was much better than at Ash Close and had an acceptable level of specification for the time. So in April of 1922 Rose and the children left Swaffham and moved into No. 8 Burntstalks on the Sedgeford Road, one mile from the centre of the village.[67]

It is not an exaggeration to say that, at first, Rose hated it and hated it with a passion. The contrast to living in the middle of her native town with family and friends all around her could not have been greater. She knew nobody, and living on top of the hill outside the village meant that the making of friends took time. Indeed, this seemed to her to be very small thanks for the years of

---

65   His appointment, unbeknown to him, was reported in the *London Gazette* which at the time listed all Government appointments.

66   The hill is in fact the second highest point in the whole of Norfolk.

67   The number has changed over the years and now number 22 is on the door. The building has recently been converted to holiday flats and has been given the grandiose name of Norfolk Heights. However, the locals still all refer to it as "Burntstalks".

struggle and deprivation that she had tolerated throughout the war. However, this remarkable woman dug deep into her inner reserves and would eventually triumph again, just as she had during those long hard war years. She persisted, she made friends and she settled down to make a new life.

Young Phyllis hated it too. She was a teenage girl in her formative years and the move came at the wrong time for her. She never really settled in Docking. Bert, however, made friends quickly and easily and in no time at all he was one of the village lads. He always had the capability of making things work for him.

Herbert himself embraced his new life with gusto. His job suited his personality to a tee. He quickly got to know all the villagers and they became used to his cheery smile as he rode on his bicycle around the country lanes. He joined the Docking Manor Bowls club and did eventually become both their Captain and President. He joined the village branch of the British Legion and became a very active member. At the back of his house, he designed and developed a garden and he enjoyed long happy hours growing all manner of fruit and vegetables. His output was prodigious, enough to keep Rose happy, with some left over to give away to neighbours. The closest he ever got to gunfire was when he did some "beating" to help at the local shoots around Docking Hall.

The war was over. The killing in the trenches was a thing of the past. The carnage and bloody battles must be forgotten, pushed into the deepest recesses of his mind. They had no part to play in this new life and they must not be allowed to blacken his contented world. He would bury his memories. He would never speak of them again. They were not to be discussed with anyone and they were not to be recalled. The war was gone. It was behind him. It was finished.

As the years went by, the family, so close and tightly knit during those war years at Ash Close grew up and went their separate ways. Alf stayed at the Grammar School at Swaffham and completed his sixth form. He then went on to train as a teacher in Sheffield. It is a strange quirk of fate that he married Connie, the adopted daughter of Herbert's sister Mary who he thought in his early years was his cousin (Appendix One). The little girl that Herbert had seen up in Edinburgh when recovering from his last wound would become his daughter-in-law. They settled down and lived in the fenland village of West Walton where Alf spent over 30 years teaching at the local school, eventually becoming the headmaster. They had four children of their own, the eldest being Mary who was accompanying Herbert on his post round (described at the beginning of this chapter) and the youngest being the author of this narrative. Phyllis had a harder life. She left Docking for London where she married and gave birth to two children. Her husband was tragically killed in the last few days of the Second World War. She successfully raised both children in the London suburb of Harrow and never married again. She became a head cook in a school canteen. She still had time to travel the world. She educated herself and became a well-read woman. If Herbert and Rose had been able to afford it, Phyllis too would have gone on to university.

Bert completed his schooling at Docking. He too went to London to make his way in the world and married a Welsh girl, Queenie Reid, who was as bouncy as bubbly as Bert was himself. They had two children. Bert spent most of the Second World War in the Army on the Seychelle Islands, which he always considered an incredible piece of good fortune. He had a series of jobs on the land and on the railways. In his later years, he and Queenie became local celebrities as the "Pedalling Pensioners" when, in their 70s, they twice cycled across the United States, once across Europe and once around the coastline of the UK. It was an extraordinary achievement and attracted the attention of television and radio and was typical of Bert's spirit which Herbert had always admired.

Little Teddy also completed his schooling at Docking Primary School. He became a chef in the Royal Air Force and was captured in Singapore when the Japanese overran that island in 1941. He spent four long terrible years in a prisoner-of-war camp in Java. Herbert and Rose did not know if he was dead or alive until he was liberated, alive but badly shaken in 1945.[68] He continued his career as a chef at the RAF station at Manby in Lincolnshire. He never married and never had children.

---

68   It is for this reason that the author of this book is named after him.

Ivy, conceived during that brief home leave in 1917, also went to school in Docking before leaving the village for London. During the war she joined the Woman's Royal Air Force and was posted out to India where she met and married a medical officer in the RAF. They had one child before divorcing. Ivy then lived with her brother Ted in Lincolnshire and together they brought up and educated the young lad. She was for many years the administrative secretary in a secondary school in Louth where she was also a member of the local choir.

The family was now scattered all over the country. In addition to his five children, Herbert and Rose had nine grandchildren, all of whom they doted on. Every year, year after year, at Christmas they made the pilgrimage back to Burntstalks to spend a few magical days with their Grandparents. The tradition, started during Herbert's fleeting home leave in 1917, was only broken by exceptional circumstances. Burntstalks replaced Ash Close as the family home and holds that position to this day.

Herbert's brother Alf, with whom he had experienced so much, had a high profile career in keeping with his flamboyant character. On being demobbed, he resumed his career as a decorator. More importantly, he entered local politics for the blossoming Labour Party, became a member of Swaffham District Council and was made a magistrate where he shared the bench with the great and good of the area. He then became the agent for Mr Sidney Dye, the high profile Member of Parliament for South West Norfolk and was very visible in local affairs for many years. He became what we would call today a local dignitary. In 1936 he became involved in a very unusual court case where, at the Norfolk Assizes, he was accused of enticing a woman away from her husband against her will. He was, in effect, indicted for practising some kind of witchcraft over her. He was acquitted but irreparable damage was done to his reputation and he was forced to move away from Swaffham to a village some miles away.[69] Herbert, through it all, remained loyal to his brother. The bond with Alf forged during their childhood in Kirby Street and then again in the

---

69 The case created legal precedent in this country and ever since, no one has been accused of this offence.

trenches of the Somme was far too strong to be broken. However, Herbert was privately appalled and somewhat embarrassed by the whole business. He did everything he could not to bring the matter up in conversation. Of course, any aspirations that Alf had to becoming an MP himself had to be forgotten.

Herbert's younger brother Jack, who he had seen so much of at Felixstowe, had a far less eventful life but very fulfilling just the same. He returned, following his discharge, to his wife Alice and together they brought up their two children in Watton, a small town a few miles from Swaffham.

As Herbert cycled back up the hill from Fring to Docking, and as he listened to Mary's excited chatter, as they noted the beauty of the countryside around them, he might have wondered why he had been spared in the Great War from death by a bullet or by a bomb. So many men, more deserving and more talented than he, had been killed. Sometimes it seemed to him almost perverse that he had survived. He would occasionally search for a reason. Right here he had his answer. It was so that he could have this life with Rose, his girlfriend, lover and wife, since they had been little more than 15 years old. It was so that he could bring up his five children, educate them as best he could, entertain them and send them out into the world to make of life what they would. It was so he could play, entertain and enjoy his nine grandchildren, enjoy their laughter and be a part of their wide eyed surprise as they discovered a new world. It was so he could, as a humble village postman, serve and help the community of which he was an integral part.

The reason might be that he was spared so that he could ride up this hill with Mary on this beautiful summer's day.

CHAPTER 16

EPILOGUE

Herbert Barnes never went back to France. Indeed he never left the shores of these islands again. Like many of his colleagues, his only journeys abroad were when he crossed the Channel to fight for his country. When he was carried ashore on a stretcher at Southampton in 1917 his overseas travel was over forever. All through his long life, he never expressed the slightest desire to revisit the places where he had fought. If he had, he would have hardly recognised the area. As the years passed, nature and agriculture reclaimed the devastated wilderness that was once a battlefield. Trenches were filled in and hedgerows grew again. No-man's-land was cleared of human remains and the discarded wreckage of war. The Somme became once more a country of rolling chalk hills and wooded valleys. Where men had fought and died, the rich golden cornfields would once again sparkle in the spring sunlight. Around Monchy near Arras, small farms now prosper and a motorway cuts through the area where Herbert and his colleagues fought their way across no-man's-land. Out of the wreckage of the village of Poelcappelle, a thriving community has grown up – small, neat Belgian farms, each one with a cluster of modern outbuildings.

Herbert never expressed a wish to revisit these places. Neither, as far as is known, did he ever go back to the hospitals and the places in this country where once he had convalesced. He did once travel north to Edinburgh and several times he went through Epsom and Shrewsbury but no-one can recall that he ever made any diversions to visit Shavington or Horton or Wemyss Castle. He was not interested in any sort of pilgrimage to all the places that must have been so vivid in his memory. Neither, for that matter, did any of his children try to trace his movements or go and see the places and buildings where their father had spent his war years. As far as Herbert was concerned the episode was closed. He had put it behind him. It was very rarely discussed and his references to that horrendous part of his life were few and infrequent.

During the First World War, 5.3 million men enlisted in the army and over 700,000 did not return from France. Herbert's war service was in many ways typical of the "average Tommy". He had spent 1,329 days in total in the British Army, always as a Private. He was retained for over nine months after the war was over so his wartime service consisted of 1,098 days, almost exactly three years. The way in which he spent his time was in no way unusual. He was in France for only 299 days, less than a year in total. Of the time that he spent in France, 82 percent of the days were spent behind the lines supporting the front line troops, sweating in work details, route marching and generally acting as a manual labourer to keep supply lines open. Eleven percent of his time (34 days) was spent in hospitals in France recovering from his wounds.

Only 6 percent of his time in France (19 days) was spent in the front line. This was very typical and reflected the British Army's sensible policy of rotating front line troops. This practice, introduced in 1915, was to have very positive results throughout the war. It involved moving battalions into the front line trenches for three or four days – sometimes more, sometimes less – before relieving them and returning them to rest and recuperate behind the lines. The men knew that after a period of time they would be relieved and this was a tremendous help to morale. The French were slow at adopting this policy with the result that crack battalions could spend weeks in the front line and incur very high casualties. Historians have reckoned that this was a contributory factor to the fact that the French Army suffered a number of mutinies while no such scourge occurred in the British Army for the whole of the war.

So Herbert was only in the front line for 19 days, six visits in all. He spent four days at Mash Valley, four days at Delville Wood and three days at Thiepval on the Somme, three days at Feuchy and three days at Monchy-le-Preux at Arras and two days at Poelcappelle during 3rd Ypres. It was a pattern of service that was repeated up and down the front line throughout the war.

Where Herbert was not typical is that he was substantially older than most of the men around him. He was 34 before he enlisted and he was 38 by the time the war was over. There were a few who were his contemporaries but the vast majority of his colleagues were not only younger, they were younger by quite a few years. He was also not typical in that in the 19 days in the front line he incurred three "blighties" to add to his hospital stay because of influenza. As we have seen, he was extremely fortunate not to have been killed – three quarters of a million of his colleagues did not make it. The pattern of Herbert's war consisted of a short, sharp visit to the front line, incurring a serious wound, being shipped back to the French coast and then to England, to recover and recuperate only to be shipped back to France for the whole sequence to happen again. In that it happened three times is somewhat exceptional and illustrates once again that fortune served him well.

The impact of these dreadful three years on Herbert is difficult to assess. He maintained a stoic silence about it all. Many thousands of peaceful, law-abiding men with young families left the comfort of their family homes and were trained to fight and kill. In France they witnessed scenes of carnage and horror that is difficult for people of this modern age to imagine. What's more, Herbert, because of his age, was probably more set in his ways than many of his colleagues. The shock of it all could only have been traumatic. His silence might cover complex feelings of shame, or guilt, or horror or any combination of emotions. The effect that it had on him will never be known – perhaps only Rose could have revealed them and she never did.

What is sure is that for the rest of his life, Herbert religiously turned his back on any form of violence. Indeed he was a most patient, considerate man. Even his children had to think hard to remember him getting angry or even raising his voice. It did happen, but it happened infrequently and was all the more impactful when it did. Violence was something he left behind in the trenches in France. It would have no part in his life. He had seen enough of what it could do. Indeed he must have felt huge despair that only 19 years after his discharge the world was at war again. In that war in which two of his sons fought, he lost a son-in-law. There can be no doubt he must have questioned the futility of it all.

Indeed, the one characteristic that he showed in abundance was that of humour. He had a quick wit and was very fast to see the funny side in any situation. He had a contagious chuckle that would on occasions break out into a hearty laugh and his friends and relations knew him for a man who enjoyed a joke or two.

Herbert had no lasting health effects from the battering his body took during those three years. He walked with a slight limp in his right leg and he had extensive scars on his neck and both legs that were not visible. The shellshock that saved him from a fourth spell in the trenches seemed to have no lasting impact. He showed no signs of being of a particularly nervous disposition. He did suffer from minor irritation with his eyes and used reading glasses but there was nothing too unusual about that. In spite of all his wounds, he lived a healthy outdoor life.

There were some ill effects. In 1948 he experienced what we today would call a "breakdown" which lasted for just a few days. He had recently retired from his job as a postman and for the first time in over 30 years, he found himself without an imposed structure in his life. He became disorientated, very depressed and acted completely out of character. He left his home in Docking and turned up three days later at his daughter Phyllis's house in London. On returning to Docking, he recovered and continued as if nothing had happened. It never happened again. As very few of his family knew the details of his war service, they were at a loss to explain what had happened. However, it is possible that this "breakdown" was in some way a delayed reaction to the trauma that he had experienced 30 years before. If that was indeed the case, it would be the only time that his years in France were to demonstrably impinge on his later life.

Herbert did not appear to carry any lasting bitterness towards either the Germans or to the senior officers who directed the war. Indeed bitterness was the one characteristic that he rarely demonstrated. Outwardly he seemed to hold no-one to blame for the things he had witnessed. Acrimony was not part of his make-up. All his brothers and sisters became involved to varying degrees in political activities in pursuit of working class causes. His brother Alf and his sister Mary were particularly active. What is more, all his children, especially Alf, Phyllis and Bert were particularly active in left wing organisations of one sort or another. Herbert himself was the exception. He never did get involved with politics. He held no malice towards the "officer class" who had, by dint of their birth, led men into battle and to their deaths. Many of course did hold a grudge but Herbert never voiced this sentiment. On the rare occasion that he was tackled on the question, he had responded that he had seen too many brave men of all ranks and classes mown down by machine-guns or blown up by bombs. These weapons were no respecter of social status. Indeed the statistics show that the casualty rates amongst battalion officers in the front line were the highest of any group in the war. In his job as a postman, Herbert called in on the Hare family at Docking Hall and on Mr and Mrs Dusgate at Fring Hall. He shared his humour and friendliness with everybody whoever they might be. He had perhaps seen too much of what bitterness could do to retain much of it himself.

He did retain some of the language of the Western Front. Before putting them to bed, he would on occasions order his grandchildren to "get their boots off". They initially found the words confusing but quickly understood what he meant. He would on occasions refer to a hole in the ground as a "dugout" and would call a small building a "shelter". He once used the word "billet" to describe a small apartment where a relation had got digs. Occasionally when out walking with his Grandchildren and when legs were getting weary, he would encourage everybody to sing "it's a long way to Tipperary" just as, no doubt, he had as he marched to the front at Arras or at Thiepval. There was an occasion during the Second World War when a string of bombs was dropped from a German aircraft onto Burntstalks at Docking. One landed in his garden and he created some amusement in the local community by calmly knocking on all his neighbours' doors to ask whether they were OK and to inquire as to whether they had found any of his rhubarb. Bombs going off around him were not a new experience.

Finally, he was all his life in contact and was involved with the British Legion. He was a stalwart member of the Docking branch and religiously attended the Armistice Day parade celebration held at the War Memorial. He attended every year, always with Rose by his side. Some of the names on the Memorial were in the Norfolk Regiment and were men that Herbert might well have known and with whom he probably fought.

Most of all he retained from the war a sense of camaraderie and a desire to care for others. Learnt from his childhood in the two up, two down in Kirby Street with his Mum and Dad and six brothers and sisters; honed in the trenches, in the dug-outs and billets in France with soldiers half his age; developed in the RAMC in Blackpool Hospital with men with shattered limbs and broken bones; Herbert's sense of caring would be directed for the rest of his life to his family and to the community in which he lived.

To his family, he was just a lot of fun. He was good with a joke, he told them stories, he taught them how to play cards especially crib and he loved to play games of all sorts. He took them for walks and cycle rides and he gave them those magical Christmases. It is true that the more serious side of living was nearly always left to Rose. Herbert became the epitome of a much loved Granddad, sitting next to the fire with his pipe in his mouth, chuckling away at the antics of the young people around him.

To the community he was the "genial" postman. Everybody knew his cheery face. He delivered the mail and did much more besides. In the days when he was among the few who had a bicycle he ran errands for them. He gave them vegetables and fruit from his garden and would get back in return perhaps a sausage or a pheasant or just a rabbit pie. Occasionally he was asked for his advice on some minor problem and he would give the question the serious consideration that it deserved. He and Rose played a very full part in village life.

Neither the family, nor the community knew that this friendly, cheerful man had come within a whisker of losing his life not once but three times. They did not know that his laughing hello and pleasant demeanour hid beneath it the horrors of Somme, Arras and Ypres. They could not have guessed the sights that he had seen or the experiences that had come his way.

This is, perhaps, Herbert's ultimate victory and the victory of thousands of Tommies like him. In spite of what he had seen, and in spite of what he had done, he was able through a conspiracy of silence to triumph over those memories. He was able to play a full and constructive part in building a life for himself and his family. Herbert had survived and his life after the war was no more than the victory he and his colleagues deserved. It was a life that they had made together. He had won in the end.

The other hero of this story is, undoubtedly, Rose. She was not only the love of Herbert's life; she was far, far more. She was his rock. This small, almost diminutive, woman was inwardly much stronger than Herbert. And she was more competent too. When he was called away to war, it was Rose who stepped into the breach to "keep the home fires burning". She took over the reins of the family, provided for the children, cared for them and raised them. She educated them not only in the ways of life, but also in the arts of music and poetry – and did it very well indeed. She disciplined them and taught them wrong from right, to such a degree that none of them ever did her anything but proud in later life. She was the one who put in the long hours, preparing food, mending clothes and doing the household chores. She rarely complained – hers was as strong a sense of duty as Herbert's but in a different way and to a different end. She loved them all and they loved her back in return for the rest of their lives. In the end, Rose won too.

Friday, March 25 1960 was a cloudy but dry spring day. The clocks had changed the previous weekend and the promise of light evenings and long days in the garden beckoned for Herbert. He was approaching his 79th birthday. Although he did everything more slowly now, he was still sprightly and able to do most things. His limp occasionally bothered him but it was not a serious problem and he did not let it get him down. Two years previously, he and Rose had celebrated their 50th Wedding Anniversary (see Photo 66). They had had a few friends round on the day but the true celebration had come when the whole extended family had gathered together. Herbert had been "tickled pink" by all the grandchildren coming to be with him. Rose enjoyed it immensely too but in a different way. She busied herself with cups of tea and generous slices of some of her very best cake. To mark the anniversary, the family had clubbed together and had paid for the couple to go on holiday to Bournemouth. The strolls along the front in sunny weather must have brought back memories of their early days visiting Hunstanton. Herbert perhaps would occasionally look across the water of the English Channel and recall the three times he had been ferried over to the other side and the memories that he had left in France. But that was a long time ago and part of another life.

That March afternoon, Rose and Herbert were due to go together to the Docking Good Friends Club at the Village Institute. It met nearly every Friday and the Barnes were regular attendees. They set off from Burntstalks on foot to cover the mile or so along the Hunstanton to Fakenham Road. It was a good stiff stroll but they had done it many times before and in spite of the advancing years still enjoyed walking in the fresh spring air.

Airman 2nd Class Ronald Joel Beseda was late to get on parade at the United States Air force base at Sculthorpe, a few miles to the east of Fakenham. He had only 42 days to complete his four years of service when he would return home to his native California where he was going to an excellent job in civvy street. He had up until that day built himself an excellent reputation and was described by his officers as an "above average" airman. On that day he had been to Hunstanton and had had far too much to drink. Indeed, it later transpired that he had consumed at least five and a half pints of beer and probably more. He had also had some wine. He found it difficult to walk, let alone drive a car. Nevertheless he only had one thing on his mind – to get back to Sculthorpe. Driving at speeds of up to 70 miles an hour, he was seen careering from one side of the road to another, occasionally mounting verges, the car horn blaring out as he went. On entering the village of Docking at about 1.45 in the afternoon he lost control of the car completely, mounted the nearside pavement, hit a wall, careered across the road, hit an electricity pole and embedded the car into a wall.

TED BARNES

Herbert and Rose Barnes were both killed instantly (see Photo 67). They had stood no chance as Beseda's car mowed them down from behind. It is possible that they might have heard the car approaching behind them but there was no time to get out of its way. Their death was both violent and instant. There was some consolation that they would have felt no pain. There was some consolation in that, just as they had spent nearly all their lives together, so they had died together. There was some consolation that Herbert at 78 years old and Rose at 76 had lived a good long life together and when they died they were both in excellent health, enjoying life to the full.

At the time, none of this was any consolation at all. It was a family tragedy. All the grandchildren were abject with grief and Alf, Phyllis, Bert, Ivy and Ted fought hard to keep their emotions under check. The village was shocked at the pointless passing of this much-loved couple. The local press descended on Docking and the national dailies started to run with the story. The existence of American air bases in the United Kingdom was a sensitive political issue at the time and there were any number of people who wished to make Herbert and Rose's death a "cause célèbre". The Daily Mirror screamed out the headline "drunken driver kills two" (see Photo 68). The newspapers made full use of the fact that Beseda had been "very drunk, very aggressive and very truculent and wanted to fight with the police".

Beseda was tried on 20 May 1960, charged with driving a car under the influence of drink and causing the death of Rose Barnes and Herbert Barnes. He was found guilty of all charges and jailed for two years.[70]

The family was too grief-stricken to be over-concerned with wider political issues. Alf and Bert went through the gruesome business of identification and they also led the process of organising the funeral which was held a few days later at the Methodist Church in the village. Herbert and Rose had lived in Docking for nearly 40 years so the funeral was heavily over-subscribed. All the family was there of course – the children and grandchildren all came and

---

70   Whether he served much of his sentence is not known as he was returned to the United States very soon afterwards. There he married, had children and lived on in California until 2006 when he died in Redondo Beach.

were joined by Herbert and Rose's surviving brothers and sisters. His brother Alf came as did Jack. The third brother Charlie was also there. Friends and neighbours from Burntstalks and people from Docking thronged the small church. The Bowls Club, the Over 60s Club, the British Legion, the Methodist Church, and the Parish Council were all represented. The Post Office staff also came as did old friends from Swaffham. Even the United States Air force sent their senior officers to try and appease the impact the terrible tragedy had had on the local community. Sitting in the back of the church were the representatives of the press, still pursuing what looked to them to be a promising story.

Herbert and Rose would have been bewildered by the fuss of it all. They would have been strangely touched too. They had lived their life in a humble modest way and were not ones for the big occasion. However they would have been gratified by the love that was shown them in death by their family for which they had done so much. They would have been touched by the outpouring of grief from the people of the village and they would have been pleased to see the respect in which they were held. They would have been flattered but also a little surprised. They had never asked for anything in return for all their kindness and they were always a little surprised to learn that they were appreciated.

All the family returned to Burntstalks after Herbert and Rose were laid to rest in Docking churchyard. The cups of tea and pieces of cake were served again but, this time, not by Rose. There was a hollow empty feeling in the room. It pervaded everybody who collected there. Sitting in the corner sipping his drink was 81 year old Alfred Negus Barnes, brother of Herbert, formerly of the 7th Battalion the Suffolk Regiment and a veteran of Delville Wood, Thiepval and Ypres. Sitting next to him was 76 year old Jack Barnes, formerly of the 8th Battalion of the Norfolk Regiment, also a veteran of Delville Wood. Both still wore the same moustaches that they had worn in the trenches in 1916, just as Herbert had done. Both puffed on their pipes, just as Herbert had done. Both wore heavy dark suits that typified their generation. For the entire world, they looked just like Herbert and a young 16 year old grandchild could be forgiven for thinking that his Granddad had come back from the dead. Their strong Norfolk drawl rang out around the room as the two men talked about times gone by. They both had so much in common with their brother Herbert. All three had fought together in the trenches. They had been at the Somme. They had been at Arras. They had been at Ypres. Places whose names had faded in the memory and which many a modern schoolboy would not recognise now. They had all been seriously wounded, partially disabled, shot to within an inch of their lives. They had all survived to live a full life until this tragic day.

The lasting impression of Herbert is of him standing every year in front of the Docking War Memorial on Armistice Day – the 11th hour of the 11th day of the 11th month. In November the air was invariably cold and you could see his breath. As the Last Post was played, Herbert would stand to attention; looking straight forward into an empty space. As the service proceeded, something in his eyes would become a little moist. He would drop his hand down to his pocket, take out a handkerchief and wipe something away from his eyes. He would then stand once more, erect, looking straight ahead. He did not smile and he did not frown. He was just remembering his colleagues with whom he fought. He was remembering them.

We will remember them too.

APPENDIX ONE

Family Tree of Herbert Barnes and Rose Drake

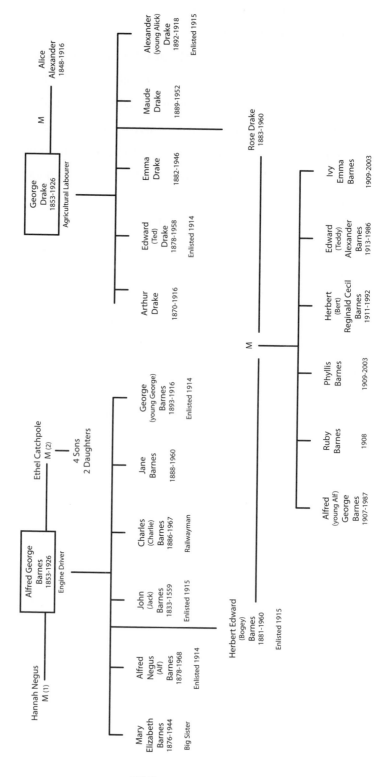

APPENDIX TWO

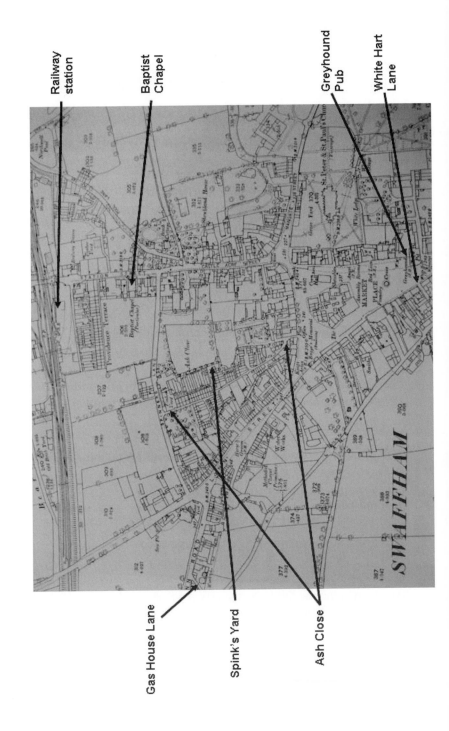

Railway station

Baptist Chapel

Greyhound Pub

White Hart Lane

Gas House Lane

Spink's Yard

Ash Close

APPENDIX THREE

Extract from "Old Maid" by Rose Drake

Late one Autumn evening, near a russet wood
Gazing at the sunset, two young lovers stood

How carefree and happy, they had stood there before
But now there was sadness, for both hearts were sore

For that terrible summons which all England knew
Had come over the ocean, and he had heard it too

War clouds had gathered, wrong overpowering right
And that call he must answer, he was going to fight

She was sad and weeping, how could she let him go
He was young and she loved him, and this parting hurt her so

But her fears soon she conquered, he must fight for the right
And through her tears she promised she would wait come what might

And so these two parted and love conquered pain
And oh! How we cheered them as they marched down the street

And again at the station one last cheering shout
And then there was silence as the train steamed out

And then came the letters so eagerly read
Love and hope, but of hardship not a word was said

And his letters she answered with love true and deep
And always she told him her promise she would keep

APPENDIX FOUR

The Attestation of Herbert Barnes on his enlistment at Norwich on 22 November 1915

APPENDIX FIVE

**Letter sent by Private George Barnes in France
to his sister Mary in Swaffham**

Sunday May 28–1914

Dear Mary,

I hope you got my p/c alright which I sent from Tidworth. I suppose when you see the writing on the envelope you will soon conclude where I have got to. Well of course I can not tell you where I am but this I will tell you, mind you keep it secret I am "somewhere in France" and not very fond of it either but at the same time I am not downhearted and live in hopes of better times later on. We are within sound of guns and it seems rather creepy but I shall no doubt get use to it in time. We are billeted in barns with a number of rats for company but I sleep outside at night as I fancy there are other live things about besides rats. And I expect to have enough of them when I get in the trenches. My word it was quick work though. I volunteered on the Friday we heard nothing further till last Wednesday week. We moved off to Tidworth and were attached to the 2/6 Gloucesters and we left Tidworth last Tuesday and well here I am and are likely to remain I suppose perhaps for ever but I keep a stout heart and trust to luck. I had no chance to go home nor yet see Gert before I came away. It has been all rush since I left N Walsham. There are about 100 of the old 6th in the battalion and we are all together.

How is Ernie, Connie and Ernie the second going on? I am so glad I went to see you at Gillingham and I do wish Ernie had been there as I should have liked to see him so much. One thing hits me jolly hard here and that is cigarettes. I have smoked all mine and I cannot buy Engligh fags here and the French are

300

awful. I hear they are going to hand out some tobacco to us shortly and I hope it is English stuff. Oh crumbs they are yelling to us to fall in again so must close now hoping you are quite well

From

Your Loving Brother

George

My address overleaf

No.1679 Private G.Barnes

1/6 bat Norfolk Reg

attached

2/6 Gloucesters

No.13 Platoon

"D" Company

BEF

France

C.O Glo London

GRANDDAD'S WAR

Letter sent by Private George Barnes in France to his sister Mary in Swaffham

Wednesday June 14/16

Dear Mary and Ernie,

Your kind letter & cigs duly received & I hardly know how to thank you enough. It has quite cheered me up & I am afraid I was getting a trifle downhearted as yours is the first letter I have received since I have been out here & I have written a good many & one or two before yours but of course some of them may have gone astray but I certainly thought I should have one from Gert but I wrote her again yesterday week so perhaps I shall soon hear from her. I believe there was a bit of a muddle with the letters when we first came out but I think everything is alright now. I did not know Herbert was over here. Perhaps you will send me his address when you write again and I will write to him, also Alf's if you have it. Was Alf wounded do you know or was it sickness? You are indeed right about the weather dear it has been & is wicked. We have had a spell in the trenches & it was rotten. Raining nearly all the time & as you know we are up all night and it was miserable really in the rain. Oh did I tell you I had all my hair clipped off all over. You would hardly know me now I expect. One thing dear I have seen the serious side of the war now & I should never have done so in N Walsham. I don't in the least regret having volunteered although perhaps I have compared doings out here to what I should have been doing in N.Walsham especially when I turned in my dugout wet through at about 4 am in the morning. It's a bit different to a feather bed I assure you. But I have the consolation of knowing that I am doing my little bit now dear. The cigs you sent me are the identical and thank you very much indeed. They were very welcome as English fags are scarce out here and the French are not worth smoking. Oh when you write again dear don't forget to put my number on letter (no 1679) as there are other Barnes in regiment. Remember me to Ernie and kiss the youngsters for me and I live in hopes of seeing you all again one day. Must close now with fondest love and kisses,

From your Loving Bro

George

TED BARNES

Letter sent by Private George Barnes in France to his sister Mary in Swaffham

France July 2 /16

My Dear Sister,

Many thanks for your letters and cigs received yesterday morning. It is very good of you indeed to send them as English fags are so scarce. Fancy you not knowing my writing but there we have no desks etc here to write on and have to do the best we can. Yes dear I have received several letters since last writing you and a huge parcel from Aunt Jane at Ely and as it came to me in the trenches it was lovely. There were some eggs and my chum and I had eggs and bacon in the trenches hardly creditable is it. Yes dear do write every week as it is very often impossible for me to get off the letters after I have written them as I may be on duty or not near where letters are collected and then it is no good until next day. I tell you what I do want dear and that is an indelible pencil. I cannot get one out here and ordinary black pencil is no cop for addressing envelopes as it rubs off so easily. I hope Ernest is better. It is not at all unlikely my meeting Aunt Nellie's boy as I have met Percy Hunter who was with Herbert at Swaffham and he and I went to school there together. He is in the same division as I. We hear a good deal about peace but I can not see it coming off yet but I truly believe we have got them whacked. I am feeling quite jolly today dear as I have just had such a lovely letter from Gert. Well give my love to Ernie and kiss the children for me and thank you once again for cigs with fondest love and kisses from

Your Loving Bro

George

PS /

We have been in rest billets the last ten days at a decent sized place and saw "Charlie Chaplin" last night.

BIOGRAPHY

Edward (Ted) Barnes was born in Norfolk. He was educated at King Edward VII Grammar School, Kings Lynn and at the University of London. For many years he successfully pursued a career in the commercial world, eventually becoming Head of Global Marketing Operations for a Fortune 500 company based in New York. In the course of his career, he travelled and worked with people in all four corners of the globe. On retirement, he vigorously pursued his lifelong interest in history and family genealogy. He is the founder Chairman of the Cogenhoe and Whiston Heritage Society in Northamptonshire where he lives. At the time of writing he is a Trustee of the Naseby Battlefield Project. His widespread interest in battles and battlefields prompted him to research his Grandfather's war experiences which eventually resulted in this book.

He is married and has two children.